OSCEs
for
MEDICAL
UNDERGRADUATES

VOLUME 1

PASTEST
Dedicated to your success

OSCEs
for
MEDICAL
UNDERGRADUATES

VOLUME 1

Adam Feather MB MRCP
Lecturer in Clinical Skills,
St Bartholomew's and the Royal London
School of Medicine and Dentistry
Registrar in Medicine of the Elderly,
Newham General Hospital, London

Ramanathan Visvanathan BM FRCS
Consultant Surgeon, Bronglais General Hospital, Aberystwyth
(Surgical Tutor, Royal College of Surgeons of England)
Lately Honorary Senior Lecturer in Surgery
and Assistant Director to the Professorial Surgical Unit
Medical College and Hospital of St Bartholomew, London

John S P Lumley MS FRCS
Professor of Surgery and Honorary Consultant Surgeon,
Medical College and Hospital of St Bartholomew, London
Member of Council, Royal College of Surgeons of England
Past World President, International College of Surgeons

© 1999 PASTEST
Egerton Court
Parkgate Estate
Knutsford
Cheshire WA16 8DX

Telephone: 01565 752000

First published 1999
Reprinted 2000
Reprinted 2001
ISBN: 1 901198 04 9

A catalogue record for this book is available from the British Library.

The information contained within this book was obtained by the authors from reliable sources. However, while every effort has been made to ensure its accuracy, no responsibilty for loss, damage or injury occasioned to any person acting or refraining from action as a result of information contained herein can be accepted by the publishers or authors.

PasTest Revision Books and Intensive Courses

PasTest has been established in the field of postgraduate medical education since 1972, providing revision books and intensive study courses for doctors preparing for their professional examinations.
Books and courses are available for the following specialties:

MRCP Part 1 and 2, MRCPCH Part 1 and 2, MRCOG, DRCOG, MRCGP, DCH, FRCA, MRCS, PLAB.

For further details contact:

**PasTest, Freepost, Knutsford, Cheshire WA16 7BR
Tel: 01565 752000   Fax: 01565 650264
E-mail: enquiries@pastest.co.uk**

Text prepared by **BREEZE LIMITED**, Manchester.
Printed and bound by **HOBBS THE PRINTERS**, Totton, Hampshire.

CONTENTS

PREFACE

Followers of recent literature on the assessment of undergraduate medical training could be excused for thinking that traditional methods were incomplete, if not arbitrary, and that potentially harmful doctors were being let loose on an unsuspecting public. This opinion is based on the unmeasurable nature of 'gut feeling' in the marking of an essay and assessing clinical competence. The application of objective measurement in qualifying examinations does add credibility to their outcome.

Every examination must be fair and favour the well-prepared, i.e. valid and reliable. We have discussed the relative merits of essays, SAQs and MCQs elsewhere, this book, (and its companion volume), is directed at the use of OSCEs in medicine. It provides a means of assessing practical procedures and communication skills, as well as knowledge and attitudes in most aspects of training.

The book is aimed at students preparing for their exit examination and will provide experience in this now widely-used examination technique. The book will also help those setting OSCE questions, providing a template onto which they can develop their own themes. OSCEs can assess history, examination, investigation and treatment of disease, together with practical techniques. OSCE stations can also obtain information on attitudes, interpersonal skills and ethical opinions. Some of these stations require the use of standard patients, manikin and videos. Although these media are not all reproduceable in a text book, advice is given on the way to deal with the likely questions, techniques and style of stations that may be encountered. It indicates what the examiner is looking for and how marks are being allocated for the approach to a patient and empathy with their problem. A correct diagnosis is not necessarily the key to obtaining a satisfactory mark: always remember to read the instructions very carefully.

The book follows a systems approach and each chapter includes questions from each type of OSCE station. Space is left for the student to respond to each question. Answers and additional advice are given in a separate section, allowing the students to assess their performance and identify areas needing further attention. In keeping with other books in the series, a revision checklist is given, and mock examinations are laid out: these latter can be undertaken within a prescribed time schedule and used for self-assessment.

INTRODUCTION

Traditional methods of assessing knowledge and clinical skills have been based on the essay and MCQ, for written tests, and the long cases, short cases and the viva for practical aspects. These forms of assessment have been extensively challenged as to their ability to test and rank students. The essay has come under the greatest criticism but the long and short cases have also been questioned as to their objectivity and reliability. Marking a viva can be very subjective and it provides a very patchy assessment of the curriculum.

Objective structured clinical examinations (OSCEs) have been designed to provide a broader coverage of knowledge and skills in a quantifiable, valid and reliable form. They aim to assess interpretive skills, as well as factual recall; they include task-orientated items and they can examine a candidate's powers of decision making and their behavioural attitude in simulated professional practice. The overall effect is to provide a more valid assessment of candidates for their subsequent clinical practice.

The OSCE comprises a number of stations, through which a group of students rotate. The number of students in the examination usually matches the number of stations, so that by the end of the examination, each student has visited every station. There may be more stations than candidates without disturbing the organisation of the examination. Usually the time allowed for each station is the same throughout but it can be increased by inserting rest or preparatory stations before a longer question. Rest stations may also be used to provide natural breaks and to increase the number of candidates being examined at any one time.

The time at a station is usually at least three minutes, five minutes being common; 24 stations are available for a two hour examination. For an examination to be statistically reliable there must be a minimum of 17–20 stations. Formative assessments may use a few selected stations (e.g. 5–10). The design of OSCE questions is usually only limited by the ingenuity of the examiners. However, questions should examine a specific part of the curriculum, rather than just an ability to respond to the style of the examination. Students should be exposed to all proposed designs of question format before the final examination.

Each station of an OSCE should assess a discrete skill. This may be a basic test of practical ability or knowledge, or involve a higher level of thinking. It is wise to have a range of difficulty to help discriminate within a group. A number of questions are included to assess core knowledge: all students are expected to pass these stations. The clinical skills of diagnosis and treatment can be divided up into:

- taking a history
- performing an examination
- requesting appropriate investigations
- making the diagnosis
- assessing the severity of the disease
- prescribing treatment.

The latter should incorporate all aspects of care, including medicine, surgery, nursing and other medical and paramedical disciplines.

The history may be taken from a standardised patient (SP), or presented as a written scenario or a video. SPs may be simulated or actual patients. In the former, a well individual is trained to simulate a patient's illness in a standard way, portraying a patient's problems. Some training is usually required for actual patients, to ensure that the main points are brought out on request and that a history can be covered fully within the time allowed for that station. Simulated patients are usually actors, although sometimes students may act as SPs. In so doing students learn the evaluation process by direct observation and listening to presentations. These stations are usually manned by an examiner who is watching and listening, not only to the style of questioning, but also to student/patient interrelationships, their conversational skills, interpersonal skills, behaviour, attitude and psychomotor assessment. SPs are often asked to give their marks on the student encounter. Written scenarios can form the basis of subsequent questions, along the line of structured answer questions. They can test factual knowledge, understanding and cognitive skills but assess clinical competencies to a variable extent. Well-trained actors can become skilled historians and very persuasive patients, such as when replicating a psychiatric disturbance, although the latter are often more effectively covered with video sequences.

Examination of a patient in a manned station is a very valuable form of assessment. However, it also presents a great problem to the examiner, since very few conditions can be repeatedly examined for two hours at a time, and the number of conditions that can be easily replicated is limited, particularly if there are a number of groups of students being examined simultaneously or consecutively. Fit models can be used for the demonstration of a normal examination and normal anatomy or, alternatively, manikins can be available to assess specific examination techniques such as rectal and vaginal assessment.

A text book has difficulty in reproducing a history and examination, in view of their practical nature and the requirement of simulated patients, videos and models. This book does, however, consider the likely SPs, historical scenarios and types of models and manikins, and the examination techniques that are encountered in OSCEs. Investigations and their interpretation can easily be presented in OSCE form, and candidates can expect charts, and lists of haematological and biochemical results, together with all forms of radiological investigations, with a request to interpret data and radiological abnormalities.

OSCE stations are suitable for most aspects of treatment and prognosis. It is essential to remember that treatment of a 'medical' illness should not be limited to drugs or that of a 'surgical' illness to surgery alone. They should include all forms of available and desirable intervention. This avoids the 'pigeon-holing' of disease entities into conventional specialities which is deprecated in current clinical teaching. Counselling skills and the assessment of ethical factors in clinical practice are readily tested in an OSCE setting as SPs can provide both the background and the patient's attitude to an illness.

The practical application of clinical skills and procedures are also readily assessed, usually with the aid of a manikin which allows such procedures as venous catheterization, cardiopulmonary resuscitation, securing and maintaining an air-way, wound debridement and suturing.

DESIRABLE FEATURES OF OSCEs

OSCEs bring a new dimension to the assessment of medical training. Of particular value is their ability to examine practical and other skills in a unified, measurable and reproducible fashion. This is in keeping with current trends towards performance based assessment throughout health care. OSCEs provide for an effective use of the examination time, examiners' time and commitment. They are effective in assessing knowledge and practical skills and ensure that each student is presented with the same material, thus providing a uniform evaluation with consistent marking of all those involved.

The validity of the response to each question is primarily related to the student's ability: in well constructed questions, very little variation is dependent on the examiner's responses in manned stations. The reliability of OSCEs in differentiating good from bad students and the inter-rater reliability of examiners is good, and becomes increasingly certain as the number of stations devoted to each component part is increased. Both construct and content validity have been well established.

• Construct validity is the ability of the OSCE to differentiate students' ability, or to follow a student's progress before and after a course of instruction.

• Content (criterion-based) validity assesses the value of the station in reaching its specified objective. In all these measures OSCEs have proved effective in student assessment and are accepted by staff and students as a fair and desirable form of assessment.

Well constructed questions are durable and can stand up to repeated use without weakening their value. Like many forms of assessment, effective questions represent the core curriculum material, and once a suitable bank size has been achieved, security of the questions is unnecessary as knowledge of the answers represents a passable understanding of the curriculum. Experiments on presenting a single station at a time to groups of students have not reduced their value in differentiating clinical performance. Assessment can be by the students themselves or by peer review. This modification substantially reduces the necessary space and organisation for an OSCE.

OSCEs can be a useful teaching modality. With the reduced stay of patients in hospitals and increased community-based education, medical schools often have to extend their teaching practice onto a number of sites. All these factors increase the need for uniformity of teaching methods as well as assessment. This can be effectively achieved with the use of OSCEs, and the reduced number of available patients can be addressed by the use of standard patients with good effect. One well-proven example of the use of simulated patients has been in the training and assessment of trauma, linked to the Advanced Trauma Life Support and related programmes. The use of students as SPs has proved an important and enjoyable learning experience, as well as, in some cases, providing financial rewards.

Assessment is a powerful learning tool and should be used as part of the teaching and learning processes but it must be accompanied by adequate feedback in order to benefit individual students. This process should also be used in auditing teaching methods and to stimulate any necessary changes. It is feasible to set up OSCEs in any medical school, provided appropriate staff time is allowed for their introduction. Some schools involve students in the design and development of OSCEs and it can increase their awareness of this form of assessment. The formulation of OSCEs should be closely linked with curriculum development and keyed into the curriculum objectives.

When using OSCEs to evaluate teaching methods, two types of error should be considered.

- Type I errors are those of fact, implying a deficiency of teaching and/or learning, reflecting omissions and ineffective or absent experience.
- Type II errors are defects of understanding, where a student fails to recognise or interpret a clinical situation. This reflects poor concept attainment and an inability to discriminate.

Locating these errors points to the direction that future teaching should follow.

DISADVANTAGES OF OSCEs

As discussed in the previous section, the value of OSCEs in training and assessment has been demonstrated in many fields and many such assessment packages are available. However, medical schools should not become involved in this form of assessment without allowing adequate staff time for their development and OSCEs should not become the only form of assessment.

The preparation of OSCEs requires a good deal of thought and time. The whole staff should be aware of, and preferably involved in, their development and students should have experience prior to any examination so that they can be comfortable with this form of assessment. An OSCE requires a great deal of organisation in collecting material, appropriate patients, laying out stations and making sure staff are available for manned areas. Setting up the examination can be costly on administration and on medical staff and patients, and includes the hidden costs of Faculty time in the development of the exercise.

Analysis of the data and ensuring the validity of the examination requires painstaking activity. The weighting of key questions on essential knowledge has to be resolved before any feedback to staff or students. Standard setting should be based on expected knowledge and the skills required and this relies as much on that much-criticized 'gut feeling' as it does on statistical formulae. Standardised patients, both actual and simulated have to be found and trained and an adequate pool must be available to cover expected needs. When introducing OSCEs, a school has to decide whether it is as an additional assessment or whether it should replace a previous part of the examination. If the latter, it is essential that other important areas are not diluted in the process. OSCEs are not ideal in assessing interpersonal skills: video clips or trained patients can be rather artificial in this respect. For patient examination, OSCEs do not provide a comprehensive evaluation of all aspects of a learning and educational programme and therefore should be part of a multi-component assessment in the final examination, forming a useful means of determining practical skills over a wide area.

In spite of their potential limitations, OSCEs do provide a valuable addition to the clinical exit examination and students and staff should become well acquainted with their format and appreciate their discriminatory properties.

HOW TO USE THIS BOOK

This book contains a series of OSCE questions. The chapters are arranged by organ system, and every chapter follows the same organisation of questions, i.e. history, examination, investigation, treatment, practical techniques and other issues. The second half of the book provides the answers, together with teaching notes and a marking scheme. There is no index but the contents list will direct you to the appropriate organ system.

In the history and counselling stations, you are advised to work with one to two colleagues to act as 'patient' and 'examiner'. The Introduction provides the background required to direct your enquiry or your counselling. Take a history from the 'patient', who will answer your questions using the history provided. The 'examiner' will mark your answers, using the scoring system outlines below, and ensure that the station is concluded in the allotted time.

The clinical examination stations include clinical photographs and test clinical skills which can be practised on appropriate patients on the ward. As the practical skills of examination cannot be assessed by a text book, a check list is included, indicating what the examiner is looking for in your examination of each system. The radiographic questions may be self-assessed by turning to the answer section.

Stations with radiographs or photographs may also carry statements requiring a 'true' or 'false' response. This adds variety to the station format and requires you to assess the answers given with respect to the radiograph or photograph. Similarly, stations with tables depicting clinical scenarios or treatment regimes test your knowledge in rearranging the latter to fit the disease.

At the back of the book, Appendix A explains the marking schedule used for the stations, and Appendix D contains six 20-station OSCE circuits: these provide typical examination scenarios.

By working through each organ system, as denoted by the chapters, you will cover most of the OSCE station scenarios and variations that you can expect to encounter in the undergraduate course.

Scoring your performance

We have chosen not to weight individual questions or items. Good is allocated 3 marks and adequate 2. In the poor/not done column the assessor can differentiate between a reasonable but inadequate mark and poor or not done. This differentiation can direct future study requirements. Each station is allocated the same mark, item scores are added in three column answers. Two of three correct responses or a mean score of 2 is a pass. A 60% correct response rate is required in two column answers. In the mock examinations two-thirds of stations should be passed to pass the examination.

GLOSSARY

A-level	Advanced level General Certificate of Education – School leaving examination, UK
ABGs	Arterial blood gases
ACE inhibitors	Angiotensin converting enzyme
ACTH	Adrenocorticotrophic hormone
ADH	Anti-diuretic hormone
AF	Atrial fibrillation
aGBM	Anti-Glomerular Basement Membrane
Alk Phos	Alkaline phosphatase
ALT	Alanine amino-transferase
ANCA	Anti neutrophil cytoplasmic antibody
Anti dsDNA	Double stranded deoxyribonucleic acid
Anti-Jo	Specific antigen
Anti-La	Specific antigen
Anti-RNP	Ribonucleic protein
Anti-Ro	Specific antigen
Anti-Scl70	Specific antigen
AP	Antero-posterior
APTT	Activated partial thromboplastin time
ASO(T)	Anti streptolysin-O-titre
AST	Aspartate amino-transferase
ATLS	Advanced trauma life support
AV	Arterio-venous
AV	Atrio-ventricular
AXR	Abdominal X-ray
BBB	Bundle branch block
Bd	Bis die – twice daily
BHL	Bilateral hilar lymphadenopathy
BM stix	Blood monitoring
BM	Bone marrow
BMI	Body mass index
BP	Blood pressure
Bpm	Beats per minute
C	Cervical
Ca	Cancer
cAMP	Cyclic AMP
Ca^{2+}	Calcium
CAPD	Chronic ambulatory peritoneal dialysis
cANCA	Cytoplasmic anti-neutrophil cytoplasmic antibody
CAGE questionnaire	Cut down Annoyed Guilty Eye-opener

Glossary

CD4	A surface antigen principally found on helper-inducer T-lymphocyte
CEA	Carcinoembryonic antigen
CIN I II III	Cervical intraepithelial neoplasia
CK	Creatinine phosphokinase
Cl⁻	Chloride
CLL	Chronic lymphocytic leukaemia
CLO	Campylobacter-like organisms
CMV	Cytomegalovirus
CNS	Central nervous system
CO_2	Carbon dioxide
COMT	Catechol O-methyl transferase
CPN	Community psychiatric nurse
Cr	Creatinine
CREST	Crest syndrome – calcinosis; Raynaud's; oesophageal dysmotility; sclerodactyly; telangiectasia
CSF	Cerebro-spinal fluid
CSU	Catheter specimen of urine
CT	Computerised tomography
CVA	Cerebro-vascular accident
CVP	Central venous pressure
CXR	Chest radiograph
DDAVP	Desmopressin, synthetic vasopressin
DIC	Disseminated intravascular coagulopathy
DIP joints	Distal inter-phalangeal joints
DKA	Diabetic keto-acidosis
DNA	Deoxyribonucleic acid
DVT	Deep vein thrombosis
DVLA	Driving vehicle licensing authority
EUA	Examination under anaesthesia
ECG	Electrocardiogram
ESR	Erythrocyte sedimentation rate
FBC	Full blood count
FEV_1	Forced expiratory volume in one second
FFP	Fresh frozen plasma
5-FU	5-fluoro-uracil
5HT	5-hydroxy-tryptamine
fT_4	Free thyroxine
FVC	Forced vital capacity
GCS	Glasgow coma scale

GCSE	General Certificate of Secondary Education
GI	Gastrointestinal
GIT	Gastrointestinal tract
GP	General Practitioner
GPI	General paralysis of the insane
GTN	Glyceryl trinitrate
GU	Genito-urinary
G6PD	Glucose 6-phosphate dehydrogenase
Hb	Haemoglobin
HB Alc	Glycosylated haemoglobin
HBV	Hepatitis B virus
HCV	Hepatitis C virus
HCG	Human chorionic gonadotrophin
HCO_3^-	Bicarbonate
HDL	High density lipoprotein
HIV	Human immunodeficiency virus
HLA	Human leucocyte antigen
HONK	Hyper-osmolar non-ketotic (coma)
HRT	Hormone replacement therapy
HSV	Herpes Simplex virus
IBD	Inflammatory bowel disease
ICP	Intra-cranial pressure
IDDM	Insulin dependent diabetes mellitus
Ig	Immunoglobulin
IgM	Immunoglobulin M
IHD	Ischaemic heart disease
INR	International ratio
IQ	Intelligence quotient
ISMN	Iso-sorbide mono-nitrate
IV	Intravenous
IVU	Intravenous urogram
K^+	Potassium
Kg	Kilogramme
Kpa	Kilopascals
KUB	Kidneys/ureters/bladder
LDL	Low density lipoprotein
LFT	Liver function tests
LH	Luteinising hormone
LHRH	Luteinising hormone releasing hormone
LNMP	Last normal menstrual period
MAOI	Mono-amine oxidase inhibitor
MCH	Mean corpuscular haemoglobin

MCP	Meta-carpophalangeal
MCV	Mean corpuscular volume
Mg^{++}	Magnesium
MI	Myocardial infarction
Mmol	Millimoles
MRI	Magnetic resonance imaging
MSU	Mid stream urine
Na^+	Sodium
NG	Neoplasia (new growth)
NIDDM	Non insulin dependent diabetes mellitus
NSAID	Non steroidal anti-inflammatory drug
O_2	Oxygen
OA	Osteoarthritis
OCP	Oral contraceptive pill
Od	Omni die, once a day
OSCE	Objective structured clinical examination
PA	Postero-anterior
PAN	Polyarteritis nodosa
pANCA	Perinuclear anti-neutrophilic cytoplasmic antibody
PCR	Polymerase chain reaction
PE	Pulmonary embolism
PEFR	Peak expiratory flow rate
pH	Puissance d'Hydrogen = - log (H^+)
Plats	Platelets
PMH	Previous medical history
PND	Paroxysmal nocturnal dyspnoea
PNS	Peripheral nervous system
PO_4^-	Phosphate
PUO	Pyrexia of uncertain origin
Prn	Pro re nata, as required
PSA	Prostatic specific antigen
PVD	Peripheral vascular disease
Qds = qid	Quaque die/quarter in die, four times a day
Retics	Reticulocytes
ROM	Range of movement
RTA	Road traffic accident
RTA (I – IV)	Renal tubular acidosis
SACD	Subacute combined degeneration of the spinal cord
SAH	Subarachnoid haemorrhage
SDH	Subdural haemorrhage

SHBG	Sex hormone binding globulin
SIADH	Syndrome of inappropriate antidiuretic hormone secretion
SLE	Systemic lupus erythematosus
SSRI	Selective serotonin reuptake inhibitors
Substance P	Vasoactive peptide and sensory neurotransmitter found in nerve cells and specialist gut endocrine cells
SVT	Supraventricular tachycardia
SXR	Skull X-ray
TB	Tuberculosis
TBM	Tuberculous meningitis
TFTs	Thyroid function tests
T_3	Tri-iodo thyronine
T_4	Tetra-iodo thyronine (thyroxine)
Tds	Ter die sumendum, to be taken three times a day
T Helper	Thymus (lymphocytes)
TIA	Transient ischaemic attack
TKco	Transfer coefficient
TPA	Tissue plasminogen activator
TPHA	Treponema pallidum haemagglutination assay
TPN	Total parenteral nutrition
TSH	Thyroid stimulating hormone
U&Es	Urea and electrolytes
Ur	Urea
USS	Ultrasound scan
UTI	Urinary tract infection
UV	Ultra violet
VDRL	Venereal disease research laboratory
V/Q scan	Ventilation/perfusion scan
WCC	White cell count

1: NEUROLOGY AND PSYCHIATRY

NEUROLOGY

History

Headache
- **Site**
- **Radiation**
- **Character**
  Dull, severe, sharp
- **Duration and onset**
  Sudden: subarachnoid haemorrhage, meningitis, migraine
  Insidious: raised intracranial pressure, migraine
- **Exacerbating factors**
  Early morning or after periods of lying down
  Straining at stool
  Laughing
  Coughing: associated with raised intracranial pressure
- **Relieving factors**
  Analgesia: paracetamol, NSAIDS, opiates
- **Precipating factors**
  Stress
  Oral contraceptive pill (may precipitate several causes of headache including migraine, saggital vein thrombosis and benign intracranial hypertension)
  Specific foods
  Alcohol
- **Associated factors**
  Nausea and vomiting, photophobia, neck stiffness
  Fever
  Rashes
  Pharyngitis, cough, sputum, myalgia, arthralgia
  Seizures
  Decreased level of consciousness/coma

Blackouts
May be caused by seizures, TIAs, CVAs and decreased cerebral perfusion.

- **Seizures**
  Pre warning aura
  Urinary incontinence
  Tongue biting
  Amnesia
  Facial appearance – cyanosed or pale
  Tonic-clonic episodes
  Head injury / trauma
  One should try to find witnesses to the 'fit' to corroborate the history.
- **TIAs/CVAs**
  Associated motor/sensory deficit
- **Vertebro-basilar insufficiency**
  Classically loss of consciousness associated with looking upwards and/or cervical spondylosis
- **Carotid hypersensitivity**
  Classically associated with tight collars and ties

Speech/comprehension problems
- **Dysphasia**
  Receptive/expressive
- **Dysarthria**
  These may be associated with swallowing problems and nasal regurgitation of food.

Visual disturbances
- **Amaurosis fugax**
  Sudden 'curtain of darkness' or black spots covering the visual field. It is associated with thromboembolic phenomenon: Loss of visual fields, e.g. tunnel vision, bitemporal hemianopia, blurring/ loss of vision, zig zag lines preceding migraines

Motor/Sensory deficit
Motor weakness may be described as global, hemiparesis, paraparesis, proximal or distal; lower motor neurone disorders are associated with wasting and fasciculation.

It is traditional, in cases of weakness to start a neurology clerking by mentioning the dominant hand of the patient, i.e. **This 34-year-old right handed man...**

In patients presenting with weakness in the lower limbs it is important to exclude symptoms of cord compression. The weakness and associated symptoms are usually acute but may be insidious in onset.

Associated symptoms include:
- **Paraparesis**
  Weakness of the lower limbs
- **Sensory loss**
  A sensory level should be defined:
  T4 – nipples
  T10 – umbilicus
  T12 – above the inguinal ligament
  L1 – below the inguinal ligament
- Constipation
- Urinary retention

Sensory changes include parasthesiae and numbness. Peripheral sensory neuropathy classically occurs in a 'glove and stocking' distribution.

Dizziness
Associated with vestibular, brain stem and cerebellar disorders. It is important to determine associated hearing loss, tinnitus and vomiting.

PSYCHIATRY

The history in psychiatry plays an important part in making the correct diagnosis.

It is important to ask broad, open questions within the framework of a specific history. The OSCE format can be limiting in this respect, as time constraints may force a more concise, directed approach. However, the student must try to bring into the histories a sense of empathy associated with this directioned approach, without losing sight of making a diagnosis.

PRESENTING COMPLAINT

Psychosis versus neurosis

Insight
This is the principal differentiating factor between psychosis and neurosis. Neurotics rarely lose sight of reality and normally have good insight into their illness and problems.

First rank symptoms
psychotic symptoms displayed by schizophrenics
• Auditory hallucination
• Thought withdrawal and insertion
• Thought broadcasting
• Delusional perception
• Somatic passivity
• External control of emotions

The differential diagnosis of acute psychosis includes recreational drug abuse, which must be excluded in the history.

Depression
Low mood; depressed view of present and future, early morning wakening, poor/disturbed sleep patterns, poor appetite, loss of enthusiasm, lack of self-interest and interest in the environment.

Self-harm/suicidal thoughts
All patients should be asked about suicidal thoughts and ideation (i.e. formulation of suicide attempt).

Mania
Elevated mood, increased energy, decreased sleep,
grandiose ideas; delusions of grandeur, forced speech, flight of ideas, increased libido.

Suicidal intent
It is extremely important to be able to make an accurate assessment of suicidal intent. The consequences of an incorrect assessment can be fatal. All patients presenting with deliberate self-harm should have a formal psychiatric assessment prior to discharge from hospital. Important factors include:

- Age – deliberate self-harm is rarely just a cry for help in the elderly. They are, therefore, often successful in attempts to commit suicide and rarely present to hospital.
- Planning
- Method
- Suicide note and content
- Premorbid events – precipitating factors, (e.g. loss of job, marital split, bereavement)
- Family/personal history of deliberate self-harm
- Family/personal history of psychiatric illness
- Present view of suicidal attempt
- View of the future
- Symptoms of depression

Drug and alcohol abuse
- Alcohol abuse – duration
  Units of alcohol per 24 hours (1 unit = 1 glass of wine, 1 measure of spirits, 1/2 pint of regular strength beer or lager)
  Always ask about all 3 types of alcohol – wine, beer and spirits
- View of alcohol excess - patients must see drinking as a problem and be prepared to accept help offered. Their view may be judged by the CAGE questionnaire.
- Drinking patterns – drinking alone, in the mornings, to relieve symptoms of withdrawal.
- Previous attempts at 'drying out'/withdrawal – formal and informal.
- Previous admissions for delirium tremens, GI bleeds or pancreatitis.

Recreational drug use
- Type – amphetamines, sedatives, cannabis, opiates
- Method – tablets, intravenous injection, smoking
- Duration of abuse
- View of drug taking
- Understanding of withdrawal
- Alcohol, cigarette smoking and illicit drug abuse are often associated and one should always ask about the others when taking a history.

Other important elements of the psychiatric history
- Premorbid personality
- Perceptions of their present illness

- View of the future
- Family history – particularly psychiatric illness
- Previous medical and psychiatric history
- Medications
- Childhood, schooling, further education
- Occupational history
- Criminal history
- Sexual history (may be relevant in certain cases)
- Major life events – bereavement, economic hardship, unemployment, divorce.

STATION 1.1   *(Answers – page 168)*

History

> You are a medical student attending a neurology outpatient clinic. The first patient is a 21-year-old woman who has been referred by her GP with headaches.
>
> Please take a history of the presenting complaint and any other relevant history with a view to making a diagnosis.
>
> *(5 minute station)*

STATION 1.2

History

> You are a medical student attached to a GP practice. The next patient is a 19-year-old man with headaches.
>
> Please take a history of the presenting complaint and any other relevant history with a view to making a diagnosis.
>
> *(5 minute station)*

STATION 1.3

History

> You are a house officer attached to a busy medical firm. The registrar has asked you to take a history in the Accident and Emergency Department from a 23-year-old woman with a severe headache.
>
> Please take a history of the presenting complaint and any other relevant history with a view to making a diagnosis.
>
> *(5 minute station)*

STATION 1.4

History

You are a medical student attending a neurology outpatient clinic. The next patient has been referred by his GP for 'funny turns'.

Please take a history of the presenting complaint and any other relevant history with a view to making a diagnosis.

(5 minute station)

STATION 1.5

History

You are a house officer attached to a neurology firm. The next patient has been admitted from the consultant outpatient clinic for investigation of 'weakness'.

Please take a history of the presenting complaint and any other relevant history with a view to making a diagnosis.

(5 minute station)

STATION 1.6

History

You are a medical student attached to a neurology firm. The next patient is a 62-year-old man who has been referred by his GP complaining of swallowing problems, weakness and weight loss. He is described as being very 'wasted'.

Please take a history of the presenting complaint and any other relevant history with a view to making a diagnosis.

(5 minute station)

STATION 1.7

History

You are a house officer attached to a neurology firm. The next patient is a 24-year-old professional football player who has been referred by his GP with numbness and parasthesiae in the hands and feet associated with blurring of his vision.

Please take a history of the presenting complaint and any other relevant history with a view to making a diagnosis.

Following the consultation, name three investigations you would request for this patient.

(5 minute station)

STATION 1.8

History

You are a medical student attached to a GP practice. The next patient is a 54-year-old man who whilst out shopping yesterday had a strange turn where his left arm and leg went 'suddenly weak and dead' but recovered within 30 or 40 minutes.

Please take a history of the presenting complaint and associated risk factors with a view to counselling this man about lifestyle changes.

(10 minute station)

STATION 1.9

Investigation

Each of the following patients had suffered an intracranial vascular event. Please match the haematological results with the patients' histories and diagnoses.

(5 minute station)

Patient history	Haematology result	Diagnosis
1. 69-year-old man with severe chronic airways disease	(A) INR 2.8 Plats 22	(a) Drug induced coagulopathy
2. 37-year-old woman with spontaneous bruising, recurrent infection and intracerebral haemorrhage	(B) INR 9.4	(b) Autocoagulation and thrombocytopenia
3. 51-year-old woman with recent DVT and thrombosis of the right upper limb	(C) Hb 19.2 Hct 0.59	(c) Pancytopenia secondary to aplastic anaemia
4. 41-year-old alcohol abuser	(D) Hb 11.4 WCC 5.9 Plats 2076	(d) Secondary polycythaemia
5. 39-year-old woman with a prosthetic mitral valve on erythromycin for chest infection now presenting in coma	(E) Hb 6.2 WCC 2.1 Plats 6	(e) Primary thrombocythaemia

Answers

1. ( ) ( )
2. ( ) ( )
3. ( ) ( )

4. ( ) ( )
5. ( ) ( )

STATION 1.10

Investigation

The following patients have presented with seizures. Please match the patient histories with the most likely biochemical abnormality and diagnosis.

(5 minute station)

Patient history	Biochemical abnormality		Diagnosis
1. A 64-year-old man with a known small cell carcinoma and cerebral metastases	(A) Na⁺ 121 K⁺ 6.7 Ur 56.8 Cr 1098	Glucose 21.3 CCa⁺⁺ 1.98	(a) Hypomagnesaemia
2. A 32-year-old woman two days postparathyroidectomy	(B) Na⁺ 134 K⁺ 3.7 Ur 2.3 Cr 67	Glucose 1.2 CCa⁺⁺ 2.43	(b) Decompensated hepatic failure
3. A 49-year-old man on high doses of frusemide	(C) Na⁺ 123 K⁺ 3.4 Ur 1.9 Cr 49 Bili 43	Glucose 3.8 Albumin 23 AST 435 Alk phos 598	(c) Hypoglycaemia
4. A 34-year-old man with end stage renal failure secondary to diabetic nephropathy	(D) Na⁺ 103 K⁺ 3.9 Ur 8.9 Cr 108	Glucose 6.4 CCa⁺⁺ 2.56 Mg⁺⁺ 0.69	(d) Hypocalcaemia
5. A 41-year-old alcohol abuser who presents with confusion and melaena	(E) Na⁺ 141 K⁺ 4.0 Ur 5.9 Cr 123	Glucose 5.7 CCa⁺⁺ 1.38 Mg⁺⁺ 0.73	(e) SIADH
6. A 59-year-old NIDDM controlled on gliclazide tablets	(F) Na⁺ 136 K⁺ 4.9 Ur 6.1 Cr 76	Glucose 4.6 CCa⁺⁺ 2.08 Mg⁺⁺ 0.42	(f) Uraemia

Answers

1. ( ) ( )
2. ( ) ( )
3. ( ) ( )

4. ( ) ( )
5. ( ) ( )
6. ( ) ( )

STATION 1.11

Investigation

Please answer the questions below about the 3 CSF samples A, B and C. The normal values are shown for comparison.

(5 minute station)

CSF	Normal values	Sample (A)	Sample (B)	Sample (C)
Appearance	Clear	Turbid	Clear	Turbid/purulent
Mononuclear (cells/mm³)	< 5	290	57	12
Polymorph (cells/mm³)	Nil	180	Nil	2460
Protein (g/l)	0.2–0.4	2.63	0.67	1.55
Glucose	> 0.5 plasma glucose	< 0.33 plasma glucose	> 0.5 plasma glucose	< 0.33 plasma glucose

Please indicate the correct answers by ticking the appropriate boxes. There may be more than one correct answer per question.

		A	B	C
(a)	Which of the patient(s) should have contact tracing?	❑	❑	❑
(b)	Which patient(s) must receive antibiotic therapy?	❑	❑	❑
(c)	Which patient(s) should be nursed in a dark, quiet room?	❑	❑	❑
(d)	Which of the patient(s) is most likely to present in DIC?	❑	❑	❑
(e)	Which of the patient(s) is most likely to be from the Indian subcontinent?	❑	❑	❑
(f)	Which patient(s) may have significantly raised ASO titres?	❑	❑	❑
(g)	Which patient(s) may have significant changes on their CXR?	❑	❑	❑
(h)	Which patient(s) are most likely to suffer with hydrocephalus?	❑	❑	❑
(i)	Which patient(s) will have a clear Gram stain?	❑	❑	❑
(j)	Which patient(s) may have a positive Kernig's sign?	❑	❑	❑

STATION 1.12

Please match the patient histories with the correct diagnosis and CSF findings.

(5 minute station)

Patient history	CSF	Diagnosis
1. 23-year-old woman with painful blurring of vision and numbness in the hands	(A) Xanthochromia	(a) Meningococcal meningitis
2. A neonate with diarrhoea and vomiting, 'off feeds' and extreme irritability	(B) High red cell count in all 3 CSF bottles	(b) Tertiary syphilis
3. 12-year-old schoolgirl with purpura, DIC and severe headache, photophobia and neck stiffness	(C) VDRL, TPHA, FTA positive	(c) Subarachnoid haemorrhage
4. 78-year-old man with recurrent falls and confusion	(D) Raised protein Low glucose Gram-negative coccobacillus	(d) Multiple sclerosis
5. 27-year-old woman with sudden onset of severe headache and coma	(E) Raised protein Low glucose Gram-negative diplococci	(e) Subdural haemorrhage
6. 61-year-old woman with increasing confusion and a previous history of pelvic inflammatory disease	(F) Oligoclonal bands	(f) *Haemophilus influenzae* meningitis

Answers

1. ( ) ( )   4. ( ) ( )
2. ( ) ( )   5. ( ) ( )
3. ( ) ( )   6. ( ) ( )

STATION 1.13

Investigation

Please identify the labelled structures in these anteroposterior and lateral radiographs of a normal skull (Figures 1.13a and b).

(5 minute station)

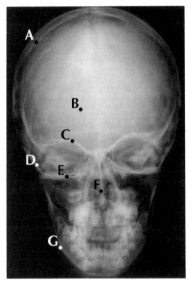

Answers
A
B
C
D
E
F
G

Fig. 1.13a

Answers
A
B
C
D
E
F
G

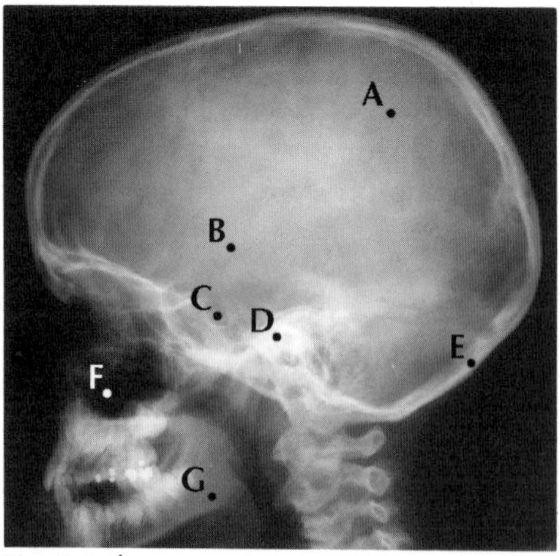

Fig. 1.13b

STATION 1.14

Investigation

Please indicate whether the statements regarding the three skull radiographs, figures 1.14a, b and c, shown below are **True** or **False.**

(5 minute station)

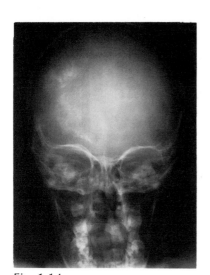

Fig. 1.14a

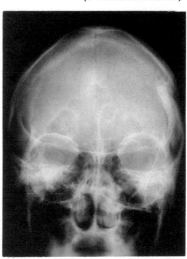

Fig. 1.14b

1.	*(Figure 1.14a)*	True	False
(a)	This is an AP view of the skull	❑	❑
(b)	The sinuses appear normal	❑	❑
(c)	The cortex is normal	❑	❑
(d)	There is evidence of intracerebral calcification	❑	❑
(e)	The disorder shown is associated with seizures	❑	❑

2.	*(Figure 1.14b)*	True	False
(a)	This is a lateral skull X-ray	❑	❑
(b)	There is evidence of cortical thickening	❑	❑
(c)	There is evidence of intracerebral calcification	❑	❑
(d)	There is a depressed parietal fracture		❑ ❑
(e)	This patient requires surgical elevation of the fracture	❑	❑

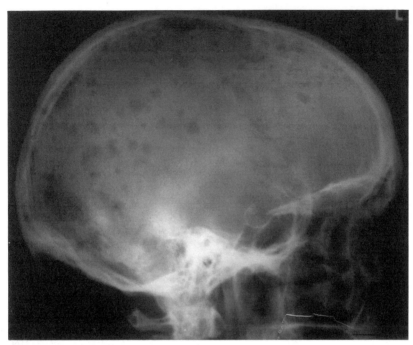

Fig. 1.14c

3.	*(Figure 1.14c)*	True	False
(a)	This is a lateral skull X-ray	❏	❏
(b)	The patient has multiple osteosclerotic lesions	❏	❏
(c)	This patient will be expected to have hypocalcaemia	❏	❏
(d)	The patient will have a paraproteinaemia	❏	❏
(e)	This disorder is associated with amyloidosis	❏	❏

STATION 1.15

Investigation

Please identify the structures labelled below in the CT scans of the head shown in Figures 1.15a and b.

(5 minute station)

(a) CT head scan – level of the orbits

Answers
A
B
C
D
E
F
G
H
I
J

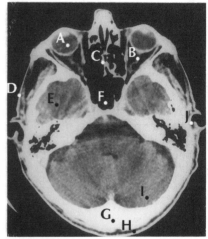

Fig. 1.15a

(b) CT head scan – level of the lateral ventricles

Answers
A
B
C
D
E
F
G
H
I
J

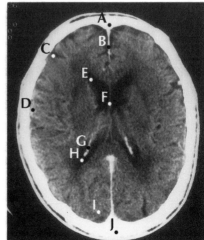

Fig. 1.15b

STATION 1.16

Investigation

Please indicate whether the statements regarding the three CT head scans shown in Figures 1.16a, b and c are **True** or **False**.

(5 minute station)

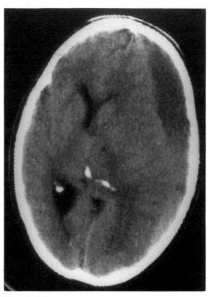

Fig. 1.16a

1.	*(Figure 1.16a)*	**True**	**False**
(a)	The patient should be given warfarin	❏	❏
(b)	The patient has hydrocephalus	❏	❏
(c)	There is evidence of midline shift	❏	❏
(d)	There is an extradural haemorrhage	❏	❏
(e)	The patient requires neurosurgical intervention	❏	❏

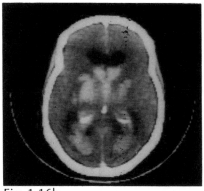

Fig. 1.16b

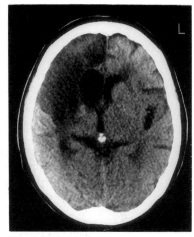

Fig. 1.16c

2.	*(Figure 1.16b)*	**True**	**False**
(a)	The scan shows interventricular blood	❏	❏
(b)	The headache associated with this disorder is classically insidious in onset	❏	❏
(c)	Xanthochromia is a feature of delayed lumbar puncture in this disorder	❏	❏
(d)	The patient should always have neurosurgical intervention	❏	❏
(e)	The patient should receive nimodipine	❏	❏

3.	*(Figure 1.16c)*	**True**	**False**
(a)	The patient will have a right-sided extensor plantar response	❏	❏
(b)	The patient is likely to be hypertensive on admission	❏	❏
(c)	There is evidence of a left occipital infarct	❏	❏
(d)	There is evidence of midline shift	❏	❏
(e)	The prognosis in this case will be improved by dipyridamole SR therapy	❏	❏

STATION 1.17

Investigation

Please indicate whether the statements below regarding the investigations (Fig.s 1.17a, b and c) are **True** or **False**.

(5 minute station)

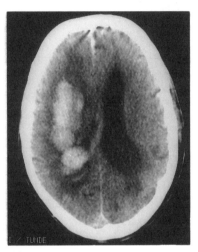

Fig. 1.17a

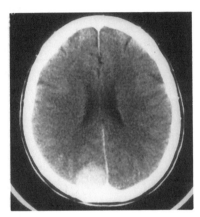

Fig. 1.17b

		True	False
1.	*(Figure 1.17a)*		
(a)	This is a CT scan with contrast	❑	❑
(b)	There is evidence of hydrocephalus	❑	❑
(c)	There is evidence of midline shift	❑	❑
(d)	This appearance is consistent with a primary malignant tumour	❑	❑
(e)	This patient is a candidate for radiotherapy	❑	❑

		True	False
2.	*(Figure 1.17b)*		
(a)	There is evidence of raised intracranial pressure	❑	❑
(b)	The ventricles are normal	❑	❑
(c)	This contrast-enhanced scan shows evidence of an intracranial haemorrhage	❑	❑
(d)	This patient will be blind	❑	❑
(e)	This patient is a candidate for neurosurgery	❑	❑

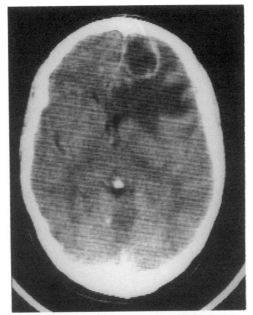

Fig. 1.17ci

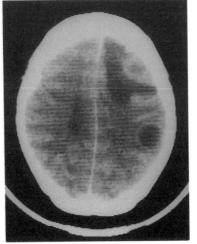

Fig. 1.17cii

3.

		True	False
(a)	There is evidence of cerebral oedema	❑	❑
(b)	There is a frontal infarct	❑	❑
(c)	There is a ring enhancing lesion	❑	❑
(d)	There is evidence of midline shift	❑	❑
(e)	This patient should receive nimodipine	❑	❑

STATION 1.18

Therapeutics

Preparation

You have 5 minutes to read the information shown below before attempting the next station.

(5 minute station)

You are a house officer in the outpatient clinic of a specialist neurology firm. The next patient is a 23-year-old fashion model who was diagnosed as having epilepsy 6 months ago. Since then she has been having increasingly frequent fits, with 6 or 7 in the last two weeks. She lives a very hectic life because of her work and she claims that she 'needs' to drive a car, (which she is still doing). She is on no medications other than the oral contraceptive pill. She drinks 20 to 30 units of alcohol per week but occasionally drinks a lot more at parties. She also admits to occasionally using recreational drugs, including cannabis and cocaine. She is very keen to accept any help with stopping her fits but is reluctant to take medications.

Please discuss the possible changes she may need to make to her lifestyle and the pros and cons of drug therapy for her epilepsy.

After reading this information please continue with the next station.

STATION 1.18a

Therapeutics

The patient in the outpatient clinic is the 23-year-old fashion model with poorly controlled epilepsy. Please discuss the lifestyle changes that she may need to make to help with her control and the pros and cons of starting drug therapy.

(10 minute station)

STATION 1.19

Treatment

Please match the patient history with the correct diagnosis and therapy.

(5 minute station)

Patient history	Diagnosis	Therapy
1. 24-year-old man with parasthesiae of his hands and feet and painful blurring of his vision	(A) Alzheimer's disease	(a) Selegiline and L-dopa
2. 18-year-old woman with exertional weakness and a thymoma	(B) Normal pressure hydrocephalus	(b) Prednisolone
3. 71-year-old man with a festenating gait and a resting tremor	(C) Multiple sclerosis	(c) Donepezil
4. 63-year-old man with progressive confusion and disability	(D) Myasthenia gravis	(d) Ventriculo-peritoneal shunt
5. 43-year-old woman with angina, jaw claudication and headaches	(E) Parkinson's disease	(e) Physostigmine
6. 79-year-old man with increasing confusion, gait dyspraxia and urinary incontinence	(F) Giant cell arteritis	(f) Beta interferon

Answers

1. ( ) ( )
2. ( ) ( )
3. ( ) ( )

4. ( ) ( )
5. ( ) ( )
6. ( ) ( )

STATION 1.20

Procedure

Consent for lumbar puncture

You are the medical house officer attached to a general medical firm. You have been asked by the registrar to consent a 23-year-old woman with a poorly resolving headache for a lumbar puncture. A CT head scan was unremarkable and she has no papilloedema.

Please obtain verbal consent for the procedure and answer any questions she may have.

(5 minute station)

STATION 1.21

History

You are a medical student attached to a psychiatry firm. The next patient in the outpatient clinic is a 43-year-old woman who has been referred by her GP with 'feeling very low'.

Please take a history of the presenting complaint and any relevant history with a view to making a diagnosis.

(10 minute station)

STATION 1.22

History

You are a medical student attached to a psychiatry firm. You have been asked by the duty psychiatrist to clerk a patient in the Accident and Emergency Department. The patient is a 23-year-old man who has been brought in by his family after several episodes of 'very strange behaviour'.

Please take a history of the presenting complaint and any further relevant history with a view to making a diagnosis.

(10 minute station)

STATION 1.23

History

You are a house officer attached to a general medical firm. You have been asked to see a patient in the Accident and Emergency Department who has been referred after trying to kill herself. Please assess this patient's suicidal intent with a view to admitting her to hospital.

(10 minute station)

STATION 1.24

History

You are a medical student attached to a GP practice. A patient has come to see the doctor about a 'private matter concerning her husband'. She has agreed to talk to you.

Please take a history of the presenting complaint and any other relevant history with a view to making a diagnosis.

(10 minute station)

STATION 1.25

History

You are a house officer attached to an alcohol dependency unit as part of your psychiatry attachment. The next patient is a 43-year-old football manager who has been referred by his GP for alcohol detoxification.

Please take a history of his alcohol abuse and any other relevant history with a view to admitting him onto the detoxification programme.

(5 minute station)

STATION 1.26

History

You are a medical student attached to a GP practice. The next patient is a 27-year-old woman who has come to see the doctor because she cannot stop washing her hands.

Please take a history of the presenting complaint and any other relevant history, with a view to making a diagnosis.

(5 minute station)

STATION 1.27

History

You are the medical house officer on call. You have been called to see a 72-year-old woman, who is demanding to go home, despite the fact it is 3 o'clock in the morning.

Please assess this patient's mental state and decide whether she can be allowed to go home. A routine set of observations has recently been performed by the nursing staff.

(5 minute station)

STATION 1.28

Investigation

The following patients have presented with acute confusion. Please match the histories with the most appropriate diagnosis and investigation results.

(5 minute station)

Patient history	Investigations		Diagnosis
1. 39-year-old alcohol abuser with liver flap and jaundice	(A) Na^+ 122 K^+ 6.1 Ur 9.6 Cr 135	Albumin 36 CCa^{++} 2.45 Glucose 3.2 Bili 14	(a) End stage renal failure
2. 56-year-old man with known metastatic carcinoma of lung	(B) Na^+ 126 K^+ 6.9 Ur 67 Cr 1067	Albumin 13 Bili 12 CCa^{++} 1.98 Glucose 4.8	(b) Diabetic ketoacidosis
3. 24-year-old woman with polydypsia, polyuria and a chest infection	(C) Na^+ 125 K^+ 3.4 Ur 1.9 Cr 67	Albumin 23 Bili 48 Glucose 3.8	(c) SIADH secondary to *Legionella pneumophila*
4. 49-year-old woman on long-term steroids for polymyalgia rheumatica presenting with 3 days of vomiting	(D) Na^+ 115 K^+ 4.3 Ur 5.6 Cr 67	Albumin 38 CCa^{2+} 2.38 PO_4^- 0.36 Glucose 5.9	(d) Ectopic parathyroid-like hormone production
5. 34-year-old woman with peripheral oedema, shortness of breath, a flap and 'frosted' skin	(E) Na^+ 139 K^+3.6 Ur 12 Cr 123	Albumin 31 CCa^{++} 2.17 Glucose 45.7	(e) Addisonian crisis
6. 27-year-old woman who has just returned from holiday in Spain, presenting with dry cough and diarrhoea	(F) Na^+ 124 K^+ 4.6 Ur 3.9 Cr 124	Albumin 29 CCa^{++} 4.31 PO_4^- 0.58 Glucose 4.9	(f) Hepatic encephalopathy

Answers

1. ( ) ( )
2. ( ) ( )
3. ( ) ( )

4. ( ) ( )
5. ( ) ( )
6. ( ) ( )

STATION 1.29

Investigation

You are a medical student attached to a psychiatry firm. Over the weekend several of the inpatients have become acutely confused. Please match the patient histories with the most appropriate investigation and diagnosis.

(5 minute station)

Patient history	Investigation	Diagnosis
1. 29-year-old schizophrenic recently started on new treatment. Now he is rigid and has a temperature of 41°C	(A) Na^+ 119 CCa^{++} 4.02 K^+ 3.9 Ur 3.8 Cr 78	(a) Lithium toxicity
2. 69-year-old being investigated for recent aggressive behaviour and change in personality	(B) Na^+ 112 CCa^{++} 2.64 K^+ 4.2 Ur 4.2 Cr 102	(b) Delirium tremens
3. 31-year-old manic depressive with polyuria	C) Na^+ 134 Hb 11.4 K^+ 5.0 MCV 108 Ur 1.6 WCC 4.3 Cr 78 Plats 64	(c) SSRI induced hyponatraemia
4. 41-year-old alcohol abuser admitted for alcohol withdrawal	(D) Na^+ 153 K^+ 3.6 Ur 5.8 Cr 112	(d) Neuroleptic malignant syndrome
5. 77-year-old demented woman with depression	(E) Na^+ 142 CK 2067 K^+ 4.7 Ur 12.2 Cr 135	(e) SIADH secondary to metastatic carcinoma of the lung

Answers

1. ( ) ( )
2. ( ) ( )
3. ( ) ( )

4. ( ) ( )
5. ( ) ( )

STATION 1.30

Investigation

You are the medical student attached to a psychogeriatric firm. The patients below have been labelled as having dementia. Please match the patient histories with the most appropriate investigation and diagnosis.

(5 minute station)

Patient history	Investigation	Diagnosis
1. A 69-year-old man with hypertension and several strokes and MIs in the past	(A) TSH 22.5 fT4 3.5	(a) Creutzfeldt -Jakob disease
2. A 79-year-old man with ataxia, confusion and urinary incontinence	(B) CCa^{++} 1.57	(b) Neurosyphilis (GPI)
3. 83-year-old woman with slow relaxing reflexes and a husky voice	(C) CT head – multiple small infarcts	(c) Subacute combined degeneration of the cord
4. 77-year-old man with weakness in the lower limbs, hyporeflexia and a previous history of treponemal disease	(D) CSF – Prion protein identified by PCR	(d) Hypopara-thyroidism
5. A 70-year-old woman with anaemia, peripheral neuropathy and leg weakness	(E) CT head scan – grossly dilated ventricles; CSF opening pressure =10 cm	(e) Multi-infarct dementia
6. A 78-year-old man with ataxia, seizures and rapidly progressive confusion	(F) B12 = 2.7 Folate = 15	(f) Hypothyroidism
7. A 69-year-old woman with insidious worsening confusion and tetany	(G) CSF – FTA/TPHA positive	(g) Normal pressure hydrocephalus

Answers

1. ( ) ( )
2. ( ) ( )
3. ( ) ( )
4. ( ) ( )

5. ( ) ( )
6. ( ) ( )
7. ( ) ( )

STATION 1.31

Therapeutics

Please read the following information before attempting the next station.

(5 minute station)

You are the medical student attached to a psychiatry firm. The registrar has asked you to explain to a relatively well controlled schizophrenic about depot injections for the administration of his antipsychotic medication. He has left you the following information to relay to the patient.

Reasons to change from tablets: after initial adjustments it will mean only one injection every 2 to 4 weeks instead of daily tablets. Depot injections often increase compliance, which in turn improves control.

What it involves: initially a small test dose is given to ensure no adverse effects.

- If this is successful then injections are given with a slow reduction in tablets.
- Regular deep intramuscular injections are given every 2 to 4 weeks.
- Injections are 2 to 3 ml of oily solution.
- Injection sites are rotated to reduce local side-effects.

Side-effects

- Local: pain, bruising, swelling, erythema, nodules.
- Systemic: increase Parkinsonian and extrapyramidal symptoms.

Caution: response to treatment is variable and may require several months of adjustment of the dose before a suitable regime is found.

STATION 1.31a

Therapeutics

The patient in the outpatient clinic is the relatively well-controlled schizophrenic who would like to go on depot injections for his antipsychotic medication. Please explain the treatment to him.

(5 minute station)

STATION 1.32

Therapeutics

Please match the medications with the most appropriate investigation and side-effect.

(5 minute station)

Medication	Investigation	Side-effect
1. Lithium	(A) WCC = 2.1	(a) Galactorrhoea
2. Fluoxetine	(B) CK = 3078	(b) Cholestatic jaundice
3. Amitriptyline	(C) Pyridoxine levels grossly reduced	(c) SIADH
4. Haloperidol	(D) Prolactin = 934	(d) Agranulocytosis
5. Chlorpromazine	(E) TSH 25.6 fT4 2.4	(e) Peripheral neuropathy
6. Phenelzine	(F) Na^+ = 112	(f) Neuroleptic malignant syndrome
7. Flupenthixol	(G) AST 434 Alk phos 621 Bili 43	(g) Hypothyroidism

Answers

1. ( ) ( )
2. ( ) ( )
3. ( ) ( )
4. ( ) ( )
5. ( ) ( )
6. ( ) ( )
7. ( ) ( )

2: OPHTHALMOLOGY AND OTOLARYNGOLOGY

EYES

The eye is affected in many local and systemic diseases and is a sensitive monitor of their progress, since relatively mild disease can produce severe loss of function. The healing process itself can interfere with vision, as revascularisation and scarring can opacify vital optically clear tissues. The retina and optic nerve are derivatives of the central nervous system and do not regenerate.

Disease may affect all or part of the ocular apparatus, examples of the former are trauma and infection. Trauma includes physical and chemical agents, and systemic toxins; the latter include lead, arsenic, insecticides, and some antibiotics and antimalarial agents. Infection may be limited to the conjunctiva but extension into the globe can cause perforation and the aqueous and vitreous humors are good culture media. Systemic diseases affecting the eye include thyrotoxicosis, diabetic retinopathy and a number of autoimmune conditions producing scleritis and iridocyclitis. These include rheumatoid arthritis, inflammatory bowel disease, sarcoid, Reiter's syndrome and ankylosing spondylitis. The lens may opacify with age, dislocation occurring in Marfan's disease. Tumours may involve the globe or the retro-orbital tissues.

Eye symptoms include abnormalities of vision, abnormal appearance and pain. The problem may be uni- or bilateral, and focal or general.

Abnormalities of vision

- **Congenital**
  Myopic, hypermetropic and defective colour vision, changing acuity with age. Blurring of vision may be due to infection and inflammation of any part of the globe.
- **Retinal abnormalities**
  Such as diabetic retinopathy, hypertension, papilloedema, and increased ocular pressure as in glaucoma. Glaucoma may produce a halo around objects, as well as blurring of the vision.
- **Loss of vision**
  In neurological abnormalities of the optic nerve and tract: pituitary tumours produce bitemporal hemianopia; lesions of the tract and cortex produce a homonomous hemianopia. Optic nerve damage may be due to trauma and optic neuritis, as in multiple sclerosis.

- **Vascular abnormalities**
  Can give rise to ischaemia of the retina or the optic nerve, as in central artery or central venous thrombosis. Emboli from sites such as the carotid bifurcation produce amaurosis fugax, and untreated giant cell arteritis can produce blindness.

Abnormal appearances

The eyelid becomes **oedematous**, due to infection of the conjunctiva and orbital cellulitis. Local blockage of glands or follicles may produce infection or cysts, such as a stye or chalazion. Protrusion of the eyeball (**exophthalmos**) is found in thyroid eye disease, ocular and orbital tumours, caroticocavernous fistulae and carotid sinus thrombosis. Thyroid eye disease also produces upper and lower lid retraction, lid lag, nystagmus and, in severe cases, conjunctivitis and exophthalmic ophthalmoplegia, often accompanied by diplopia. Horner's syndrome produces **enophthalmos**, **myosis** and **loss of sweating** on the ipsilateral face.

Entropion and **ectropion** produce discomfort and associated conjunctival infection. Blockage of lachrymal drainage can produce discomfort, discharge and local swelling, sometimes with an associated mucocoele. A **squint** may be congenital or secondary to ocular or cerebral damage and accompanied by diplopia. A defective iris may be congenital (coloboma) or acquired in the treatment of glaucoma. Wide **dilatation** of the pupil can be due to damage of the optic nerve and ocular pathways, and the pupil may be non-responsive. It may also be due to atropine-like drugs. Small pupils can be linked with opiates and may be irregular in tabes dorsalis. An intra-ocular tumour can alter the normal red eye reflex, a typical white or yellow **cat's eye** reflex being observed in children with retinoblastoma.

The conjunctiva may be stained **yellow** in jaundice: **red eye** is most commonly due to conjunctivitis but is also associated with trauma, infection and inflammation within the eye, raised intra-ocular pressure and retro-orbital disease. Conjunctivitis is produced by a wide variety of organisms, as well as allergy, trauma, chemicals and ultraviolet light. Infection is associated with oedematous **swelling** and **discharge**. This may be inflammatory with lachrymation, the patient complaining of a gritty feeling within the eye, and sticky eyelids.

Itchyness

Itchyness is associated with conjunctival injection and is present in allergic and bacterial conjunctivitis.

Pain

Pain in the eye accompanies infection and trauma but is also a warning sign in glaucoma, uveitis and keratitis. Pain is often accompanied by **photophobia.**

Examination of the eye and orbit

Compare the appearances of the two sides.
Assess visual acuity, e.g. counting fingers at three feet, or Snellen and colour vision charts.

- **Eyelids:** injury/oedema, discharge, deformity, ptosis, lid lag or retraction
- **Orbital rim:** palpate for the presence of a fracture
- **Globe:** examine for any displacement (exophthalmos, enophthalmos) and normal ocular movement
- **Pupil:** assess shape and pupillary reflex
- **Cornea:** examine for foreign bodies or abrasions with fluorescein and an ultraviolet light
- **Conjunctiva:** examine for haemorrhage, chemosis and sub-conjunctival emphysema (indicating fracture of the orbit into an adjacent sinus), jaundice, anaemia
- **Anterior chamber:** examine for depth and for presence of hyphaema or foreign bodies
- **Iris:** examine for pupil shape, deformity or defect
- **Lens:** assess transparency and displacement or dislocation
- **Vitreous:** vitreous haemorrhage obscures normal transparency on fundoscopy, look for opacities and foreign bodies
- **Retina:** examine with an ophthalmoscope for haemorrhage, discoloration, tears or detachment, papilloedema and vessel pattern, size, nipping and aneurysms, tumours.

EARS

Earache/otalgia

As with all causes of pain, the character including site, radiation, onset, duration, severity, and exacerbating and relieving factors need to be defined.

Causes

- **External ear**
  Injury, haematoma of the pinna
  Otitis externa, bacterial or fungal
  Perichondritis – rare
- **Middle ear**
  Acute suppurative otitis media, principally *Streptococcus* and *Haemophilus* infections
  Chronic secretory otitis media – 'glue ear'
  Acute mastoiditis
- **Referred pain**
  Derived from structures sharing a common innervation with the ear. These include oro and laryngopharynx – tonsillitis, carcinoma
  Teeth – upper molars, impacted wisdom teeth, poor-fitting dentures.
  Temporomandibular joint
  Parotid swelling
  Cervical spondylosis (C2,3)

Associated symptoms
Fever
Upper respiratory tract symptoms
Cervical lymphadenopathy

Discharge from the ear-otorrhoea
Purulent or mucopurulent – often indicates acute otitis media
Serous fluid – otitis externa
Clear or blood-stained fluid after a head injury should be treated as a CSF leak until proven otherwise
Smelly/offensive – cholesteatoma, associated deafness and vertigo

Hearing impairment/deafness
This severe disability leads to problems with communication and language

Defined by – rate of onset, age of onset, degree of impairment, uni- or bilateral ear involvement.
Causes are divided into conductive and sensorineural.

- **Tinnitus:** the perception of hearing noises
  Defined by - onset, duration, severity and character of the noise. It is often associated with hearing impairment.
- **Vertigo**: the perception of movement either of the patient with respect to their surroundings, or *vice versa*. Patients often describe the feeling as 'being drunk'.
  Defined by – onset – acute, e.g. vestibular neuritis, trauma, vertebrobasilar ischaemia
  Postural change – benign postural vertigo
  Chronic onset – Ménière's disease, cholesteatoma.

Associated symptoms
Nausea and vomiting
Auditory symptoms – tinnitus, deafness
Central nervous causes have associated neurological symptoms (e.g. ataxia, dysarthria, diplopia).

NOSE

Loss of smell – hypo/anosmia

Causes

Smoking
Coryza
Cribriform plate fracture
Frontal meningioma

Pain
By defining the character of the pain, the cause is usually obvious.

- **Acute/severe**
  Infection
  Trauma
- **Chronic/dull**
  Sinusitis (may become severe)
  Tumours of the nasal passage/sinuses

Discharge

- **Defined by – character**
  Bloody
  Mucopurulent
  Serous
  Clear – after trauma one should suspect CSF leak
- **Unilateral**
  Foreign body
  Tumour – carcinoma
  Polyps
- Post nasal drip – discharge from the back of the nose into the oropharynx; can lead to an odd taste in the mouth and halitosis

Causes

Infection
Foreign body

Obstruction

- Defined by uni- or bilateral involvement, permanent or intermittent

Causes

Allergic rhinitis
Coryza
Polyps
Trauma
Foreign body
Tumour

Bleeding – epistaxis

Causes

- **Trauma**
  Iatrogenic, accidental
  Spontaneous/idiopathic < 30 years old – common: anterior septum
  (Little's area)
  > 30 years old – less common: posterior
  septum

- **Tumours**
  Benign – polyps, angiofibroma
  Malignant: carcinoma – nasal sinuses
               Lymphoma
  Miscellaneous
               Wegener's granulomatosis
- **Hereditary haemorrhagic telangiectasia**
  (Osler–Weber–Rendu syndrome)
- **Hypertension**
- **Coagulopathy**
- **Iatrogenic** – warfarin, heparin

THROAT

Hoarseness
Partial loss of the voice may lead to complete voice loss; prolonged hoarseness should always be investigated.

Causes

Acute/chronic laryngitis
Recurrent laryngeal nerve palsy
Vocal cord (glottic); supra and subglottic carcinoma

Stridor
Obstruction of the upper respiratory tract leads to difficulty in breathing and 'whistling/wheezing' breath sounds.

Causes

Acute epiglottitis
Trauma
Large goitre
Upper respiratory tract tumours

Dysphagia
The feeling of food or liquid sticking within the oropharynx or oesophagus.

- Defined by – level: oropharynx, upper, mid, lower oesophagus.

Associated symptoms
Aspiration
Regurgitation
Dysarthria

Causes

Neuromuscular disorders
Motor neurone disease
Poliomyelitis
Syringobulbia
Brain stem CVA
Multiple sclerosis
Pharyngeal pouch
Large goitre
Benign/malignant strictures of the oesophagus
Achalasia of the cardia

Examination of the external ear

This consists of examination of the external ear, the auditory meatus and the eardrum.
The external meatus is swabbed clear of wax, discharge or blood before auroscopic inspection of the meatal walls and the drum.
Foreign bodies in the meatus may be identified and removed.
The characteristics of the drum (i.e. tears, tension, discoloration, may indicate middle ear disease).

STATION 2.1 *(Answers – page 222)*

History

A 13-year-old boy presents to you, a GP trainee, with inflamed, red and watering eyes.

Please take a history and suggest the most likely diagnosis.

(5 minute station)

STATION 2.2

Examination

Please match the causes of a red eye with the most appropriate symptoms, disorder and disease marker.

(5 minute station)

Eye disorder	Symptoms	Systemic disorder	Systemic disease marker
1. Keratoconjunctivitis sicca	(A) Sticky discharge in itchy red eye, redness of both the eye and inside lids	(a) Rheumatoid arthritis	(F) Icosahedral DNA virus
2. Anterior uveitis/ iritis	(B) Severe pain with intense redness, occasionally bluish eye	(b) *Herpes simplex* virus	(G) *Shigella* infection
3. Bacterial conjunctivitis	(C) Pain, photophobia, watering, sectorial redness	(c) Reiter's syndrome	(H) aRo and aLa
4. Scleritis	(D) Dry, discomfort	(d) Ankylosing spondylitis	(I) IgM against IgG
5. Keratitis	(E) Pericorneal pain and photophobia, visible corneal precipitates	(e) Sjögren's syndrome	(J) HLA B27

Answers

1. ( ) ( ) ( )
2. ( ) ( ) ( )
3. ( ) ( ) ( )

4. ( ) ( ) ( )
5. ( ) ( ) ( )

STATION 2.3

History

A 42-year-old man presents to the Accident and Emergency Department complaining of pain in his left eye.

Please take a history from this patient with a view to making a diagnosis.

(5 minute station)

STATION 2.4

Examination

The four figures (Figures 2.4a – 2.4d on page 163) show eye conditions following blunt trauma.

(5 minute station)

1. Please name the injury-induced pathology in each of the illustrations.
2. Please list eight other ocular injuries caused by blunt trauma.
3. Please tick the correct response to the following.
   You would identify an intra-ocular foreign body by:

		True	False
a.	Ophthalmological examination	❑	❑
b.	Fluorescein staining of the conjunctiva	❑	❑
c.	Radiograph of the orbit	❑	❑
d.	Ultrasonography of the orbit	❑	❑
e.	Presence of intraocular haematoma	❑	❑

STATION 2.5

Examination

Refer to the figures 2.5a – 2.5d on page 164 which relate to the following questions.

Figure a. What is the diagnosis in this 9-year-old boy?
How would you initially correct this condition?
Figure b. What is the diagnosis in this 30-year-old man, who was exposed to chemical fumes in an industrial accident?
How would you initially treat this condition?
Figure c. What is the diagnosis in this 58-year-old man?
State two complications to the eye from this condition.
Figure d. This is the eye of a 7-year-old boy. What is the probable diagnosis and a diagnostic feature that is demonstrated?

(5 minute station)

STATION 2.6

Examination

Figure 2.6 shows a woman who complains of progressive visual symptoms.

(5 minute station)

1. What disease is affecting the eyes of this patient?
2. What is the associated eye condition called?
3. List three eye complications that may result.
4. How would you treat the eye lesion if it threatens vision?

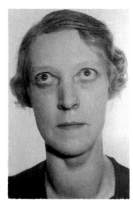

Fig. 2.6

STATION 2.7

Examination

Figure 2.7a (on page 164) shows a painful swelling in the upper eye-lid of a 24-year-old woman.
Figure 2.7b (on page 164) shows a surgical instrument tray prepared to treat this lesion.

(5 minute station)

1. What is the diagnosis?
2. Name the items labelled in figure 2.7b to treat this condition.
   A.
   B.
   C.
   D.
3. How would you use these items in treating this lesion?

STATION 2.8

Examination

Figure 2.8 on page 165 shows the left eye of a 69-year-old man, who complained of failing vision on that side.

(5 minute station)

1. What is the cause of his visual impairment?
2. List four predisposing causes of this condition.
3. State one absolute indication for treating this condition.
4. How would you treat this condition?

STATION 2.9

Examination

Please examine visual acuity and peripheral vision in this 29-year-old woman (simulated patient). A Snellen chart (Figure 2.9) is provided, please report your findings.

(5 minute station)

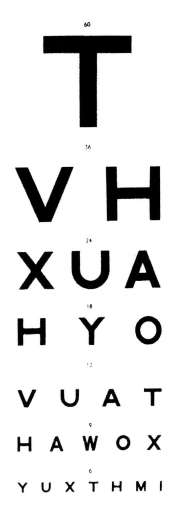

Fig. 2.9

STATION 2.10

Examination

Please match the eye signs with their associated inherited disorder and disease markers.

(5 minute station)

Eye disorder	Inherited disorder	Disease marker
1. Kayser–Fleischer rings	(A) Marfan's syndrome	(a) Glucocerebrocidase deficiency
2. Brushfield spots	(B) Tuberous sclerosis	(b) Yellowish reticulate plaques around the flexures
3. Superior dislocation of the lens	(C) Pseudoxanthoma elasticum	(c) Abnormal collagen gene
4. Pingueculae	(D) Wilson's disease	(d) TSC gene
5. Retinal phacoma	(E) Osteogenesis imperfecta	(e) Trisomy 21
6. Angioid streaks	(F) Tay–Sachs disease	(f) Abnormal fibrillin gene – chromosome 15
7. Macular cherry red spot	(G) Gaucher's disease	(g) Serum copper/ caeruloplasmin
8. Blue sclera	(H) Down's syndrome	(h) Hexosaminidase deficiency

Answers

1. ( ) ( )
2. ( ) ( )
3. ( ) ( )
4. ( ) ( )

5. ( ) ( )
6. ( ) ( )
7. ( ) ( )
8. ( ) ( )

STATION 2.11

History

You are a medical student attached to an ENT outpatient clinic. You have been asked to obtain a history from a 65-year-old man with a history of dizziness.

Please take a history of the presenting complaint and any other relevant history with a view to making a diagnosis.

(5 minute station)

STATION 2.12

History

A 40-year-old woman is seen in the Accident and Emergency Department with a severe nose bleed.

Please take a history with a view to making a diagnosis.

(5 minute station)

STATION 2.13

History

A woman holidaying with her family in a coastal resort brings her five-year-old daughter to the Accident and Emergency Department complaining that the child is ill with pain in her throat.

Please take a history with a view to making a diagnosis.

(5 minute station)

STATION 2.14

Examination

(5 minute station)

A. The patient in figure 2.14 (page 165) has a facial abnormality.

1. What is the diagnosis?
2. How would you test for facial muscle weakness?

B. Tick the appropriate column:

Causes of facial palsy are:	True	False
a. CVA	❑	❑
b. Acoustic neuroma	❑	❑
c. Polyneuritis	❑	❑
d. Middle ear infection	❑	❑
e. Parotid tumours	❑	❑
f. Sarcoidosis	❑	❑
g. Ear pain may precede facial weakness in Bell's palsy	❑	❑

STATION 2.15

Examination

The swelling on this patient's face (Figure 2.15, page 165) is asymptomatic and has been present for 5 years.

(5 minute station)

1. What is the probable diagnosis and the pathological features of the swelling?
2. How would you treat this condition?
3. Please name a significant complication of treatment, and how would you avoid this?
4. What would be the likely diagnosis if facial pain or facial palsy were a recent feature of the swelling?

STATION 2.16

History

A three-year-old boy with fever and pain in his ear is brought by his foster-mother to the GP surgery to see you, a GP trainee. Please take a history with a view to making a diagnosis.

(5 minute station)

STATION 2.17

Examination

1. Please examine the ear of this patient (or manikin) with the instrument provided (Figure 2.17, see page 165).
2. List four lesions of the ear that are diagnosed by using this instrument.

(5 minute station)

3: CARDIOVASCULAR DISEASES AND HAEMATOLOGY

SYMPTOMS

Chest Pain

This is one of the most common presenting symptoms that a doctor will come across and it is, therefore, very important to try to differentiate the causes from the history.

All causes of chest pain must be defined by:

- **Character**
  Dull, sharp, severe, pleuritic, burning
  Common descriptions – 'like a knife'; 'like a weight on my chest'
- **Site**
  Retrosternal, anterior, unilateral, can it be defined by one point on the chest wall?
- **Radiation**
  To the upper limbs, the neck, the jaw
  Epigastric – inferior ischaemic cardiac pain
  Interscapular/back – dissecting thoracic aortic aneurysm, posterior cardiac pain
- **Exacerbating factors**
  Exertion – need to define exercise tolerance in minutes or metres
  Respiration – pain worse with inspiration implies pleuritic pain
  Coughing/movement of the chest wall – pleuritic or musculoskeletal
- **Relieving factors**
  Stopping any exertion
  Glyceryl trinitrate (GTN) spray or tablets
  Oxygen – often given by paramedics in the ambulance
  NSAIDs
- **Associated factors**
  Nausea and vomiting
  Shortness of breath
  Clamminess/sweating
  Dizziness/faint
  Loss of consciousness
  Palpitations
  Haemoptysis, cough, sputum
  Recent chest wall trauma

Differential diagnoses
- Ischaemic cardiac chest pain, angina or myocardial infarction
- Pericarditis: sharp, anterior chest pain, relieved with sitting forward, worse on lying down
- Myocarditis: may be angina or pericarditis type pain
- Musculoskeletal chest pain – variable in characteristics, depends on the cause
- Pleuritic pain: worse with inspiration and coughing, patient can often define the exact location on the chest wall by pointing with one finger
- Costochondral pain: worse with pressure over the costochondral joints, coughing and movements of the chest wall (viral costochondritis is eponymously known as Tietze's syndrome)

Dyspnoea or shortness of breath

Associated with:
- Exertion: define exercise tolerance (walking) in minutes or metres; exertion may be limited to activities of daily living (e.g. washing or transferring between pieces of furniture) if dyspnoea is severe
- Cough, sputum, haemoptysis
- Wheeze
- Peripheral oedema

Paroxysmal nocturnal dyspnoea (PND)
This is a manifestation of heart failure; the patient describes waking feeling short of breath. The feeling is relieved by sitting up, sitting on the edge of the bed or getting up out of bed.

Orthopnoea
This is the sensation of breathlessness on lying flat. It should be defined by the number of pillows that the patient sleeps with. Patients with extreme orthopnoea will often sleep in a chair or sitting upright in bed as they are unable to lie down at all.

Peripheral oedema
Swelling of the ankles, calves and thighs
Ascites, pleural effusion

Differential diagnoses
Renal failure/nephrotic syndrome
Hepatic failure

Palpitations
- Defined as fast or slow; regular or irregular
- The patient should be asked to beat out the palpitations on the table or bed
- 'Sinister' symptoms associated with palpitations: dizziness, loss of consciousness, nausea, sweating/clamminess and dyspnoea

These symptoms may be the result of either haemodynamic compromise or are due to associated autonomic changes. Patients often describe a feeling of 'being aware of their heart beat in bed or whilst sitting quietly'. Unless this is associated with any of the symptoms above, it is normal and the patient may be reassured.

STATION 3.1   *(Answers – page 246)*

History

You are a house officer attached to a general medical firm. The registrar has asked you to take a history from a 43-year-old man with chest pain who has been referred by the casualty officer.

Please take a history of the presenting complaint and any other relevant history with a view to making a diagnosis.

(5 minute station)

STATION 3.2

History

You are a medical student attached to a general medical firm. You have been asked by the on call SHO to take a history from a 29-year-old man complaining of chest pain.

Please take a history of the presenting complaint and any other relevant history with a view to making a diagnosis.

(5 minute station)

STATION 3.3

History

Preparatory

Please use the next 5 minutes to read the information below. You may then proceed to Station 3.3a.

You are a GP. The next patient is a 33-year-old man, who has asked to see you because he is worried about some chest pains he has been experiencing lately. His father died 6 weeks ago of a myocardial infarction, aged 62 years old, and he is worried he is at risk of angina. He recently went for a routine life assurance examination and investigations taken at the time are shown below.

FBC; U+Es; Glucose; TFTs – normal
Cholesterol – total 6.9; LDL 5.0; HDL 1.2
(Target total cholesterol < 5.5 mmol/l)
CXR; ECG – within normal limits
BMI – 29.5 (normal limits 22–28)

(5 minute station)

STATION 3.3a

Counselling

You are a GP. The patient referred to above has come to see you regarding the recent onset of chest pain which he is particularly worried about because of the death of his father 6 weeks ago of an acute MI.

Please assess his chest pain and risk factors for ischaemic heart disease and counsel him with regard to any lifestyle changes you think may be necessary.

(5 minute station)

STATION 3.4

History

You are a GP. The next patient is a 67-year-old woman who has come to see you because she is having palpitations.

Please take a history of the presenting complaint with a view to making a diagnosis.

(5 minute station)

STATION 3.5

History

You are a GP. The next patient is a 63-year-old man who has come to see you complaining of exertional dyspnoea.

Please take a history of the presenting complaint and any relevant history with a view to making a diagnosis.

(5 minute station)

STATION 3.6

Examination

This 72-year-old patient complains of pain in his left calf and thigh on walking 30 metres on the flat.

(5 minute station)

1. Clinically assess the vascularity of the lower limbs.
2. Demonstrate how you would obtain the ankle:brachial pressure index on the symptomatic limb.

Equipment provided: sphygmomanometer, hand-held Doppler machine and couch.

STATION 3.7

Investigation

The table below lists six coagulation disorders. Please indicate the correct results of the screening tests (I, II, III) as normal, raised or lowered and identify the appropriate treatment for each of these conditions by rearranging the last column.

Coagulation Disorder	I: T T	II: P T	III: A P P T	IV: Treatment
1. Thrombocytopenia				A Factor VIII concentrate
2. Haemophilia				B Protamine sulphate
3. Disseminated intravascular coagulation				C Platelet concentrate
4. Patient on heparin therapy				D Fresh frozen plasma (FFP)
5. Massive transfusion of stored blood				E Phytomenadione (Vitamin K) (Synkavite) plus Factors II, IX, X and VII
6. Patient on warfarin therapy				F Whole blood, crystalloid or red cell concentrates. Treat underlying cause (e.g. sepsis, FFP, platelet concentrates)

T T   Thrombin Time
P T   Prothrombin Time
A P P T Activated Partial Thromoplastin Time

(5 minute station)

STATION 3.8

Investigation

All of the patients below are suffering from haemolytic anaemia. Please match the patient histories with the correct diagnoses and markers of their disease.

(5 minute station)

Patient history	Diagnosis	Disease marker
1. 29-year-old Italian man presenting with haemolytic anaemia after a meal containing fava beans	(A) Sickle cell disease	(a) Warm antibodies (IgG) Coomb's positive AIHA
2. 34-year-old man with a cough, fever, bullous myringitis and erythema multiforme	(B) β-thalassaemia	(b) Hb β chains have glutamine rather than valine at position 6
3. 7-year-old Greek girl with transfusion siderosis and frontal bossing of the skull	(C) G6PD deficiency	(c) Hb electrophoresis shows increased Hb F
4. A 24-year-old woman with butterfly malar rash; renal failure secondary to glomerulonephritis and anti-double stranded DNA Ig antibodies	(D) Mycoplasma pneumonia	(d) Heinz bodies in the blood
5. A 21-year-old Afro-caribbean man with abdominal and bone pain	(E) SLE	(e) Cold antibodies (IgM) Coombs' positive AIHA

Answers

1. ( ) ( )
2. ( ) ( )
3. ( ) ( )

4. ( ) ( )
5. ( ) ( )

STATION 3.9

Investigation

You are the house officer covering the routine anticoagulation clinic. The patients' current INR results are shown below. Please match the patients with the most appropriate advice.

(5 minute station)

Patient history	INR	Management advice
(A) 29-year-old woman with mitral valve replacement	1.9	1. Stop warfarin therapy
(B) 21-year-old woman previously on the OCP presenting 3 weeks after admission for a right calf DVT	2.5	2. Admit; omit warfarin Consider FFP if active bleeding
(C) 41-year-old man with known biventricular cardiac failure and atrial fibrillation	10.1	3. Check compliance Increase the dose of warfarin
(D) 61-year-old man on warfarin for previous thrombo-embolic CVA	3.5	4. Omit warfarin for 2 days Remind GP and patient to check the INR and the need for care with erythromycin
(E) 47-year-old woman with proven PE 7 months ago	2.8	5. Continue same dose of warfarin
(F) 31-year-old man with recurrent PE, now presenting after a course of antibiotics for a chest infection	5.9	6. Decrease the dose of warfarin

Answers

(A) ( )

(B) ( )

(C) ( )

(D) ( )

(E) ( )

(F) ( )

STATION 3.10

Investigation

The blood bottles shown in Figure 3.10 (page 165) are the standard bottles used in the NHS in the UK. Please indicate which bottle is used for the investigations listed below.

(5 minute station)

	Blood test	Blood bottle
(a)	Check Hb post transfusion	
(b)	Blood glucose	
(c)	Serum lipids	
(d)	Cross match	
(e)	Serum potassium	
(f)	Auto antibody screen	
(g)	Malaria screen	
(h)	Atypical pneumonia screen	
(i)	Thyroid function tests	
(j)	Platelet count – thrombocytopenia	
(k)	INR	
(l)	Amylase	
(m)	FDPs (fibrinogen degradation products)	
(n)	Serum osmolality	
(o)	ESR	

STATION 3.11

Investigation

The patients below have all been found to have a raised serum creatine phosphokinase (CPK). Please match the patient history with the correct diagnosis.

(5 minute station)

Patient history

1. A 27-year-old schizophrenic man recently started on droperidol, now presents with muscle rigidity and pyrexial illness

2. A 69-year-old woman with bilateral subdural haemorrhages on CT head scan

3. An endurance marathon runner admitted post 300 km race, with leg pains and renal failure

4. A 43-year-old Scottish man 6 weeks post MI now presents with proximal limb pains

5. A 46-year-old smoker with severe central chest pain. ECG shows ST elevation in leads V1 to V4

6. A 52-year-old man with proximal limb wasting, a skin rash and a suspicious mass on the chest X-ray

7. A 17-year-old woman brought in from a 'rave party' with hyperpyrexia and muscle rigidity

Diagnosis

(A) Anterior myocardial infarction

(B) Simvastatin induced myositis

(C) Dermatomyositis

(D) Neuroleptic malignant syndrome

(E) Ecstasy overdose

(F) Rhabdomyolysis

(G) Recurrent falls

Answers

1. ( )
2. ( )
3. ( )
4. ( )

5. ( )
6. ( )
7. ( )

ECGs

This section deals with how to interpret an ECG; it is by no means comprehensive and assumes the student has a basic knowledge of the ECG.

We recommend the following steps every time you read an ECG. In this way you will not miss the simple abnormalities that can be easily overlooked.

Rate

Measurement of the rate of the ECG (i.e. the heart rate) is determined by the speed of the machine. Always check that the ECG is running at 25 mm/second. 25 mm are equal to 5 large squares, therefore in 1 minute the paper travels (5 x 60) = 300 large squares. To ascertain the heart rate, one measures between two consecutive points (e.g. two R waves) and divides this figure into 300. Thus, if there are 4 large squares between two R waves the heart rate is 75 beats per minute (bpm). Independent of the rhythm, tachycardia is defined as a rate greater than 100 bpm, and bradycardia below 60 bpm.

Rhythm

The rhythm is determined by the presence or absence of a P wave. Once you have determined the presence or absence of a P wave, you need to decide whether the rhythm is regular or irregular.

- **P wave present**
  Regular: sinus rhythm
  Irregular: sinus arrhythmia, Wenckebach

- **P wave absent**
  Regular: narrow QRS complexes
  Nodal: junctional/idioventricular
  Atrial flutter with 2:1, 3:1 block
  Broad complexes
  Ventricular tachycardia: SVT with aberrant conduction (i.e. bundle branch block)
  Irregular: narrow complexes – atrial fibrillation (AF)
  Atrial flutter with variable block
  Broad complexes
  Ventricular fibrillation
  AF with bundle branch block

P Wave Morphology
This can only be commented on if there are P waves present!

- **P Mitrale**: this is a broad M-shaped P wave which is a sign of left atrial hypertrophy. It may be accompanied by a sine wave shaped P wave, particularly in leads V1 and V2.

- **P Pulmonale**: this is a tall, peaked P wave which is associated with right atrial hypertrophy and right heart strain. It is often seen in patients with chronic airflow limitation and associated right heart failure.

PR Interval
The normal PR interval is < 5 mm or 0.20 seconds. It should be measured from the **start** of the P wave to the **start** of the QRS complex (i.e. it should include all of the P wave). A prolonged PR interval represents a delay in conduction through the AV node. Calcium channel blockers, β blockers and amiodarone are common causes.

Axis
The axis is estimated by using the vectors of the standard leads I, II and III.

aVR: limb lead attached to the right upper limb
aVL: limb lead attached to the left upper limb
aVF: limb lead attached to the left lower limb
Neutral lead: attached to the right lower limb

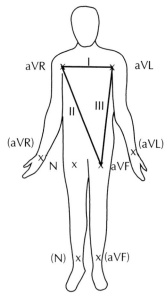

Fig. 3A

Leads I, II and III are 'virtual' leads derived from the vectors of the leads aVR, aVL and aVF. Lead I is made up by the vectors of aVR and aVL, Lead II from aVR and aVF and Lead III from aVL and aVF. Chest leads (V1–6) are shown in Station 3.12.

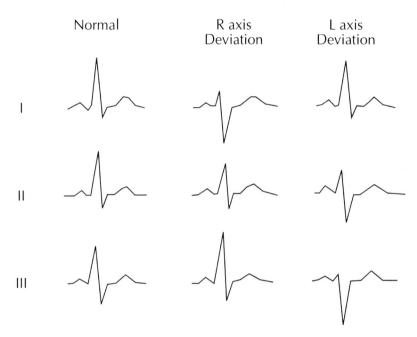

| Normal | R axis Deviation | L axis Deviation |

Fig. 3B: Leads I, II and III showing normal, right and left axis deviation.

There are several ways to 'calculate' the axis. Most experienced physicians are able to state the axis through pattern recognition. Until those heady days, one needs to be able to work it out from first principles. The axis is derived from leads I, II and III. First choose which of the 3 leads is the most isoelectric, i.e. when one adds the positive and negative deflections of the QRS complex the sum is nearest to zero. The axis is said to rotate around this lead, which is often lead II. Then work out whether the sum of the positive and negative deflections in the other two leads leaves a net positive or negative deflection for each of the leads. A net positive deflection for lead I moves the axis to the left; likewise a net positive deflection in leads II or III moves the axis to the right. The two patterns of abnormal axis deviation are shown in figure 3B.

QRS Complexes

These should be no more than 3 mm or 0.12 seconds wide. Any complexes wider than 0.12 seconds indicate an intraventricular conduction defect or bundle branch block.

To work out Right and Left Bundle Branch Block (RBBB and LBBB):
RBBB: remembered by **M** a **RR** o **W**
LBBB: remembered by **W** i **LL** i a **M**

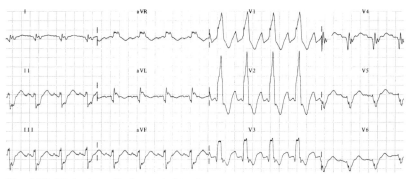

Fig. 3Ci: Right bundle branch block

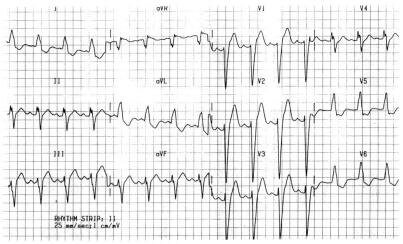

Fig. 3Cii: Left bundle branch block

In practice these simplifications represent
RBBB: Dominant R wave in V1, and a dominant S wave in V6 and Lead I
LBBB: Dominant S wave in V1, and a dominant R wave in V6 and Lead I

Lead Territories
All of the leads, except aVR, represent specific areas of myocardium supplied by the two coronary arteries and their major branches.

II, III and aVF: Inferior leads – right coronary artery lesions or (dominant left circumflex)
V1 and V2: Anterior leads: left main stem or left anterior descending lesions
V3 and V4: Septal leads: left anterior descending lesions
V5 and V6: Lateral leads: left circumflex lesions
I and aVL: High lateral leads: left circumflex lesions

Signs of Ischaemia
Non critical: ST segment depression; T wave inversion
Critical: Q waves, ST segment elevation, T wave inversion
New LBBB

Signs of an acute pulmonary embolism – sinus tachycardia
Dominant R wave in V1 (represents a right heart strain pattern) right axis deviation
Classically, (although rarely seen) a dominant S wave in lead I and a Q wave and inverted T wave in lead III, termed $S_1Q_3T_3$

STATION 3.12

Investigation

You are the house officer on call. You have been asked to perform an ECG on a patient complaining of chest pain.

(5 minute station)

1. On the diagram below please indicate the positions of the leads:
    aVR, aVL, aVF
    V1, V2, V3, V4, V5, V6

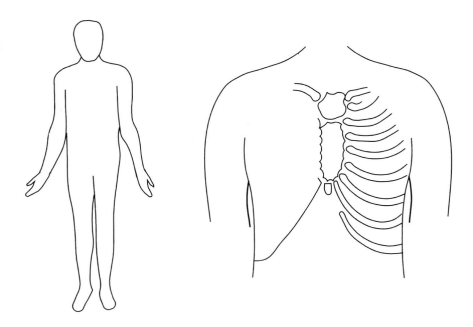

Fig. 3.12a

2. On performing an ECG on the patient, the trace shown in Figure 3.12b was obtained. Please answer the questions below.

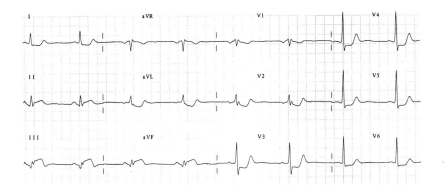

Fig. 3.12b

(a) What is the rate?
(b) What is the rhythm?
(c) What is the axis?
(d) Is the P wave morphology normal?
(e) Is the PR interval normal?
(f) Are the QRS complexes normal?
(g) What is the major abnormality?

STATION 3.13

Investigation

Please indicate whether the statements below are **True** or **False**.

(5 minute station)

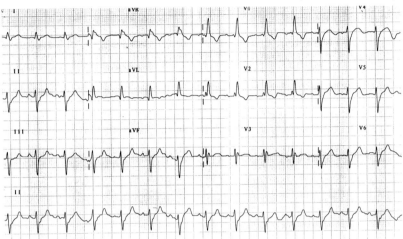

Fig. 3.13a

		True	False
1.	*(Figure 3.13a)*		
(a)	There is first degree heart block	❑	❑
(b)	There is left axis deviation	❑	❑
(c)	The rate is 66 bpm	❑	❑
(d)	There is evidence of left ventricular hypertrophy	❑	❑
(e)	There is a left bundle branch block pattern	❑	❑

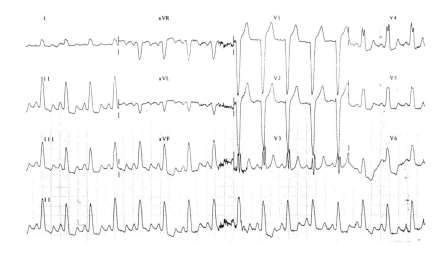

Fig. 3.13b

2.	*(Figure 3.13b)*	**True**	**False**
(a)	There is P pulmonale	❏	❏
(b)	There is a normal axis	❏	❏
(c)	The rate is 96 bpm	❏	❏
(d)	There is a left bundle branch block pattern	❏	❏
(e)	The pattern shown is a normal variant seen in healthy people	❏	❏

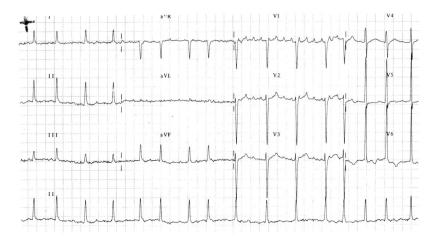

Fig. 3.13c

3.	*(Figure 3.13c)*	True	False
(a)	There is a normal axis	❑	❑
(b)	There is evidence of right ventricular hypertrophy	❑	❑
(c)	There is evidence of an old inferior infarct	❑	❑
(d)	The patient is at increased risk of stroke	❑	❑
(e)	Cardioversion should be attempted if this is a new sustained rhythm	❑	❑

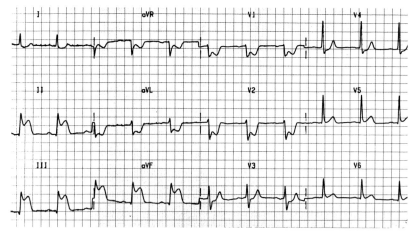

Fig. 3.13d

4.	(Figure 3.13d)	**True**	**False**
(a)	The patient is in sinus rhythm	❏	❏
(b)	The axis is normal	❏	❏
(c)	There is evidence of pericarditis	❏	❏
(d)	The patient should be given thrombolytic therapy	❏	❏
(e)	This patient is at increased risk of complete heart block	❏	❏

Fig. 3.13e

5.	(Figure 3.13e)	**True**	**False**
(a)	There is a sinus tachycardia	❏	❏
(b)	The axis is deviating to the left	❏	❏
(c)	There is evidence of an inferior MI	❏	❏
(d)	There is a left bundle branch block pattern	❏	❏
(e)	This patient will classically demonstrate a respiratory alkalosis	❏	❏

STATION 3.14

Investigation

Please state whether the following statements regarding the radiographs shown opposite are **True** or **False**.

(5 minute station)

		True	False
1.	*(Figure 3.14a)*		
(a)	This is a PA chest radiograph	❏	❏
(b)	There is fluid in the horizontal fissure	❏	❏
(c)	The patient is wearing a cardiac monitor	❏	❏
(d)	There is a right-sided chest drain in situ	❏	❏
(e)	This patient should be given intravenous diuretics	❏	❏

		True	False
2.	*(Figure 3.14b)*		
(a)	This is an AP chest radiograph	❏	❏
(b)	There is upper lobe blood diversion	❏	❏
(c)	There are Kerley B lines	❏	❏
(d)	The cardiothoracic ratio is normal	❏	❏
(e)	This patient will characteristically have cannon waves of the JVP	❏	❏

		True	False
3.	*(Figure 3.14c)*		
(a)	This CXR is overpenetrated	❏	❏
(b)	There are hyperexpanded lung fields	❏	❏
(c)	There is loss of the atrial appendage	❏	❏
(d)	There is cardiomegaly	❏	❏
(e)	These radiological findings are associated with mitral stenosis	❏	❏

		True	False
4.	*(Figure 3.14d)*		
(a)	This is an AP chest X-ray	❏	❏
(b)	There is a left pleural effusion	❏	❏
(c)	The cardiothoracic ratio is increased	❏	❏
(d)	The cardiac silhouette is normal	❏	❏
(e)	A cause of this appearance is lead toxicity	❏	❏

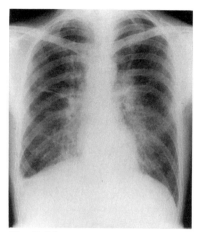

Fig. 3.14a

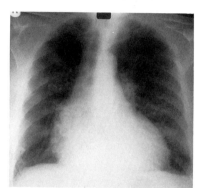

Fig. 3.14b

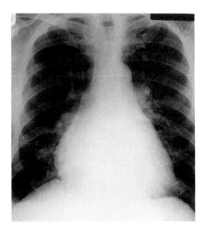

Fig. 3.14c

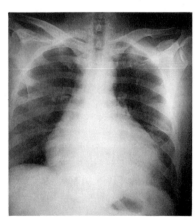

Fig. 3.14d

STATION 3.15

Investigation

The coronary angiogram shown in figure 3.15b is taken from a 43-year-old man who has recently had an acute myocardial infarction.

(10 minute station)

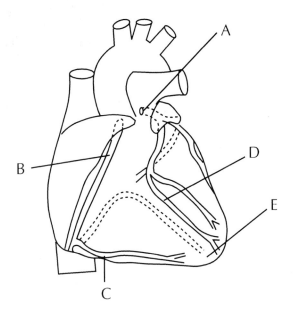

Fig. 3.15a

Please label the structures (A) to (E) in Figure 3.15a and (F) in Figure 3.15b: then answer the following questions.

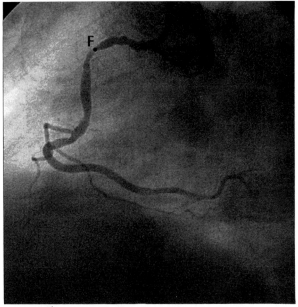

Fig. 3.15b

1. From the angiogram (Figure 3.15b), which ECG leads would demonstrate the infarct?
2. What other changes associated with this type of infarct may be seen on the ECG?
3. What intervention would you recommend for this patient?

STATION 3.16

Investigation

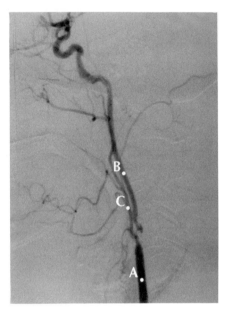

Fig. 3.16

This is a radiograph of a 61-year-old man with a 6-month history of transient ischaemic attacks.

(5 minute station)

A. 1. Name the investigation performed
   2. Name the structures labelled A, B and C
   3. State the abnormality shown
   4. State the principles of treating this condition

B.   Answer the following questions by ticking '**Yes**' or '**No**'

		Yes	No
1.	Amaurosis fugax is caused by:		
(a)	diminished blood supply to the brain	❑	❑
(b)	increased intra-ocular pressure	❑	❑
(c)	microemboli to the retinal artery	❑	❑
(d)	spasm of the retinal artery	❑	❑

		Yes	No
2.	A carotid angiogram is commonly performed by accessing through:		
(a)	the common carotid artery	❑	❑
(b)	the brachial artery	❑	❑
(c)	the abdominal aorta	❑	❑
(d)	the common femoral artery	❑	❑

		Yes	No
3.	Carotid artery disease is associated with:		
(a)	Raynaud's phenomenon	❑	❑
(b)	diabetes mellitus	❑	❑
(c)	hypercholesterolaemia	❑	❑
(d)	smoking	❑	❑

		Yes	No
4.	Carotid artery disease may lead to:		
(a)	blindness on the affected side	❑	❑
(b)	slurring of speech	❑	❑
(c)	cerebral atrophy on the affected side	❑	❑
(d)	stroke on the affected side	❑	❑

STATION 3.17

Investigation

Figure 3.17 is a radiograph of a 68-year-old man with peripheral vascular disease (PVD).

(5 minute station)

1. (a) What is this investigation called?
   (b) State the abnormality shown
   (c) State two risk factors for this lesion
   (d) List two presenting symptoms in this patient

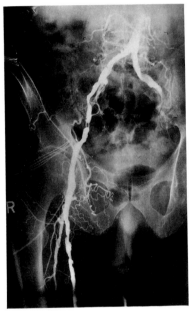

Fig. 3.17

2. Answer the following questions by ticking the appropriate answer.

	True	False
(a) PVD is rarely associated with smoking	☐	☐
(b) Diabetes mellitus is a risk factor for PVD	☐	☐
(c) Surgery is usually indicated for PVD	☐	☐
(d) Surgical treatment of PVD is usually palliative	☐	☐

STATION 3.18

Therapeutics

You are a house officer on a general medical firm. You have been asked to explain to a 47-year-old woman with newly diagnosed angina how and when to use her GTN spray.

(5 minute station)

STATION 3.19

1. Please label the diagram of the nephron (A) – (K)

(5 minute station)

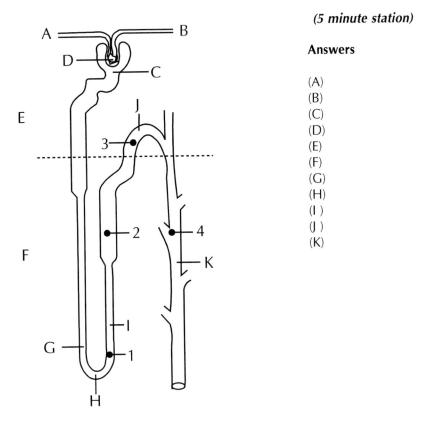

Answers

(A)
(B)
(C)
(D)
(E)
(F)
(G)
(H)
(I)
(J)
(K)

Fig. 3.19

2. Please indicate at which site, (1) – (4), the following diuretics act

		Site
(a)	Spironolactone	( )
(b)	Frusemide	( )
(c)	Bendrofluazide	( )
(d)	Amiloride	( )
(e)	Metolazone	( )
(f)	Bumetanide	( )

STATION 3.20

Therapeutics

Please match the patient histories with the most appropriate medication and its described side-effect.

(5 minute station)

Patient history	Drug	Side-effect
1. A 71-year-old man with paroxysmal atrial fibrillation complaining of grey skin, feeling jittery and disliking the hot weather	(A) Atenolol	(a) Xanthopsia
2. A 41-year-old woman with bradycardia and atrial fibrillation on her ECG complaining of nausea and 'yellow vision'	(B) Nifedipine	(b) Peripheral neuropathy
3. A 61-year old man who is 36 hours post acute myocardial infarction now complaining of dyspnoea and worsening wheeze	(C) Sotalol	(c) Fluid retention and vasodilatation
4. A 79-year-old woman with hypertension complaining of flushing, headaches and swollen ankles	(D) Amiodarone	(d) Worsening heart failure and postural hypotension
5. A 27-year-old woman with Wolff-Parkinson-White syndrome complaining of parasthesiae in the fingers	(E) Digoxin	(e) Skin pigmentation and thyrotoxicosis
6. A 51-year-old woman with atrial fibrillation complaining of increasing exertional dyspnoea,and PND, associated with dizziness on standing	(F) Flecainide	(f) Bronchospasm/ asthma

Answers

1. ( ) ( )
2. ( ) ( )
3. ( ) ( )

4. ( ) ( )
5. ( ) ( )
6. ( ) ( )

STATION 3.21

Therapeutics

You are the house officer on call for general medicine. In the hospital in which you work it is policy to obtain verbal consent prior to giving a patient thrombolysis. Please obtain verbal consent from a 46-year-old man who has been 'fast tracked' from the Accident and Emergency Department with an acute anterior myocardial infarction.

(5 minute station)

STATION 3.22

Therapeutics

Mrs Debra Thomas is an 88-year-old woman with known myelodysplasia. She has been admitted for a 'top up' transfusion under the Care of the Elderly firm on which you are the house officer. Her last transfusion was 2 weeks ago and the notes confirm she is blood group A rhesus positive. No abnormal antibodies have been reported. Her Hb, checked yesterday by her GP, was 5.2 g/dl. She is on Flemming ward in St. Peter's Hospital under the care of Dr Little. Her DOB is 13/09/09 and unit number is 123432. She is to have four units of packed cells to start this afternoon.

Please fill in the cross match form (the transfusion form where details of blood units would be entered by the laboratory personnel and cross-checked by you is shown in Figure 3.22a opposite) and then write up the blood transfusion on the IV fluid prescription chart (Figure 3.22b, page 84) provided.

(5 minute station)

HEALTH AUTHORITY .... HOSPITAL

REQUEST FOR BLOOD FOR TRANSFUSION AND/OR GROUPING

Patient's surname	first name(s)	sex	date of birth	Ward/dept.	Hospital No.	Ethnic orig.

Consultant..   Signature of doctor
                                                                    making this request

Patient identified and blood taken by.......................... at .... hours on *(date)*......................

Clinical Diagnosis.. Hb .... g/dl.

Nature of operation or other reason for Transfusion ....

Previous Transfusions?.. Group (if known) ....

Reactions?...

Pregnancies?.. E.D.D. ....

Have Antibodies been reported?...

REQUEST FOR:
Please tick or number box as appropriate

☐	Group Only *Serum will be kept for 7 days*
☐	packs immediately unchecked to save life ⎫
☐	packs urgent ⎬ *Telephone Hospital Blood Bank*
☐	packs whole for use at .... a.m./p.m. on...
☐	concentrated cells for use at .... a.m./p.m. on...

For other blood products telephone Hospital Blood Bank
Blood will be issued only if this form is properly completed and is accompanied by a correctly labelled specimen of the patient's blood.

RECORD OF TRANSFUSION   Complete in ward. At end of transfusion affix to notes.

PATIENT'S BLOOD GROUP...............   RHESUS (D).......................
The following packs are compatible with patient's serum **ANTIBODIES:**.................................
They will be returned to stock at .... hours on (date) ....

PACK NUMBER	GROUP	RHESUS	EXPIRY DATE	PACK PUT UP BY		COMMENTS	SIGNATURE
				TIME	DATE		

BLOOD TRANSFUSION   In the event of a reaction stop transfusion and notify laboratory

Signature...
Date...

14498 GHRJ

Fig. 3.22a – Blood transfusion request form

HEALTH AUTHORITY   **24 HOUR INTRAVENOUS FLUID PRESCRIPTION CHART**

DATE					FOR PATIENTS WITH MORE THAN ONE INTRAVENOUS LINE					
CONSULTANT			WARD		Use computer label if available Unit No.					
HOUSE OFFICER			HOSPITAL		Surname			Forenames		
DRUG IDIOSYNCRASY					Address			Sex . M/F		
								D of B		
								Weight		

					PRESCRIPTION FOR DRUGS TO BE ADDED TO FULL BOTTLE					
TYPE OF IV FLUID	VOLUME	INFUSION RATE	TIME STARTED	NURSES SIGNATURE	DRUG ADDED AND SOLVENT	DOSE OF DRUG	H.O's SIG	ADDITION TIME	ADDED BY	PHARM

INTRAVENOUS LINE 1 ; SPECIFY TYPE (eg CVP, Peripheral)   LABEL LINE

INTRAVENOUS LINE 2 ; SPECIFY TYPE (eg CVP, Peripheral)   LABEL LINE

INTRAVENOUS LINE 3 ; SPECIFY TYPE (eg CVP, Peripheral)   LABEL LINE

INTRAVENOUS FLUID THERAPY SHOULD BE REVIEWED EVERY 24 HOURS AND ALL PREVIOUS REGIMENS CANCELLED
NOTE: THE PRESCRIPTIONS FOR INTRAVENOUS FEEDING MUST BE COMPLETED BY NOON TO ALLOW PHARMACY TO PREPARE THE PRODUCT.

Fig. 3.22b – Intravenous fluid form

STATION 3.23

Therapeutics

You are the house officer on call. You have been called to the ward by the nursing staff to see a patient who has become pyrexial and is having rigors whilst receiving their second unit of a 3 unit blood transfusion. Please explain to the examiner what you would do at the bed side and what instructions you would give the nursing staff.

(5 minute station)

Varicose veins

Varicose veins are thin-walled, tortuous, dilated and lengthened, with incompetent valves. The incompetence may be primary, often with a family history, or secondary to deep venous thrombosis. On rare occasions the veins are part of a congenital vascular malformation or an acquired arteriovenous fistula. Incompetence gives rise to venous hypertension when standing, and this increases tissue fluid, with swelling and subsequent trophic skin changes. The latter are due to poor skin nutrition with slow healing of any minor trauma and, eventually, ulceration.

Symptoms are very variable, often worse in warm weather and during pregnancy. In the history it should be established whether the veins are primary, starting in the teens with a family history, or postphlebitic with or without anticoagulation. The presenting problem is often cosmetic, and there may be aching, particularly at the end of the day, after prolonged standing with heaviness, cramps and swelling. Note symptoms of eczema, itching, pigmentation, bleeding or chronic ulceration.

On examination note the distribution of the veins; long saphenous varices outnumber short saphenous by about seven to one. There may be skin changes of eczema, pigmentation or ulceration. The features of ulceration and the differential diagnoses are considered in station 3.25. Look and feel for cough impulses over the saphenofemoral and the saphenopopliteal junctions, and see if there is a propagated tap impulse distally along a length of abnormal vein, denoting incompetence.

The use of a tourniquet at sites along a limb, after emptying the veins, indicates where dependent filling can be controlled or whether there is leaking of blood from the deep to superficial veins, through incompetent perforators below the level of the tourniquet.

Apply a below-knee venous tourniquet and ask the patient to stand on tip-toes ten times. If the deep veins are blocked the muscle pump forces blood into the superficial varices, whereas, with normal deep veins, the pump empties the superficial system. The use of a doppler ultrasonic probe is an effective means of identifying reversal of the superficial venous flow, incompetent perforators and abnormalities of the deep system.

Deep venous thrombosis (DVT)

Thrombosis is characteristically attributed to Virchow's triad of venous stasis, coaguable states and endothelial injury; however it is usually due to more than one of these contributing factors. A number of conditions predispose to this problem; they include operative procedures, particularly of the hip joint, pregnancy and female gender, ageing (> 40), obesity, malignancy and previous DVT. The most common site of origin of a DVT is in the soleal plexus of the calf. Propagation occurs into the popliteal, femoral and, occasionally, ilial veins. Symptomatically DVT may go unnoticed but suspicion should be raised by any leg pain or swelling in patients at risk, particularly in the post-operative period.

In patients with no identifiable risk, a procoagulant or thrombophilia screen should be undertaken. This should include FBC, INR, APPT, Protein C and S levels, factor V Leiden and anti-cardiolipin antibody.

On examination there may be a low grade pyrexia and swelling. Tenderness in the calf and along the length of the lower limb veins may be slight or marked and, in extreme cases, result in venous gangrene. However, the signs, like the symptoms, may be minimal, requiring careful examination for traces of peripheral oedema, and palpation of the length of the calf and popliteal fossa, and along the anteromedial thigh, for tenderness. The diagnosis can usually be confirmed by ultrasonic doppler scanning.

The clinical importance of DVT is the danger of pulmonary embolism during the developing phase and the late sequelae of the postphlebitic syndrome (Station 3.25). For this reason prophylactic subcutaneous heparin is prescribed in high risk patients with anti-embolic compression stockings; proven DVT is treated with full anticoagulation.

STATION 3.24

Examination

A 38-year-old lady attends your surgery complaining of aching in her legs. She has had varicose veins for 20 years, starting after the first of her three pregnancies, the symptoms have recently been getting worse: there is no history of DVT. Please outline how you would examine this lady's legs, indicating sites of interest on the leg diagram (Figure 3.24) provided.

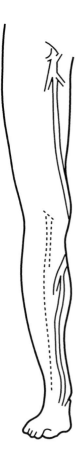

Fig. 3.24

STATION 3.25

Examination

You are a medical student in a surgical outpatient department, when a 67-year-old lady is referred with recurrence of her leg ulcer (Figure 3.25 on page 165): this has been present intermittently for over 8 years.

Please comment on the ulcer, and state what additional symptoms and signs you must look for in this patient.

(5 minute station)

STATION 3.26

Therapeutics

Preparatory Station

You are the house officer on a medical firm, caring for a 23-year-old woman who has been treated for an OCP induced right lower limb DVT.

(5 minute station)

You should mention the following

1. Compliance: important to take dose prescribed as this will keep patient's blood at the correct dilution; stress importance of not missing doses.
2. Effect: 'thins blood'
3. Side-effects
   a Haemorrhage: if there are any problems with ongoing bleeding the patient should seek medical attention immediately.
   b Easy bruising
   c Others – rare: nausea, rashes
4. Warfarin/anticoagulant clinic: visit 1 x fortnight. Warfarin book will explain treatment.
5. Duration of therapy: 3–6 months

6. Contraception: must not use OCP; other methods, seek guidance from G.P.
7. Interactions with other drugs: antiepileptics, antibiotics, you should attempt to answer any questions she may have.

STATION 3.26a

Therapeutic

You are the house officer attached to a general medical firm. You have been asked to explain warfarin treatment to a 23-year-old patient, who was admitted 5 days ago with a right ileo femoral DVT. She was previously on the OCP. Please discuss the treatment, side-effects and any other relevant information with the patient.

(10 minute station)

4: RESPIRATORY MEDICINE

SYMPTOMS

Shortness of breath (dyspnoea)
Clarify whether dyspnoea occurs on exertion or at rest. The exercise tolerance should be quantified in terms of:

- Distance patient can walk – on the flat/up a hill/up a flight of stairs
- If immobile – define by activities of daily living (e.g. washing themselves, dressing, eating, transferring from bed to chair)
- What causes the patient to stop, i.e. is it shortness of breath; angina; claudication?

The cause of dyspnoea is usually characterised by its associations.
- **Cough**
  Productive or non-productive
  Nocturnal – may be a sign of asthma or aspiration
- **Sputum**
  Colour
  Consistency
  Volume
- **Haemoptysis**
  Volume
  Fresh or altered blood

Haemoptysis is a sinister symptom, particularly in smokers, and should always be taken seriously. Persistent haemoptysis requires investigation.

Causes of haemoptysis
- **Upper respiratory tract**
  Epistaxis; upper respiratory tract infection
- **Pharyngeal lesions**
  Carcinoma
- **Lower respiratory tract**
  Benign and malignant tumours of the lung:
      Pneumonia and tuberculosis
      Bronchiectasis
      Abscess
      Pulmonary embolism
      Trauma

- **General causes**
  Blood dyscrasia and coagulopathy

Wheeze
This is a sign of bronchospasm. Causes include asthma, chronic airflow limitation, pulmonary oedema (cardiac asthma) and allergic response.

Orthopnoea
This is defined by the number of pillows that the patient sleeps with. Always ask why the patient sleeps with this number of pillows; not every patient with four pillows is breathless when lying flat!

Chest pain
Principally pleuritic pain, i.e. sharp pain which is worsened by deep inspiration and is said to catch the patient as they take a breath. Define the pain in terms of character, site, radiation and relieving/exacerbating factors.

Stridor
This is an upper airways symptom of obstruction; it may be caused by lesions or severe infection from the pharynx to the carina of the trachea.

Causes of shortness of breath
- **Respiratory**
  Asthma, chronic airways disease, pneumonia, pulmonary embolism, pulmonary fibrosis, lymphangitis carcinomatosis
- **Cardiac**
  Silent angina, arrhythmia, pulmonary oedema
- **Neuromuscular**
  Guillain-Barré, motor neurone disease, muscular dystrophy
- **Miscellaneous**
  Anaemia, obesity, hysteria, ketoacidosis

STATION 4.1   *(Answers – page 282)*

History

You are the house officer on a general medical firm. You have been asked to see a 23-year-old asthmatic man who has presented with acute shortness of breath. He is breathless but able to speak in stilted sentences. His PEFR is 220 l/min.

Please take a history of the presenting complaint with any other relevant history you feel is necessary.

(5 minute station)

STATION 4.2

History

You are a medical student attached to a GP practice. The next patient is a 49-year-old man with a cough.

Please take a history of the presenting complaint and any other relevant history with a view to making a diagnosis.

(5 minute station)

STATION 4.3

History

You are a medical student attached to a respiratory unit. You have been asked to take a history from a 61-year-old new patient in the chest clinic who has been sent by his GP with 'worsening shortness of breath–chronic airways disease'.

Please take a history of the presenting complaint and other relevant history with a view to making a diagnosis.

(5 minute station)

STATION 4.4

History

You are the house officer on a busy respiratory unit. You have been asked to admit a 63-year-old man from the outpatient clinic with haemoptysis.

Please take a history of the presenting complaint and other relevant history with a view to making a diagnosis.

(5 minute station)

STATION 4.5

History

You are a medical student attached to a GP practice. The next patient is an 18-year-old female A-level student who has come to see the GP with acute shortness of breath and chest pain.

Please take a history of the presenting complaint and any other relevant history, with a view to making a diagnosis.

(5 minute station)

STATION 4.6

History

You are a medical student attached to a GP surgery. The next patient is a 16-year-old schoolboy who is complaining of shortness of breath.

Please take a history of the presenting complaint and any other relevant history, with a view to making a diagnosis.

(5 minute station)

STATION 4.7

Investigation

The patients listed below complain of shortness of breath Please match the patient history with the most appropriate diagnosis and FBC result.

(5 minute station)

Patient history	FBC	Diagnosis
1. A 72-year-old smoker with chronic type II respiratory failure	(A) Hb 12.2 WCC 12.2 Plats 2507	(a) Haemolytic anaemia secondary to sickle cell disease
2. A 61-year-old woman with rheumatoid arthritis on Naproxen	(B) Hb 7.2 MCV 104 WCC 4.7 Plats 211 Film - lymphopenia, reticulocytosis	(b) Thrombocytosis
3. A 79-year-old woman with confirmed PE on V/Q scan	(C) Hb 5.4 MCV 65 WCC 6.4 Plats 201	(c) Polycythaemia
4. A 22-year-old woman with mycoplasma pneumonia	(D) Hb 5.4 MCV 102 WCC 12 Plats 173 Film - reticulocytosis, red cell fragmentation	(d) Microcytic anaemia
5. A 27-year-old African man with bony pain and pneumonia	(E) Hb 20.6 Hct 57.2 WCC 20.2 Plats 416	(e) Haemolytic anaemia secondary to atypical pneumonia

Answers

1. ( ) ( )
2. ( ) ( )
3. ( ) ( )

4. ( ) ( )
5. ( ) ( )

STATION 4.8

Investigation

The patients below all have pulmonary lesions on their CXR. Please match the patient histories with the most appropriate biochemical marker and diagnosis.

(5 minute station)

Patient history	Biochemical marker	Diagnosis
1. A 49-year-old man with dyspnoea, wheeze, flushing and diarrhoea	(A) Na⁺ 145 K⁺ 2.1	(a) Liver metastases
2. A 56-year-old woman with vomiting and confusion	(B) Albumin 31 AST 57 Alk Phos 567	(b) Ectopic ACTH
3. A 61-year-old man with confusion and seizures	(C) 5-HIAA	(c) Ectopic parathormone
4. A 68-year-old woman with jaundice and 8 cm hepatomegaly	(D) CCa⁺⁺ 4.07	(d) SIADH
5. A 47-year-old man with striae, hypertension, proximal myopathy and oedema	(E) Na⁺ 106 K⁺ 3.9	(e) Carcinoid syndrome

Answers

1. ( ) ( )   4. ( ) ( )
2. ( ) ( )   5. ( ) ( )
3. ( ) ( )

STATION 4.9

Investigation

Match the patient histories with the most appropriate diagnosis and immunological marker.

(5 minute station)

Patient history	Immunological marker	Diagnosis
1. A 27-year-old Afro-caribbean woman with shortness of breath and erythema nodosum	(A) anti DS - DNA antibody	(a) Churg-Strauss syndrome
2. A 39-year-old man with shortness of breath, nasal discharge and renal failure	(B) pANCA - anti-myeloperoxidase antibody	(b) Progressive systemic sclerosis
3. A 29-year-old woman with asthma, eosinophilia, purpura and peripheral neuropathy	(C) antiglomerular basement antibody	(c) Rheumatoid arthritis
4. A 67-year-old man with dyspnoea and acute renal failure 2 weeks after a flu-like illness	(D) antiSCL - 70 antibody	(d) Systemic lupus erythematosus
5. A 43-year-old woman with a symmetrical polyarthropathy and fibrosing alveolitis	(E) cANCA - anti-proteinase 3 antibody	(e) Goodpasture's syndrome
6. A 24-year-old woman with a butterfly rash, pleurisy and bilateral pleural effusions	(F) CD4 helper cell proliferation	(f) Wegener's granulomatosis
7. A 35-year-old woman with Raynaud's syndrome, dysphagia, renal failure and pulmonary fibrosis	(G) IgM directed against IgG	(g) Sarcoidosis

Answers

1. ( ) ( )
2. ( ) ( )
3. ( ) ( )
4. ( ) ( )

5. ( ) ( )
6. ( ) ( )
7. ( ) ( )

Arterial blood gases

Comment

How to interpret blood gas results
Before attempting to interpret blood gas results it is important to know the normal values and what they tell us.

- **pH 7.35–7.45;** pH < 7.35 – acidosis, pH > 7.45 – alkalosis.

- **PaCO$_2$ 4.6–6.4 Kpa.** Think of this as the **RESPIRATORY** component of pH.

- **PaO$_2$ > 10.6 Kpa;** If the pO$_2$ is less than normal, i.e. hypoxia is present, this implies respiratory failure. To decide whether this is type I or type II failure, one must look at the pCO$_2$ (see example below).

- **Saturation 96–98%.** You should refer to the O$_2$ dissociation curve to interpret desaturation.

- **HCO$_3^-$ 22–28 mmol/l.** Think of this as the **METABOLIC** component of pH.

- **Base excess ± 2.0.** This figure gives an indication of how deranged the pH has become. Negative figures imply a net loss of HCO$_3^-$ (i.e. an acidosis). This negative value indicates the amount of base (i.e. alkali) necessary to correct the acidic plasma to normal. Likewise a positive value implies an excess of alkali.

The most important elements of the arterial blood gases are summed up below.

Henderson Hasselbach equation:

$$pH \, \alpha \quad \frac{HCO_3^-}{PaCO_2} \quad = \quad \frac{\textbf{METABOLIC}}{\textbf{RESPIRATORY}}$$

If the HCO$_3^-$ is raised this causes a metabolic alkalosis. To compensate this would mean one would have to produce a respiratory acidosis, i.e. one would have to retain CO$_2$ (slow the respiratory rate significantly) which is impossible. However, in a patient with a chronic respiratory acidosis, i.e. CO$_2$ retainers, there may be a compensation by the kidneys with a resultant retention of HCO_3^-. Therefore the pH may be normal. This is termed a compensated respiratory acidosis.

Respiratory failure

Students often get very confused at the mere mention of respiratory failure. Hopefully this simple explanation will dispel the mysticism on this subject!

By definition if the PaO_2 is subnormal, i.e. < 10.6 Kpa, this implies respiratory failure.

One must then decide whether the respiratory failure is type I or II.

Type I respiratory failure

Subjects with a normal respiratory drive use an increase in $PaCO_2$ to increase their respiratory rate, i.e. hypercapnic drive. Type I failure can be thought of as failure of gaseous exchange, i.e. anything that may disrupt the passage of oxygen from the alveolar space to the red blood cells.

If they become hypoxic they can be given high flow oxygen, i.e. 35–100%.

Causes of type I respiratory failure

- Pneumonia – particularly atypical pneumonias
- Asthma
- Pulmonary oedema
- Pulmonary fibrosis, pulmonary embolism

Remember: all causes of type I failure may cause type II failure when the patient becomes tired or the pathological process in the lungs becomes overwhelming.

Type II respiratory failure

These patients have an abnormal respiratory drive. They are chronic CO_2 retainers and therefore the respiratory centres in the brain stem have converted to hypoxic drive. These patients, if given high flow oxygen, will slow their respiratory rate, eventually leading to apnoea and CO_2 narcosis. Such patients should be given 24–28% O_2, remembering the O_2 content of air is approximately 20%.

Causes of type II respiratory failure
- Chronic airflow limitation (chronic bronchitis and emphysema)
- Obesity (Pickwickian syndrome)
- Chest trauma
- Neuromuscular disease – Guillain-Barré, muscular dystrophy, myasthenia gravis
- Drug overdose – opiates, sedatives

Clinically, patients may be divided into 'pink puffers' and 'blue bloaters'. Pink puffers are thin, pink and classically have type I failure caused by emphysema. Blue bloaters are obese, cyanosed and have type II failure caused by chronic bronchitis. Blue bloaters are the patients that get sleep apnoea (Pickwickian syndrome). Although this division is still applicable clinically, post mortem examination has revealed that many pink puffers have chronic bronchitis and, likewise, many blue bloaters have emphysema.

Consider this example
A 27-year-old man with poorly controlled asthma presents in the Accident and Emergency Department with severe dyspnoea. His wife says he has been unwell for 3 days with a 'cold' and has been coughing up green sputum.

His arterial blood gases, taken on air, are shown below:
> pH 7.21
> $PaCO_2$ 6.98
> PaO_2 7.2
> Sats 82%
> HCO_3^- 17
> Base excess – 5.2

These are the steps you should follow when interpreting any blood gases.

- **Does the patient have respiratory failure?**
  The patient has PaO_2 of 7.2 which by definition means he does have respiratory failure.
- **If respiratory failure is present, is it type I or II?**
  The $PaCO_2$ is greater than 6.4 therefore this patient is retaining CO_2 and has type II failure. This patient has a low HCO_3^- but if it were raised it would imply chronic CO_2 retention with a compensatory metabolic alkalosis.

- **Is the patient acidotic or alkalotic?**
  The pH is below 7.35, therefore there is an acidosis present.
- **Is the pH derangement due to respiratory or metabolic problems?**
  The respiratory element, i.e. the $PaCO_2$, is raised therefore there is a respiratory acidosis. The metabolic element, the HCO_3^-, is low which means there is a metabolic acidosis as well.

This patient has type II respiratory failure with a mixed respiratory and metabolic acidosis. In an asthmatic this is a sinister combination, implying the patient is exhausted and will require assisted ventilation.

Formal respiratory function tests
Early detection and progression of respiratory disease may be followed at the bedside using a peak flow meter. This measures the PEFR (peak expiratory flow rate) and will vary with age, sex and height.

Patients with suspected respiratory disease or with dyspnoea of uncertain cause may be sent for formal respiratory function testing. This involves spirometry which measures the FEV_1 and FVC and can be used to assess reversibility of their dyspnoea after nebulised respiratory stimulants, such as salbutamol.

The ratio of the FEV_1:FVC is normally 75%. A restrictive lung defect causes a reduction in the FEV_1 and FVC to a similar extent so that the ratio remains the same or may increase. An obstructive defect causes a relatively larger reduction in the FEV_1 compared to the FVC so that the ratio is less than normal.

i.e. FEV_1:FVC < 75%   = obstructive defect
     FEV_1:FVC ≥ 75%   = restrictive defect

The transfer coefficient, TKco, is an indication of how effectively gaseous exchange is occurring. It is therefore affected by the elements that make up alveolar/ capillary gaseous exchange:

- The effective alveolar surface – alveolar surface area integrity
- The Hb concentration
- Ventilation/perfusion matching.

Causes of a reduced transfer coefficient include emphysema, fibrotic lung disease and pulmonary oedema. Causes of an increase include asthma, sarcoidosis and pulmonary haemorrhage. The transfer coefficient is useful in distinguishing similar clinical disorders such as asthma and emphysema.

STATION 4.10

Investigation

Match the patient histories with the most appropriate set of blood gas results (taken on air) and the therapy that should be initiated. You should write the inferred diagnoses for each set of blood gas results, e.g. type II respiratory failure with a metabolic acidosis.

(5 minute station)

Patient history	Blood gases	Therapy
1. A 24-year-old man with a viral respiratory tract infection now presenting with weakness and numbness in the legs and acute breathlessness	(A) pH 7.52 $PaCO_2$ 2.1 PaO_2 14.2 sats 100% HCO_3^- 22	(a) 60% O_2/ heparin
2. A 49-year-old man with acute dyspnoea 4 hours after being admitted with a large anterior myocardial infarction	(B) pH 7.20 $PaCO_2$ 8.4 PaO_2 4.7 sats 72% HCO_3^- 36	(b) Paper bag/ reassurance
3. A 62-year-old chronic smoker with a cough, green sputum and acute dyspnoea	(C) pH 7.52 $PaCO_2$ 2.4 PaO_2 6.5 sats 86% HCO_3^- 23	(c) IPV/ plasmapheresis
4. A 26-year-old woman with acute dyspnoea, haemoptysis and pleuritic chest pain	(D) pH 7.42 $PaCO_2$ 6.9 PaO_2 8.2 sats 89% HCO_3^- 24	(d) 60% O_2/ diuretics
5. A 14-year-old schoolgirl who became acutely dyspnoeic, dizzy and has carpopedal spasm during a pop concert	(E) pH 7.20 $PaCO_2$ 4.5 PaO_2 7.5 sats 83% HCO_3^- 16	(e) 24% O_2/ nebuliser

Answers   Inferred diagnoses from ABGs

1. ( ) ( )   1.
2. ( ) ( )   2.
3. ( ) ( )   3.
4. ( ) ( )   4.
5. ( ) ( )   5.

STATION 4.11

Investigation

The three patients below have been sent from the chest clinic for investigation of shortness of breath. Their formal respiratory function tests are shown. Please answer the questions below regarding the results.

(5 minute station)

Patient (A)   27-year-old woman with rheumatoid arthritis now presenting with a 6-month history of shortness of breath
$FEV_1 = 3.0$ Oxygen saturation on air – 92%
$FVC = 3.8$ Transfer coefficient – grossly reduced

Patient (B)   69-year-old man with 2-year history of exertional dyspnoea and an episodic cough.
$FEV_1 = 2.5$ Oxygen saturation on air – 89%
$FVC = 3.7$ Transfer coefficient – reduced

Patient (C)   22-year-old woman with 2-month history of worsening shortness of breath and fatigue on exertion and repetitive movements.
$FEV_1 = 3.7$ Oxygen saturation on air – 95%
$FVC = 4.6$ Transfer coefficient – normal

Which of these patients:	A	B	C
1. Demonstrates a restrictive lung defect?	❏	❏	❏
2. Demonstrates an obstructive lung defect?	❏	❏	❏
3. Will have type I respiratory failure?	❏	❏	❏
4. Will typically demonstrate type II respiratory failure?	❏	❏	❏
5. Should be treated with nebulisers?	❏	❏	❏
6. Is most likely to have a thymoma?	❏	❏	❏
7. Is most likely to have an associated primary lung cancer?	❏	❏	❏
8. Will classically worsen their hypoxia with exertion?	❏	❏	❏
9. May benefit from steroid therapy?	❏	❏	❏
10. May derive benefit from other forms of immunosuppression?	❏	❏	❏

The Normal Chest Radiograph (CXR)

As with all radiological imaging it is important to have a structured approach to the chest radiograph and to know the normal limits. When reading a chest X-ray one must always look at the various components, i.e. the heart, the lung fields, the hemidiaphragms, the ribs and other bones and the soft tissues. **Always check the patient details are correct for your patient before proceeding on to the more technical elements.**

- **PA or AP?**
  PA (Posteroanterior) and AP (Anteroposterior) refers to the direction the X-rays travel onto the X-ray plate: a PA plate lies on the anterior chest wall of the patient with the X-rays delivered from behind. AP plates lie behind the patient, with the X-rays directed from the front. The heart appears magnified in AP views as it lies further from a plate lying posteriorly and the X-rays are dispersed over a wider area. Technically, one should not comment on the cardiac size on an AP film.

- **Rotation**
  To decide whether a film is centred and not rotated, look at the clavicles and their relationship to one another and the rest of the thorax. On a well-centred film the clavicles are horizontal, directly opposing one another, clearly seen along their entire length, perpendicular to the rest of the thoracic cavity, and equally placed on either side of the vertebral column.

- **Penetration**
  This refers to the penetration of the X-rays through the thoracic cavity. Rays that are focused in front of the X-ray plate give poorly penetrated views. The heart and lung markings appear very dense and the vertebrae are not seen. Rays focused too far through the thoracic cavity produce over-penetrated views, with the lung markings and vertebrae becoming very prominent. (Occasionally, over penetration is used to give lesions in the lung more definition.)

- **The heart**
  The left heart border is made up (from superior to inferior) of the aortic knuckle, the left pulmonary artery, the left arterial appendage and the left ventricle. It is intimately related to the lingula lobe, a part of the upper lobe, of the left lung. Therefore consolidation within the lingula lobe causes the left heart border to become hazy and difficult to define.

The right heart border is made up of the superior vena cava and the right ventricle. It is intimately related to the right middle lobe and consolidation within this lobe causes loss of definition of the right heart border.

The heart size on a PA film should be less than half of the thoracic cavity at its widest point. This is called the cardiothoracic ratio (CTR), and should be < 0.50.

- **The lungs**
  The left lung has two lobes, the upper, incorporating the lingula lobe, which lies anteriorly and the lower lobe which lies posteriorly. The right lung has three, the upper, middle and lower lobes. The right lung is divided by the horizontal fissure, which becomes visible on X-ray when fluid filled. The lungs are both divided radiologically into 3 zones. The upper zone incorporates the apices and extends from the apex to the 2nd anterior rib. The midzone extends from the 2nd to 4th anterior ribs, and the lower zones extend from the 4th to the 6th anterior ribs.

- **Hyperexpansion**
  To decide whether the lung fields are hyperexpanded, two conditions must apply.

(a) Seven or more **anterior** ribs should be visible, (however this will also apply if a patient takes a deep inspiration). The ribs, in a hyperextended view, often look 'flattened' or very horizontal, as do the hemidiaphragms.

(b) The precise way of establishing hyperexpansion is to draw a line between the costodiaphragmatic angle (A) and the cardiodiaphragmatic angle (B) (figure 4A). A perpendicular is then drawn from the mid point of the diaphragm (x). The distance from the diaphragm to the original line should be 1.0 cm or more. If this distance is less than 1.0 cm the diaphragms are 'flattened' and the lung fields are said to be hyperexpanded.

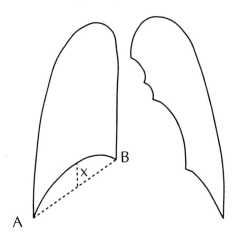

Fig. 4A

- **Bones**
  There should be no more than 6 anterior ribs seen on a PA film, unless a deep inspiration has been made or there is hyperexpansion. One should comment on whether the ribs and other bones look normal or osteopenic, whether there are any fractures or evidence of arthritis. The rib spacing is greatly reduced with underlying lung collapse and is termed 'crowding'.

- **Diaphragm**
  The right hemidiaphragm should lie 1–2 cm higher than the left. Blunting, or loss of the costodiaphragmatic angles implies an effusion. Always check both costodiaphragmatic angles are present on film. If they are not, one should repeat the film prior to commenting on it. The left hemidiaphragm usually has the gastric bubble below, do not confuse this with pneumoperitoneum caused by perforation of a viscus.

- **Soft tissues**
  Always check for calcified masses, air in the soft tissues (surgical emphysema) and, in women, the 2 breast shadows.

STATION 4.12

Please label the chest radiograph and answer the questions shown below.

(5 minute station)

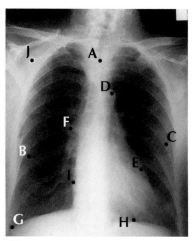

Fig. 4.12

Answers

(A)	(F)
(B)	(G)
(C)	(H)
(D)	(I)
(E)	(J)

		True	False
1.	This is a PA chest radiograph	❏	❏
2.	There is evidence of hyperexpansion	❏	❏
3.	The cardiothoracic ratio is increased	❏	❏
4.	There is calcification in the left pulmonary artery	❏	❏
5.	There is upper lobe blood diversion	❏	❏
6.	The tracheal position is normal	❏	❏
7.	The costodiaphragmatic angles are normal	❏	❏
8.	There is a fracture of the posterior part of the left 4th rib	❏	❏
9.	There is surgical emphysema	❏	❏
10.	This X-ray shows evidence of a perforated viscus	❏	❏

STATION 4.13

Investigation

Please indicate whether the statements about the radiographs shown below are **True** or **False**.

(10 minute station)

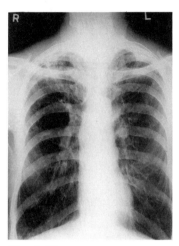

Fig. 4.13a

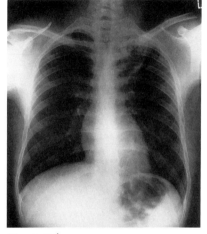

Fig. 4.13b

(a)	*(Figure 4.13a)*	True	False
1.	This is a PA CXR	❑	❑
2.	The hilar are enlarged	❑	❑
3.	There is pulmonary pruning	❑	❑
4.	There is hyperexpansion of the lung	❑	❑
5.	This patient has evidence of apical fibrosis	❑	❑

(b)	*(Figure 4.13b)*	True	False
1.	This CXR is poorly penetrated	❑	❑
2.	The X-ray is rotated	❑	❑
3.	There is cavitation in the left upper lobe	❑	❑
4.	One cause of this appearance is tuberculosis	❑	❑
5.	The patient requires a bronchoscopy	❑	❑

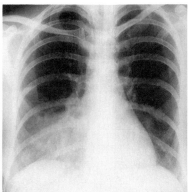

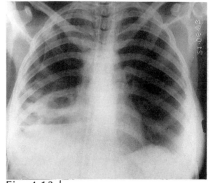

Fig. 4.13d

Fig. 4.13c

(c)	*(Figure 4.13c)*	True	False
1.	This is a well-penetrated CXR	❑	❑
2.	There is blunting of the left costodiaphragmatic angle	❑	❑
3.	There is evidence of a right lower lobe pneumonia	❑	❑
4.	The bones are osteopenic	❑	❑
5.	These appearances are characteristic of a Klebsiella pneumonia	❑	❑

(d)	*(Figure 4.13d)*	True	False
1.	This is a well penetrated CXR	❑	❑
2.	The cardiothoracic ratio is normal	❑	❑
3.	There is a right sided pneumothorax	❑	❑
4.	There is a right sided pleural effusion	❑	❑
5.	The lung fields are hyperexpanded	❑	❑

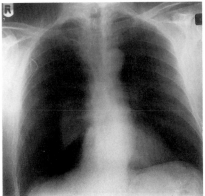

Fig. 4.13e

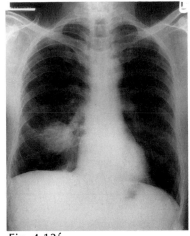

Fig. 4.13f

(e)	*(Figure 4.13e)*	True	False
1.	This is an AP CXR	❑	❑
2.	The costodiaphragmatic angles are clearly seen	❑	❑
3.	There is right midzone consolidation	❑	❑
4.	There is a chest drain in situ	❑	❑
5.	There is evidence of surgical emphysema	❑	❑

(f)	*(Figure 4.13f)*	True	False
1.	This is a well centred CXR	❑	❑
2.	There is a large right apical tumour	❑	❑
3.	There is other evidence the patient is a smoker	❑	❑
4.	There is tenting of the right hemidiaphragm	❑	❑
5.	There is evidence of bone metastases	❑	❑

STATION 4.14

Investigation

Please indicate whether the statements about the radiographs shown below are **True** or **False**.

(10 minute station)

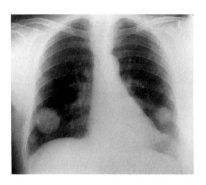

Fig. 4.14a

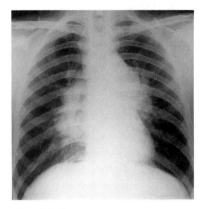

Fig. 4.14b

(a)	*(Figure 4.14a)*	True	False
1.	This is a well-penetrated CXR	❑	❑
2.	There is a left pleural effusion	❑	❑
3.	There is tenting of the right hemidiaphragm	❑	❑
4.	The multiple pulmonary lesions are consistent with cannonball metastases	❑	❑
5.	This appearance is consistent with multiple myeloma	❑	❑

(b)	*(Figure 4.14b)*	True	False
1.	This is a PA CXR	❑	❑
2.	It is rotated	❑	❑
3.	There is bilateral hilar lymph adenopathy	❑	❑
4.	There is evidence of bone metastases	❑	❑
5.	This appearance is consistent with sarcoidosis	❑	❑

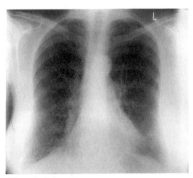

Fig. 4.14c

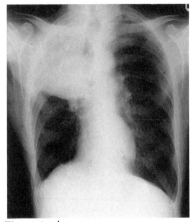

Fig. 4.14d

(c)	*(Figure 4.14c)*	**True**	**False**
1.	This is a PA chest X-ray	❏	❏
2.	The patient has made a poor inspiratory effort	❏	❏
3.	There is evidence of peribronchial thickening	❏	❏
4.	There is evidence of cardiac failure	❏	❏
5.	These appearances are caused by previous whooping cough infection	❏	❏

(d)	*(Figure 4.14d)*	**True**	**False**
1.	The cardiothoracic ratio is increased	❏	❏
2.	The left hemidiaphragm is right upper lobe collapse elevated	❏	❏
3.	There is evidence of right upper lobe collapse	❏	❏
4.	There is right middle lobe consolidation	❏	❏
5.	A cause of this appearance is a bronchogenic carcinoma	❏	❏

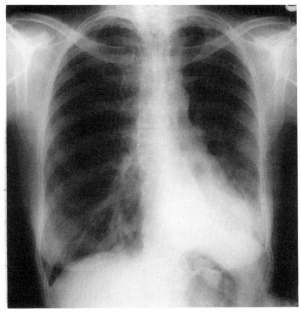

Fig. 4.14e

	True	False
(e) *(Figure 4.14e)*		
1. This patient has had a right sided mastectomy	❏	❏
2. There is evidence of mediastinal shift	❏	❏
3. There is a left apical pneumothorax	❏	❏
4. There is a 'double' left heart border	❏	❏
5. This appearance is consistent with left lower lobe collapse	❏	❏

STATION 4.15

Investigation

Please label the two CT scans of the thorax taken at the level of the clavicles and the mid thorax.

(10 minute station)

(a)

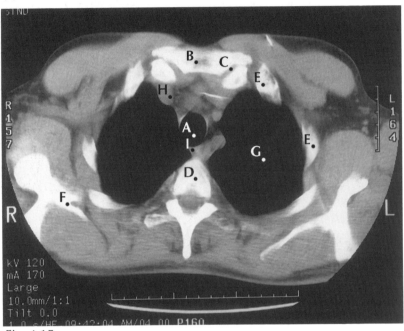

Fig. 4.15a

Answers

(A)	(F)
(B)	(G)
(C)	(H)
(D)	(I)
(E)	

(b)

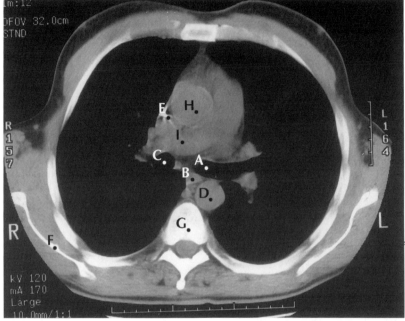

Fig. 4.15b

Answers

(A)	(F)
(B)	(G)
(C)	(H)
(D)	(I)
(E)	

STATION 4.16

Investigation

Please answer the questions about each of the investigations shown.

(5 minute station)

1. A 63-year-old woman presents with central chest pain radiating through to her back.

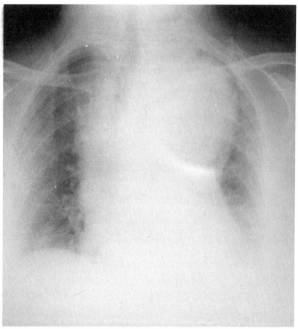

Fig. 4.16a

a. What is the investigation?
b. What does it show?

2.   A CT scan of her thorax is then performed

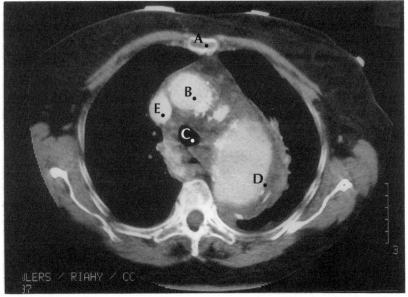

Fig. 4.16b

Label the structures A to E

(A)   (D)
(B)   (E)
(C)

3. A 27-year-old woman on the OCP is referred to the Accident and Emergency Department with pain and swelling in her left leg.

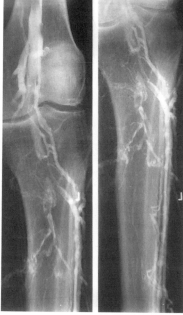

Fig. 4.16ci   Fig. 4.16cii

a. What is this investigation?
b. What does it show?
c. What is the further management?
d. List one alternative mode of investigation for this condition.

STATION 4.17

Investigation

Please answer the questions below regarding the two studies shown.

(5 minute station)

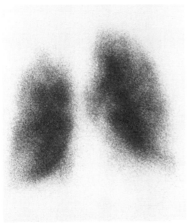

Fig. 4.17ai

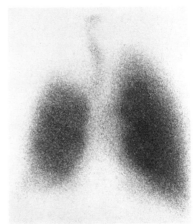

Fig. 4.17aii

(a)
1. What is this investigation?
2. What do the V and Q scans represent?
3. What do the scans show?
4. What treatment would you recommend?

(b)
1. What is this investigation?
2. What does it show?
3. What do the radio-opaque tubes represent?

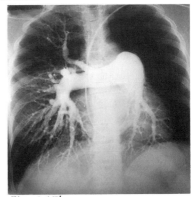

Fig. 4.17b

119

STATION 4.18

Therapeutics

> You are the house officer attached to the respiratory firm. You have been asked to explain to a newly diagnosed 22-year-old asthmatic how and when to use the inhalers.

> *(5 minute station)*

STATION 4.19

Therapeutics

> You are a GP. The next patient is a 31-year-old, poorly-controlled asthmatic, who has been placed on long-term steroids by the hospital consultant to improve her control. The patient is very worried about the steroids as she has heard 'they can do terrible things to your body'. Of note, the patient is also an insulin dependent diabetic.

> Please explain the steroid therapy to the patient, the benefits and the possible side-effects.

> *(5 minute station)*

STATION 4.20

Therapeutics

> You are a house officer attached to a chest unit. The consultant has asked you to talk to a 64-year-old chronic airways patient who is to have home oxygen therapy and does not seem to understand very much about it.

> Please explore the patient's understanding and anxieties about the therapy, and explain the benefits to her.

> *(5 minute station)*

STATION 4.21

Informed Consent

Preparatory

Please read the information below. You have 5 minutes to prepare for the next station.

You are a house officer on a respiratory firm. You have been asked to obtain informed consent from a 53-year-old man who is to have a bronchoscopy and biopsy tomorrow for a large mass in the right midzone on his CXR, which is likely to be malignant. The procedure is performed under local anaesthetic and takes about 20 minutes. The bronchoscope is about as thick as a finger and is inserted down into the 'windpipe'. The instrument is thin enough to allow the patient to breathe.

(5 minute station)

Common complications
- Sore throat postprocedure
- Some chest discomfort
- Drowsiness postprocedure

Uncommon complications
- Bleeding into the lung
- Perforation of the windpipe and smaller airways, causing pneumomediastinum, pneumothorax and surgical emphysema

If the patient incurs a significant pneumothorax or severe surgical emphysema there may be a need for insertion of a chest drain.

If asked directly, you should confirm the mass on the X-ray, may indeed be a cancer.

STATION 4.21a

Informed Consent

You have been asked to obtain informed consent from the 53-year-old man who is to have a bronchoscopy and biopsy tomorrow for a large lesion in the right lung, which is likely to be malignant.

Please obtain informed consent from the patient and address any questions he may have.

(5 minute station)

5: ORTHOPAEDICS & TRAUMA

The care of the injured patient begins in an emergency setting and the immediate response of the trauma team is directed towards keeping the patient alive, preventing exacerbation of his injuries and deterioration of his vital functions. This involves maintenance of the airway and respiration, cervical spine stabilisation, controlling external haemorrhage and supporting the circulation by obtaining vascular access. Pain relief is administered when the initial survey is completed and the general state stabilised.

Head injuries call for the immediate assessment and monitoring of cerebral function; they are diagnosed by neurological signs that localise the intra-cranial injury and confirmed by a CT head scan. Cervical spinal injury must be suspected in the unconscious patient and in those with head or thoracic injuries. Displaced limb fractures are gently realigned to alleviate pain and reduce haemorrhage.

Soft tissue injuries are explored and debrided and closed primarily or secondarily. Visceral injuries must be recognised early as they are usually life-threatening. Thoracic injuries call for ventilatory and circulatory support to ensure adequate lung perfusion and gaseous exchange. Abdominal injuries may result in peritoneal contamination and/or haemorrhage and call for urgent surgical assessment.

The management of a burn injury begins with a brief history of the accident and assessment of the extent and severity of the injury. An inhalation injury requires careful monitoring of respiratory function for signs of deterioration. The local treatment of a burn wound is debridement or excision with overgrafting. Fluid loss from the burn surface is calculated according to burn formulae and replaced. Adequate parenteral analgesia must be administered early. Prophylactic antibiotics are indicated. The emotional impact of a burn injury on the patient, relatives and carers is more evident than in other types of injury and psychological support and counselling must be given.

A survey of injuries to the various anatomic regions may be as follows:

- **Head**
  Document the level of consciousness and search for scalp lacerations or bruising that may indicate an underlying fracture. A CT scan is indicated for patients with a GCS score of 12 or less on admission.

If the patient is comatose or is rapidly losing consciousness, suspect a diffuse or focal brain injury. Intracranial bleeding from contusions or lacerations must be diagnosed early as emergency decompression is life-saving and limits the neurological sequelae of cerebral compression.

- **Face**
  Check airway patency and breathing. Examine the eyes before periorbital swelling closes the eyelids.
  Palpate for obvious maxillary or mandibular fractures.
  Obtain a radiograph of the facial bones.

- **Spine**
  Cervical or upper thoracic spinal injury is suspected if there is unconsciousness; flaccid areflexia (flaccid anal sphincter tone or loss of bladder control); diaphragmatic breathing; ability to flex but not extend the elbow; loss of sensation below the injury; hypotension with bradycardia (in the absence of haemorrhage) and priapism (an uncommon but characteristic sign).
  Obtain a lateral cervical spine radiograph showing C7 and T1 vertebrae.

- **Chest**
  The signs of a tension pneumo- or haemothorax are:
  skin bruising, cyanosis and respiratory distress
  paradoxical movements in a flail chest
  tracheal shift to the opposite side
  absent or reduced breath sounds at site of injury and soft tissue crepitus.
  Obtain anteroposterior and lateral chest radiographs.

- **Abdomen**
  The signs are seat belt skin bruising; rigid or tender abdomen with rebound and absent bowel sounds.
  Abdominal distension with hypotension suggests visceral injury and/or haemorrhage. Obtain a diagnostic peritoneal lavage or an ultrasound scan; the latter should only be performed on a stable patient.
  A pelvic ring fracture or disruption is often associated with abdominal or pelvic visceral injuries and produces significant internal haemorrhage.

- **Limbs**
  Limb fractures and joint injuries are often missed in patients with multiple or severe trauma. Long bone fractures are usually obvious from the history and local signs. Feel for pulses distal to the fracture to ensure integrity of blood flow. Exclude compartment syndrome by ascertaining sensation and perfusion distally.

  Obtain radiographs of the injured limb in two planes to include the joints above and below the fracture.

STATION 5.1   *(Answers – page 312)*

History

You are a medical student attending an orthopaedic clinic. The next patient is a 43-year-old hospital porter complaining of chronic backache.

Please take a history of the presenting complaint and any other relevant history, with a view to making a diagnosis.

(5 minute station)

STATION 5.2

History

You are a medical student in an orthopaedic clinic. The next patient complains of a wry neck with pain and stiffness.

Please take a history of her presenting complaint, and any other relevant history, with a view to making a diagnosis.

(5 minute station)

STATION 5.3

Examination

Please examine the neck of the patient whose history you took in Station 5.2 (using a simulated patient).

(5 minute station)

STATION 5.4

Examination

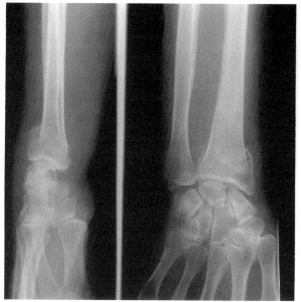

Fig. 5.4

Figure 5.4 demonstrates a left wrist fracture. What type of fracture is this? Please demonstrate the closed reduction of the fracture in the subject (manikin) and how you would apply local anaesthetic prior to reduction.

(5 minute station)

STATION 5.5

An adult who sustained a closed head injury is depicted by a manikin.

(5 minute station)

1. Please demonstrate how you would assess the level of consciousness.
2. Please demonstrate three clinical tests to detect cerebral compression/ injury.

STATION 5.6

Examination

A ship's gangway, 16 feet above ground level, collapsed during boarding, injuring four ferry passengers who were on it. Clinical observations in the Primary Survey are as follows:

(5 minute station)

Age & sex	Patient A 46-year-old Male	Patient B 34-year-old Female	Patient C 29-year-old Female	Patient D 52-year-old Male
Pulse rate	140	120	100	150
Respiratory rate	40	32	20	40
Systolic blood pressure	65	140	120	80
GCS	8	11	14	12

1. Please calculate the Revised Trauma Score (RTS) for each patient from the scoring system given below.
2. How would you prioritise these patients for treatment? Please discuss your reasons.

Revised Trauma Scoring: Score allocated

A.	Respiratory rate	10–24	4
		24–35	3
		> 35	2
		1–9	1
B.	Systolic blood pressure	> 89	4
		70–89	3
		50–69	2
		1–49	1
C.	GCS	13–15	4
		9–12	3
		6–8	2
		4–5	1

Revised Trauma Score = A + B + C

STATION 5.7

Examination

This 36-year-old woman pedestrian was run over by a motor vehicle. She complained of severe pain in her back and side and was found to have frank haematuria.

(5 minute station)

1. Please describe the features observed in Figure 5.7, on page 166
2. State the mechanism of the injury.
3. State the likely cause of the haematuria and list two imaging procedures that may demonstrate the injury sustained.
4. List three other structures that are susceptible to injury in this accident.

STATION 5.8

Examination

You are a medical student and have just taken a history of a patient complaining of pain and stiffness in her left hip. Please examine the hip joint (using a simulated patient).

(5 minute station)

STATION 5.9

Examination

You are the medical student attached to an orthopaedic firm. The next patient is a 43-year-old woman complaining of pain and stiffness in her right shoulder. Please demonstrate how you would examine the shoulder joint (using a simulated patient).

(5 minute station)

STATION 5.10

Examination

To attempt this station someone should act as the injured party. All the equipment needed can be found in the Accident and Emergency Department.

You are a medical student in the Accident and Emergency Department, when a 20-year-old woman is admitted with a suspected cervical fracture sustained in a trampolining accident. Her airway is clear, and she is breathing normally.

(5 minute station)

1. What equipment is required for emergency neck stabilisation?
2. Please stabilise the patient's neck with the equipment described.
3. Assess the integrity of the cervical spine and cord.

STATION 5.11

Examination

A patient (represented by a manikin) is brought to the Accident and Emergency Department with a closed fracture of the left femur.

(5 minute station)

1. Please carry out a clinical survey of the injured limb, stating your objectives.

Please answer the following questions by ticking the appropriate column

		True	**False**
2.	A poor pulse distal to a limb fracture should be assumed to be due to vascular injury and not spasm	❏	❏

		True	**False**
3.	Diagnostic clinical signs of a limb fracture are:		
a)	Deformity	❏	❏
b)	Swelling	❏	❏
c)	Crepitus	❏	❏
d)	Abnormal movement	❏	❏

		True	**False**
4.	Compartment syndrome in a limb may be caused by:		
a)	A fracture	❏	❏
b)	A nerve injury	❏	❏
c)	A cold injury	❏	❏
d)	A crush injury	❏	❏
e)	A burn injury	❏	❏
f)	Revascularisation of an ischaemic limb	❏	❏

STATION 5.12

Investigation

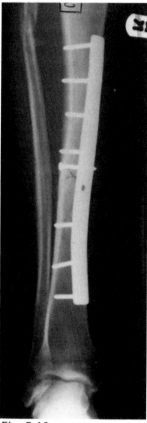

Fig. 5.12

(5 minute station)

This is a post-operative radiograph of a limb injury.

1. Name the bones involved and the components used in the treatment.
2. Name the technique used.
3. Which of the following conditions are appropriately treated with this technique.
   (Please tick the appropriate column.)

	True	False
(a) Fractures that are unstable and are prone to displacement following reduction	❏	❏
(b) Fractures that cannot be reduced without operation	❏	❏
(c) Fractures that unite poorly or slowly	❏	❏
(d) Multiple fractures that require early and definitive treatment to reduce the risk of general complications	❏	❏
(e) Compound fractures	❏	❏

STATION 5.13

Figure 5.13 on page 166 shows a fracture that has been treated surgically.

(5 minute station)

1. Name the bone(s) involved and the components A and B used in the treatment.
2. Name the technique used.
3. Answer the following questions on this technique by ticking the appropriate column.

		True	False
(a)	The patient should be encouraged to weight bear on that limb immediately following reduction	❏	❏
(b)	This method is suitable for infected or contaminated fractures	❏	❏
(c)	This method is suitable for fractures in children	❏	❏
(d)	A common complication of this method is delayed healing due to overdistraction	❏	❏
(e)	This method is suitable for compound fractures	❏	❏

STATION 5.14

Investigation

Figures 5.14a, b and c are chest, pelvic and abdominal radiographs of two adults injured in a road traffic accident.

(5 minute station)

1. Please list two positive findings in figure 5.14a.

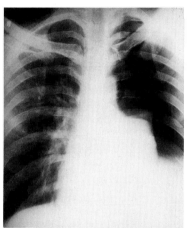

2. State a positive finding in figure 5.14b and in figure 5.14c.

Fig. 5.14a

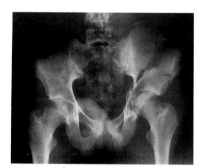

Fig. 5.14b

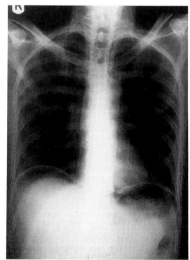

Fig. 5.14c

3. Indicate how you would conduct a primary survey of their injuries by ticking the appropriate columns in response to the following statements.

		True	False
(a)	Immediately allocate the patients to major, intermediate and minor injury categories	❏	❏
(b)	Ascertain whether they are able to walk	❏	❏
(c)	Assess their neurological status	❏	❏
(d)	Assess their breathing and ventilation	❏	❏
(e)	Ascertain the mechanism of their injuries	❏	❏
(f)	Completely undress the patient	❏	❏
(g)	Protect patients from hypothermia	❏	❏
(h)	Take a brief history of events leading to the accident	❏	❏

STATION 5.15

Investigation

This is a radiograph of a 16-year-old girl who presented with a spinal deformity.

(5 minute station)

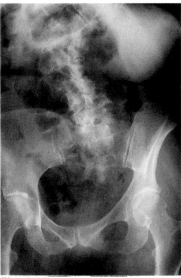

Fig. 5.15

1. (a) What is the abnormality seen?
   (b) How would you measure the spinal deformity?
   (c) Please comment on the aetiology of this condition.
   (d) State the principles of treating this condition.

2. Please answer the following questions by ticking the appropriate column.

	True	False
(a) Spinal bracing usually corrects this deformity before adulthood	❑	❑
(b) Surgical correction is feasible at any age	❑	❑
(c) Spinal cord lesions are common in this condition	❑	❑
(d) Muscle palsy is the usual cause of this condition in children and adolescents	❑	❑

STATION 5.16

The CT head scans shown below are taken from patients who have incurred a head injury.

Please indicate whether the statements below are **True** or **False**.

(5 minute station)

1.

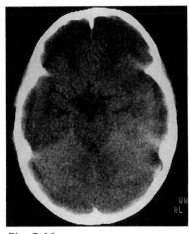

Fig. 5.16a

		True	**False**
(a)	This is a CT head scan with contrast	❏	❏
(b)	There is evidence of midline shift	❏	❏
(c)	There is evidence of hydrocephalus	❏	❏
(d)	There is evidence of cerebral oedema	❏	❏
(e)	The patient would benefit from a mannitol infusion	❏	❏

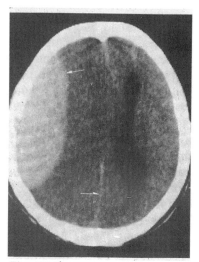

Fig. 5.16b

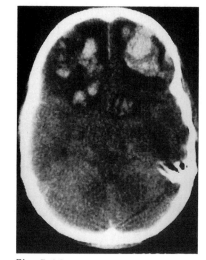

Fig. 5.16c

2.	*(Figure 5.16b)*	**True**	**False**
(a)	There is evidence of an occipital fracture	❏	❏
(b)	There is subdural haemorrhage	❏	❏
(c)	This injury can be produced by a punch in a boxing match	❏	❏
(d)	The condition shown classically produces a 'period of lucidity' prior to loss of consciousness	❏	❏
(e)	The patient would benefit from immediate neurosurgical intervention	❏	❏

3.	*(Figure 5.16c)*	**True**	**False**
(a)	This is a CT head scan with contrast	❏	❏
(b)	There is evidence of midline shift	❏	❏
(c)	The patient would benefit from Nimodipine	❏	❏
(d)	The prognosis is independent of the GCS score on admission	❏	❏
(e)	There is evidence of intracerebral bleeding	❏	❏

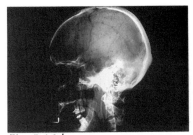

Fig. 5.16d

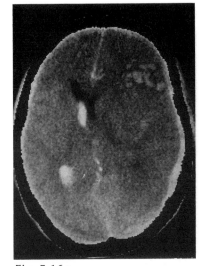

Fig. 5.16e

4.	*(Figure 5.16d)*	**True**	**False**
(a)	This is an AP skull X-ray	❏	❏
(b)	There is a frontoparietal fracture	❏	❏
(c)	This injury may produce a CSF leak	❏	❏
(d)	MRI rather than CT is a better modality to image this condition	❏	❏
(e)	This injury is likely to have been incurred through a knife wound	❏	❏

5.	*(Figure 5.16e)*	**True**	**False**
(a)	There is evidence of hydrocephalus	❏	❏
(b)	There is midline shift towards the right	❏	❏
(c)	There is evidence of intracerebral blood	❏	❏
(d)	This condition is often associated with cerebral oedema	❏	❏
(e)	This patient should have immediate neurosurgical intervention	❏	❏

STATION 5.17

Treatment

A model of an upper limb depicts a recently sustained 'clean', soft tissue wound.

(10 minute station)

1. Demonstrate, using the 'minor ops' set provided (Figure 5.17, see page 166), how you would treat the wound in a living subject.

2. The following factors increase the incidence of wound infection. Answer by ticking the appropriate column.

		True	False
a.	Wounds over one hour old at presentation	❑	❑
b.	Crush injury to surrounding tissue	❑	❑
c.	Presence of shattered glass particles	❑	❑
d.	Use of 2% lignocaine as a local anaesthetic	❑	❑
e.	Use of 1% lignocaine with adrenaline as a local anaesthetic	❑	❑
f.	Loosely-tied skin sutures	❑	❑
g.	High wound vascularity	❑	❑
h.	Inadequate haemostasis	❑	❑
i.	Chronic use of steroids	❑	❑
j.	High impact causative force	❑	❑

STATION 5.18

Treatment

An adult, 'depicted by a manikin', has sustained a right-sided traumatic tension pneumothorax.

(5 minute station)

1. Please demonstrate the steps you would take in treating this condition, using the equipment on the sterile 'set' provided. (Figure 5.18a, see page 166).
    Skin prep solution, sterile drapes and dressings
    1% lignocaine in two ampoules, with syringe and needle
    Scalpel and non-absorbable suture material
    Chest drain with introducer and artery forceps
    Water-seal bottle and connecting tubing.

2. Figure 5.18b is a radiograph of a patient with a tension pneumothorax. Identify the lesions labelled A, B and C.

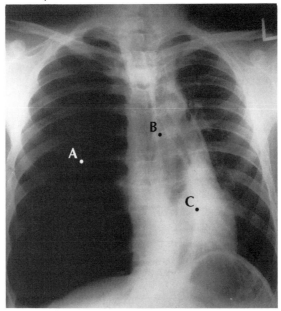

Fig. 5.18b

Answers
(A)
(B)

(C)

STATION 5.19

Treatment

Figure 5.19 on page 166 shows a tray of instruments used for central venous cannulation. A manikin simulates a patient in traumatic shock.

(5 minute station)

1. Name the items labelled A, B, C and D.
2. Demonstrate the siting, introduction and confirming of the position of a central venous catheter on the manikin.

Answers
(A)   (C)
(B)   (D)

STATION 5.20

Treatment

Please tick the appropriate column in the following questions.

(5 minute station)

		True	False
1.	The indications for diagnostic peritoneal lavage in blunt abdominal trauma are:		
a.	Unexplained hypotension	❏	❏
b.	Abdominal distension	❏	❏
c.	A 'silent' abdomen	❏	❏
d.	Abdominal skin bruising	❏	❏

2. The instruments in Figure 5.20a on page 166 are set out for diagnostic peritoneal lavage.
    Name those labelled A, B, C, D and E.

Answers

(A)   (D)

(B)   (E)

(C)

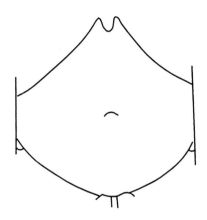

Fig. 5.20b

3. In the diagram of the abdomen above, choose the site most commonly used for diagnostic peritoneal lavage.

6: ETHICS AND LEGAL MEDICINE, INCLUDING CONSENT AND IV PROCEDURES

Ethical and legal situations and dilemmas are faced by clinicians almost every working day. Such issues often pose difficulties to the medical student or junior doctor and are, therefore, avoided. Observation of senior colleagues and acquired experience help: the following simple guidelines may make dealing with these issues a little easier.

Ethical issues are often multifaceted. Difficult emotional and interpersonal dynamics direct the various parties involved in desiring different results. As doctors, one of the most difficult areas to confront is the lack of a definitive, correct answer. Such issues are often grey, and it is this uncertainty which troubles us all.

When dealing with these issues ask yourself whether the following items have been considered and answered.

- **'Do no harm'.** This simple principle should underpin everything one does in medicine. Within this phrase lies the issue of the 'patient's best interests'. At all times the patient is the one we are all working to help, and this may need to be impressed upon relatives and other health care professionals.

  Doing no harm should also be applied to dealings with relatives and other health care professionals. Their views should be noted empathetically. It may be you who are 'wrong'! Doctors are often very poor at looking after themselves and one another. Doing no harm should also be applied to oneself and one's colleagues. Support for each other and yourself is very important. Medicine is a team game!

- **Communication**. It is always important to ensure careful documentation of discussions with colleagues, relatives and patients. Procedures and actions should be truthfully described, including mishaps and poor outcomes. This is not only a legal obligation and sensible professional practice, it also allows colleagues to follow the rationale and direction of treatment.

- **Legal aspects.** Junior doctors are often unaware of the legal aspects and implications of their actions. In difficult situations it is always wise to seek a wide range of opinion from nursing staff, colleagues and other health care professionals involved with the

case. Senior colleagues' advice, particularly that of the lead clinician, should be sought and noted.
In very difficult or awkward situations the advice of the GMC, BMA, MDU or MPS should also be sought and noted.

- **Work towards compromise.** Within the framework set out above one must work toward compromise. The setting of realistic, achievable goals, and recognition of success and results should be acknowledged. Compromise between the interested parties may often be the only way to succeed in such matters.

STATION 6.1   *(Answers – page 338)*

You are the medical SHO on call. The house officer has rung you to tell you that a 53-year-old woman in the Accident and Emergency Department is refusing treatment after being admitted with a paracetamol overdose.

On questioning the house officer, you find out that she has serious suicidal intent but appears well orientated and rational. She has no psychotic symptoms.

Unfortunately, you are dealing with an emergency on one of the wards and cannot see the woman yourself. Please advise the house officer how to proceed, protecting all the parties involved.

(10 minute station)

STATION 6.2

Preparatory

You have 5 minutes to read the information below before attempting the next station.

You are a GP in a large practice. One of your partners has left you a rather difficult situation to deal with. He has been seeing a 56-year-old woman, who had a genetic screening test for Huntington's chorea. She found out that her father committed suicide aged 50, when he was diagnosed as having the disorder. Her mother died when she was young, and neither her three brothers nor her two daughters know about their father's/ grandfather's problem.

The test indicates that she has the disorder, but when your partner told her, she refused to allow him to tell or screen her relatives. One of her daughters is your patient and is 'trying for a family'.

Please counsel the patient with a view to obtaining her consent to use this information to screen her family. Huntington's chorea is an autosomal dominant disorder, which causes progressive dementia and unwanted, involuntary movements. It is usually fatal.

(5 minute station)

STATION 6.2a

The 56-year-old woman, who is a patient of one of your partners, has come to see you for the results of her genetic screening test, which are positive for Huntington's chorea. Please counsel her with a view to obtaining her consent to use the information to screen her family.

(10 minute station)

STATION 6.3

Preparatory

You have 5 minutes to read the information below prior to attempting the next station.

You are a house officer attending a care-planning meeting for a 79-year-old man with mild dementia. The gentleman has insisted on going home but relatives, who are his primary carers, are refusing, as they say he is unsafe and is a danger to himself and his neighbours.

The salient points from the case notes are as follows:

On admission – found by Police, very confused and wandering naked in the street.
Mental test score – 1/10.
Diagnosis – UTI/confusional state.
UTI treated with good effect, using oral trimethoprim.
Mental test score now 7–8/10

Rehabilitation: Nurse's report – independent of all ADLs, very pleasant on the ward, a little slow mobilising.
Occupational therapist's report – home visit very successful, need a few minor adjustments (i.e. handrail on the stairs and in the bathroom).
Physiotherapist's report – walks independently with a stick; a little slow sometimes. Occasionally unsteady but continues to improve.
Social worker's report – the patient has accepted that the gas must be capped off and meals on wheels brought in. Home care to help with cleaning; bath attendant arranged for once a week.

(5 minute station)

STATION 6.3a

You have been asked to present the case to the relatives as to why this 79-year-old gentleman with mild dementia is safe to go home.

This station may be acted out as a group OSCE, with people playing the roles of each member of the health care team (i.e. social worker, occupational therapists and physiotherapists, and nurse).

(10 minute station)

STATION 6.4

Preparatory

You have 5 minutes to read the information below prior to attempting the next station.

You are the ITU consultant in a district general hospital. You have been called at home by your registrar for some advice. This is the dilemma that faces you both:

Case 1: In the last 5 minutes, an 83-year-old man has been admitted to the Accident and Emergency Department. He was riding his new mountain bike to see a friend, when he was hit by a hit-and-run driver. He has multiple fractures and a head injury, and was electively paralysed and ventilated at the scene by the trauma team.

There are 3 beds in your ITU, and all are occupied.

Bed 1: A 68-year-old, previously fit and well woman, who, whilst recovering from a total hip replacement, developed a severe lower respiratory tract infection, leading to ARDS. She was electively ventilated 2 days ago and is stable. She is the mother of the Care of the Elderly physician.
Bed 2: A 24-year-old HIV positive man, who has systemic candidiasis, with cerebral involvement. During the last 24 hours he has required triple inotrope support and has worsening renal and cardiorespiratory function.
Bed 3: A 54-year-old businessman and leading local councillor, who was electively ventilated for respiratory distress, secondary to pulmonary oedema following an anterior MI.

(5 minute station)

STATION 6.4a

As the ITU consultant you have to decide the most appropriate management for the four patients described in Station 6.4. Please discuss the factors that you take into account when deciding which patient to transfer to another hospital 20 miles away.

(10 minute station)

STATION 6.5

A 30-year-old man is being treated by you, his general practitioner, for tonic-clonic seizures. His wife has informed you that, contrary to your advice not to drive, he continues to drive a mini-cab. You have asked to see the patient to discuss the situation.

Please counsel the patient, with a view to reaching an agreement about his driving.

(10 minute station)

INFORMED CONSENT

Informed consent may be written or verbal. It implies that the patient agrees to the procedure to which he or she is about to be exposed which is fully explained and any anxieties addressed.

In recent years, the medico-legal implications of poor consent have become very much more prominent. House officers, who often have little knowledge or experience of technically complex procedures, have traditionally been the people required to obtain informed consent. This situation is unsatisfactory for patient, doctor and lawyer.

In recognition of these facts, the Royal Colleges have issued new guidelines which recommend that the person(s) performing the procedure should be the one(s) to obtain the informed consent.

The following stations represent common procedures that, although not directly performed in most instances by the junior doctor, are still procedures which one should be familiar with and could obtain informed consent.

Important aspects of informed consent

- **How much information?** The simple answer to this difficult question is 'as much as is necessary to impart all the information regarding the procedure, whilst answering all the patient's anxieties'.

  Students and newly-qualified/inexperienced doctors often avoid important and difficult parts of this process, as they find discussion awkward. Medico-legally this is disastrous. Experience and knowledge make this a lot easier, although never easy, and have led to the new guidelines.

  Mortality and morbidity must be clearly explained and noted.

- **Who gives consent?** If at all possible, the patient must be the one to give informed consent. Under common law, procedures may be undertaken in emergencies with the consent of two doctors. In patients less than 16 years old, a parent or guardian must give their consent. Relatives may also be used to give consent in emergencies or when the patient is unable to give consent (e.g. dementia). In all cases, the patient's wishes must always be respected, and patient confidentiality must be assured and maintained.

STATION 6.6

Informed consent

Preparatory

Please read the information below before attempting the next station.

(5 minute station)

You are the house officer on a gastroenterology firm. You have been asked to obtain informed consent from a 52-year-old woman who has been admitted for a liver biopsy to be performed by your registrar this morning.

On review of the notes you ascertain the following facts:

a. Alcohol consumption – 5 to 10 units a day
b. No risk factors for hepatitis B or C
c. The consultant has diagnosed possible haemochromatosis
d. The patient has already been clerked in pre-admission clinic

No results of FBC or INR

Common side effects of the procedure:
a. Local bruising
b. Right upper quadrant pain – mild to moderate
c. Referred pain to the right shoulder

Uncommon side-effects:
a. More severe abdominal pain due to bleeding from the liver
b. Biliary peritonitis
c. Haemobilia
These may require admission and possible surgery.

Procedure

Takes 5 to 10 minutes
Need to lie flat and take a deep breath and hold it for 10 seconds
Needle passed into the liver and a small piece taken away
Procedure performed under local anaesthetic

Post procedure

Need to lie flat for 6 to 8 hours
Can go home after this period if observations are normal
Will have blood pressure/pulse taken half- to one-hourly through this period

NOTE: This procedure cannot be undertaken until an INR and platelet count are known.

STATION 6.6a

Informed consent

Please obtain informed consent from the 52-year-old woman who has been admitted for a liver biopsy to be performed by your registrar this morning.

(10 minute station)

STATION 6.7

Informed consent

Preparatory

Please read the following information before attempting the next station.

(5 minute station)

You are the medical house officer attached to a gastroenterology firm. The next patient is a 43-year-old woman, who has been admitted to day care for an upper GI endoscopy. She was found to have a hypochromic microcytic anaemia on routine investigation.

Upper GI endoscopy – OGD = oesophagogastroduodenoscopy

Procedure

Performed under local anaesthetic which is sprayed at the back of the throat; occasionally the patient is given an intravenous sedative. Endoscope is about 1cm in diameter and is passed down through the gullet into the stomach.
It also allows biopsies to be taken.
Side-effects:
   Common: sore throat and gullet, drowsiness if sedation used
   Uncommon: Oesophageal tears – small, spontaneously heal; large – pneumomediastinum, mediastinitis – requires antibiotics.
   Larger tears may require surgery.

STATION 6.7a

Informed consent

You have been asked to obtain informed consent from this 43-year-old woman, who is being investigated for a microcytic anaemia for an upper GI endoscopy.

(5 minute station)

STATION 6.8

Informed consent

Preparatory

Please read the following information before attempting the next station.

(5 minute station)

You are a surgical house officer, and you have been asked to obtain informed consent for a colonoscopy from a 62-year-old woman who is being investigated for weight loss and intermittent constipation.

Procedure

Performed using intravenous sedation, which also has amnesiac effect.
Endoscope is about 1cm in diameter and is passed up through the anus.
The endoscope is flexible and carries a fibre optic light which allows the inside of the bowel to be seen.
It also allows biopsies to be taken.

Side-effects:

Common: Discomfort during the procedure, bleeding from bowel lining.
Uncommon: Perforation of the bowel; small – treated conservatively with antibiotics; large – may need oversewing if detected early.
A defunctioning colostomy may be required if there is peritoneal soilage.

STATION 6.8a

Informed consent

You are required to obtain informed consent for a colonoscopy from this 62-year-old woman who is being investigated for weight loss and constipation.

(5 minute station)

STATION 6.9

Informed consent

Preparatory

Please read the following information before attempting the next station.

(5 minute station)

You are a house officer attached to a gastroenterology firm. You have been asked to obtain informed consent for an ERCP from a 36-year-old obese woman. She presented 2 days ago with jaundice, and ultrasound has shown gallstones and a dilated common bile duct.
ERCP = endoscopic retrograde cholangiopancreatography

Procedure

Performed with a local anaesthetic spray in back of the throat and intravenous sedation.
Endoscope is flexible and carries a fibre optic light, allowing the operator to view inside the bowel.
Need to identify and cannulate the ampulla of Vater so that a wire basket 'cage' will be passed up around stone and the operator will attempt to remove it. A small cut may be made in the sphincter of Oddi for this purpose.
If unsuccessful, may require further attempt or operation.
Side effects:
Common: sore throat and gullet
Uncommon: pancreatitis, cholangitis

STATION 6.9a

Informed consent

You are required to obtain informed consent for an ERCP from an obese 36-year-old woman who presented with jaundice secondary to a gallstone in the common bile duct. Please obtain informed consent and address any anxieties the patient may have.

(5 minute station)

STATION 6.10

Informed consent

> Please read the information below. You have 5 minutes to prepare for the following station:-
>
> You are a house officer attached to a cardiology firm. You have been asked to obtain informed consent for a transoesophageal echocardiogram from a 43-year-old in-patient who is suspected of having infective endocarditis.
>
> You will need to mention the following information:

(a) The patient is required to be conscious for the procedure as they need to assist the operator by swallowing and moving from time to time. Normally local anaesthetic spray is used to anaesthetise the back of the throat. If the patient is anxious a small injection may be given which will make them sleepy and stops them from remembering the procedure.

(b) The instrument is about 3–4cm in diameter at its thickest and the patient is asked to swallow it down into their oesophagus/gullet.

(c) The procedure takes about 10 minutes and should be no more than uncomfortable.

Common complications :-
(a) During the procedure the patient will gag on the instrument but should NOT feel any pain.
(b) Post-procedure the patient is often left with a slight sore throat and oesophagus. This will pass in a few days.

Uncommon complications :- These are extremely rare
(a) The instrument may tear the oesophagus, causing
Pneumomediastinum (Air in the mediastinum)
Small tears will spontaneously heal over; larger tears may require surgical intervention
Surgical emphysema (Air within the soft tissues and below the skin)
Mediastinitis – severe sepsis within the mediastinum rarely this may be fatal.

(5 minute station)

STATION 6.10a

Informed consent

Please obtain informed consent from this 43-year-old in-patient who is suspected of having infective endocarditis for a transoesophageal echocardiogram.

(5 minute station)

STATION 6.11

Informed consent

Preparatory

You are a house officer attached to a cardiology firm. The next patient is a 53-year-old man who has been admitted for day case cardiac catheterisation. You have been sent to obtain informed consent from the patient who has already been clerked in the pre-admissions clinic.

(5 minute station)

Please obtain informed consent mentioning the following information:
- The procedure is performed under local anaesthetic
- An injection is given into the groin and a very thin tube is passed up to the heart
- Contrast medium is then injected in through the tube. This is a special fluid which shows up under X-ray. A cine film is taken as it passes through the blood vessels and the heart.

From this information we can tell what is causing the chest pain

The patient must lie in bed after the procedure for 4-6 hours prior to being allowed home

Must ensure the patient –
- Can lie flat for 20 minutes
- Has no previous reactions to medications or contrast medium

Common complications –
- Flushing/warm feeling as the contrast medium is circulating
- Bruising at the puncture site in the groin

Uncommon complications –
- Rupture of a coronary artery requiring immediate bypass surgery
- Arrhythmia requiring treatment
- Death – mortality is less than 1%
- Femoral false aneurysm – requiring surgery

STATION 6.11a

Informed consent

You have been asked to obtain informed consent from this 53-year-old man who has been admitted for day case cardiac catheterisation.

(5 minute station)

Generic skills
The following four stations are common to all branches of medicine from general practice to psychiatry. A mannequin arm should be available in all clinical skills centres. If you do not have access to such an arm you can still practise the stations, explaining how you would proceed.

STATION 6.12

For this station you will require a mannequin arm, a tourniquet, vacutainer, needles, syringe, blood bottles and gloves.

You are the medical student attached to a GP practice. You have been asked by the GP to obtain a full blood count sample from a 43-year-old woman, who is attending the surgery for lethargy. Please obtain a sample using the mannequin arm, explaining your actions as you proceed.

(5 minute station)

STATION 6.13

For this station you will require a mannequin arm, intravenous cannula, alcohol wipe, tourniquet, dressing for cannula, gloves, saline flush, syringe/needle.

You are the medical student attached to an obstetric and gynaecology firm. You have been requested to insert an intravenous cannula into a 23-year-old primagravida, who requires intravenous heparin for a suspected pulmonary embolism (PE). Using the mannequin arm, insert the cannula, explaining your actions as you proceed.

(5 minute station)

STATION 6.14

For this station you will require a mannequin arm with cannula in situ, a bag of intravenous fluid (you can use stickers to change the content), giving set, gloves and a drip stand.

You are the house officer attached to a general medical firm. You have been asked by the senior house officer to set up and site an intravenous drip for a 63-year-old woman, who was admitted 24 hours ago in a hyperglycaemic coma. The fluid chart is provided.

Using the mannequin arm, please set up and site the intravenous drip.

(5 minute station)

STATION 6.15

For this station you will require: a vial of antibiotic powder, gloves, appropriate mixing fluid, alcohol wipe, needles/syringes, a mannequin arm with cannula in situ (the arm should have an identity bracelet), normal saline flush, appropriate prescription chart.

You are the medical student attached to a surgical firm. You have been requested by the house officer to draw up and give a dose of antibiotic for a patient who is 24 hours post-cholecystectomy.

Using the mannequin arm and the equipment provided, draw up and give the antibiotic, explaining your actions as you proceed.

(5 minute station)

Fig. 2.4a (Page 42)

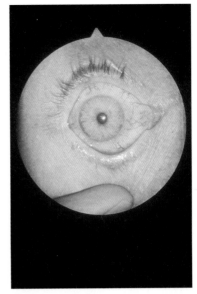

Fig. 2.4b (Page 42)

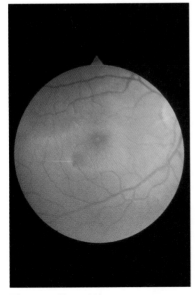

Fig. 2.4c (Page 42)

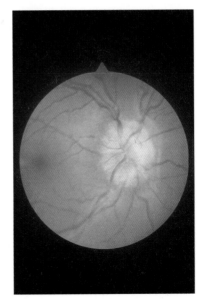

Fig. 2.4d (Page 42)

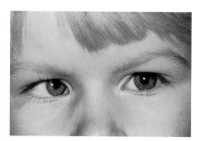

Fig. 2.5a (Page 43)

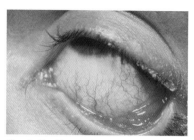

Fig. 2.5b (Page 43)

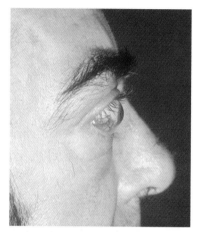

Fig. 2.5c (Page 43)

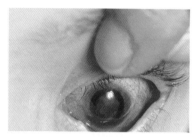

Fig. 2.5d (Page 43)

Fig. 2.7a (Page 44)

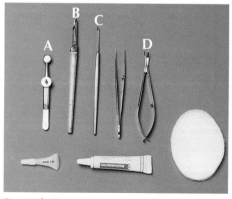

Fig. 2.7b (Page 44)

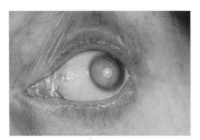

Fig. 2.8 (Page 44)

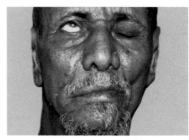

Fig. 2.14 (Page 48)

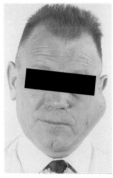

Fig. 2.15 (Page 48)

Fig. 2.17 (Page 49)

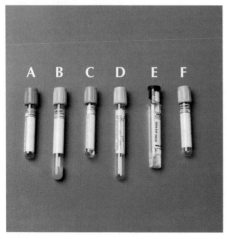

Fig. 3.10 (Page 59)

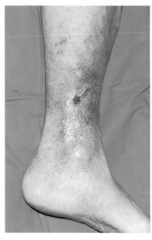

Fig. 3.25 (Page 89)

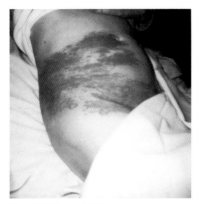

Fig. 5.7 (Page 129)

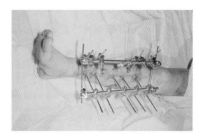

Fig. 5.13 (Page 133)

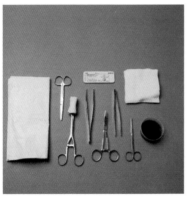

Fig. 5.17 (Page 140)

Fig. 5.18a (Page 141)

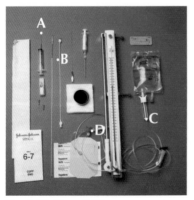

Fig. 5.19 (Page 142)

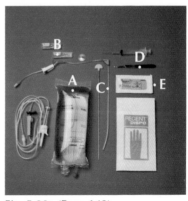

Fig. 5.20a (Page 143)

STATION 1.1

Patient history

I am 21 years old and have been well until about four months ago, when I started the oral contraceptive pill. Since then I have had a number of severe, generalised headaches. They seem to come on at any time, but especially when I have red wine. They are 'thumping' and I often get a strange feeling about 2 or 3 hours before they really start. The feeling is like muzziness and tiredness.

The headaches last about 24 hours before they finally go. I have to take four aspirin to get any relief. The headaches are made worse by loud noise but I haven't noticed that they are any worse in the morning or when crying, laughing or straining. They do ease a little if I lie down in a quiet room. I get flashing lights in my eyes, and any bright light hurts my eyes. I don't get a stiff neck. I am often very sick with the headaches and vomit throughout the period of worst pain. I have never had headaches before; no-one in my family has migraine.

Apart from this problem I am well and haven't had any blackouts, fits, weakness or loss of feeling in my limbs. My speech is not affected. I am very worried about the possibility of a brain tumour.

Assessment	Good	Adequate	Poor/not done
1. Polite introduction; establishes rapport	❑	❑	❑
2. Establishes onset of symptoms	❑	❑	❑
3. Establishes the characteristics of the headache:			
Site	❑	❑	❑
Radiation	❑	❑	❑
Nature/severity	❑	❑	❑
Relieving factors	❑	❑	❑
Exacerbating factors	❑	❑	❑
Precipitating factors	❑	❑	❑
4. Establishes associated symptoms:			
Meningism	❑	❑	❑
Nausea and vomiting	❑	❑	❑
Warning aura	❑	❑	❑
Visual disturbances	❑	❑	❑

	Good	Adequate	Poor/not done
5. Excludes previous family history of migraine	❑	❑	❑
6. Invites patient questions and answers them in a reasonable manner	❑	❑	❑
7. Makes a reasonable attempt at the diagnosis	❑	❑	❑
8. Does all in a fluent, professional manner	❑	❑	❑

Diagnosis
Migraine attacks

Comment

Treatment of migraine: once precipitants have been identified and excluded, treatment may be divided into symptom relief and prophylaxis.

Symptom relief: appropriate analgesics should be used to relieve the headache. Patients should be advised to start with simple analgesia such as aspirin and paracetamol and then move up the analgesic ladder to opiates such as codeine phosphate. Oral analgesia may be hampered by vomiting and it may be necessary to give the analgesia by intramuscular or per rectal routes. Antiemetics such as metoclopramide and domperidone are commonly used. 5-HT agonists such as ergotamine and sumatriptan may be used in acute attacks and relieve the pain and nausea in about two-thirds of patients.

Prophylaxis: this should be offered to patients having more than two attacks per month. Treatments include beta blockers, 5-HT antagonists (5-HT agonists are used in acute episodes), cyproheptadine, pizotifen, methysergide and calcium antagonists.

The many drugs used in treatment is an indication of the uncertainty of the causes of migraine. The drugs act on various receptors, including those for 5-HT, calcium channels and histamine. Their various actions include vasoconstriction, membrane stabilisation and reducing sympathetic outflow.

STATION 1.2

Patient history

I am 19 years old and am studying for my final school examinations. I was well until about 3 months ago, when I started to get increasingly severe headaches. They are mainly on the right side of my forehead, radiating to the back of the head. At first it was a dull ache, but now the headaches are extremely painful, and aspirin or paracetamol don't help. The headaches are almost constant but are much worse in the early morning when I wake up and when I am straining on the toilet, coughing or laughing.

In the last few weeks I have felt dreadful – very tired and out of sorts, with no energy. I have been nauseated and have been vomiting with blurring of my vision. In fact, I can't go on revising for my examinations. In the last two days I have had two blackouts, and have woken up feeling very battered and bruised. I have also wet myself. Over the last week my left hand and arm have felt weak, and I have dropped a few things.

What do you think is wrong with me, and what can be done about it?

Assessor: Please ask the student – "What course of action would you now take" (i.e. patient requires urgent admission).

Assessment	Good	Adequate	Poor/not done
1. Polite introduction; establishes rapport	❑	❑	❑
2. Establishes duration of symptoms	❑	❑	❑
3. Establishes the characteristics of the headache:			
Site	❑	❑	❑
Nature/severity	❑	❑	❑
Radiation	❑	❑	❑
Relieving factors	❑	❑	❑
Exacerbating factors	❑	❑	❑
Precipitating factors	❑	❑	❑

	Good	Adequate	Poor/not done
4. Establishes the associated symptoms:			
Nausea and vomiting	❏	❏	❏
Blurring of vision	❏	❏	❏
5. Establishes history of associated neurological symptoms:			
Episode of blackout	❏	❏	❏
Mild weakness in left arm	❏	❏	❏
6. Establishes systemic symptoms:			
Lethargy	❏	❏	❏
Malaise	❏	❏	❏
Weight loss	❏	❏	❏
7. Makes a reasonable attempt at the diagnosis	❏	❏	❏
8. Invites patient questions and answers appropriately	❏	❏	❏
9. Does all in a fluent, professional manner	❏	❏	❏
10. When asked implies the patient needs urgent admission	❏	❏	❏

Diagnosis

Space occupying lesion leading to raised intracranial pressure and localising signs, i.e. left arm weakness and seizures.

STATION 1.3

Patient history

I am 23 years old and have always kept well but while I was at work today I developed the worst headache in the world. I feel very frightened and upset about it. I work as a hairdresser and while I was cutting someone's hair about 3 hours ago, this terrible headache suddenly came on out of the blue. It was like a clap of thunder going off in my head. The pain is mainly at the back of my head but doesn't seem to radiate anywhere else. I have felt dizzy and unwell since the headache came on and I've vomited 2 or 3 times. Nothing seems to be making the headache any better, and I don't think it could possibly get any worse! My neck feels stiff, and I can't look into the light because it hurts my eyes. I haven't had any cold, sore throat or cough.

I've never had headaches before but I remember my mother telling me that my grandmother had kidney problems and died in child birth, aged 34, of a bleed in the brain.

Assessment	Good	Adequate	Poor/not done
1. Polite introduction; establishes rapport	❑	❑	❑
2. Establishes the duration and onset of symptoms	❑	❑	❑
3. Is sensitive to the fact patient is in severe distress; mentions the need for analgesia and antiemetic	❑	❑	❑
4. Establishes the characteristics of the headache:			
Site	❑	❑	❑
Nature/severity	❑	❑	❑
Relieving factors	❑	❑	❑
Exacerbating factors	❑	❑	❑
Precipitating factors	❑	❑	❑

	Good	Adequate	Poor/not done
5. Establishes associated symptoms:			
Neck stiffness	❑	❑	❑
Nausea and vomiting	❑	❑	❑
Mild photophobia	❑	❑	❑
6. Excludes fever and symptoms of upper and lower respiratory tract infection	❑	❑	❑
7. Establishes family history of cerebrovascular and renal disease	❑	❑	❑
8. Excludes previous history of headaches specifically migraine	❑	❑	❑
9. Makes a reasonable attempt at the diagnosis	❑	❑	❑
10. Does all in a fluent, professional manner	❑	❑	❑

Diagnosis
Subarachnoid haemorrhage probably secondary to the rupture of a Berry aneurysm.

STATION 1.4

Patient history

I am 17 years old and still at school. I have always been well but I have had 4 or 5 funny turns in the last couple of months. At least two of these were only 48 hours apart. The turns can come on at any time but I think I know when they are about to happen because I get strange feelings in my hands and feet, as if they were on fire. I get dreamy-like visions in front of my eyes. I don't remember anything about the turns but I know I become unconscious. My mother saw it happen the last time and said I fell to the floor, and began shaking, and grunting very loudly. I was frothing at the mouth and wet myself, too. The turn lasted 3 or 4 minutes and then got better. When I woke up I felt battered and bruised, and very sleepy. My mother put me to bed, and I slept for three hours. When I woke up I felt much better but had a bit of a headache.

I've never had any epileptic fits before, although my mother says I had 3 or 4 fever fits when I was a baby. As far as I know, no-one in my family has epilepsy. Apart from this I am very well and haven't had any other symptoms in the last few months. I have never had a head injury, and I am not taking any medicines. I drink less than five units of alcohol in a month. I don't smoke or use recreational drugs.

Assessment	Good	Adequate	Poor/not done
1. Polite introduction; establishes rapport	❏	❏	❏
2. Establishes the duration and frequency of the symptoms	❏	❏	❏
3. Establishes the characteristics of the 'funny turns'			
Aura – warning symptoms	❏	❏	❏
Memory of turns	❏	❏	❏
Witness accounts; limb shaking	❏	❏	❏
Post ictal symptoms and duration	❏	❏	❏
Associated			
Tongue biting		❏	❏
Incontinence of urine		❏	❏
Facial plethora		❏	❏
Loss of consciousness		❏	❏

	Good	Adequate	Poor/not done
4. Excludes other neurological symptoms:			
Headaches	❏	❏	❏
Permanent motor and sensory deficit	❏	❏	❏
Speech	❏	❏	❏
Visual and hearing loss	❏	❏	❏
Dizziness		❏	❏
5. Excludes other systemic symptoms	❏	❏	❏
6. Establishes alcohol, cigarette and illicit drug history	❏	❏	❏
7. Excludes previous/family history of epilepsy, e.g. febrile convulsions as a child	❏	❏	❏
8. Excludes previous history of head injury	❏	❏	❏
9. Makes a reasonable attempt at the diagnosis	❏	❏	❏
10. Does all in a fluent, professional manner	❏	❏	❏

Diagnosis
Recent onset of idiopathic epilepsy.

Comment

Management of epilepsy: patients presenting with seizures need to have a full metabolic screen, CT head scan and EEG to exclude other causes of seizures prior to a diagnosis of idiopathic epilepsy being made. Routine blood tests should include FBC, U+Es, corrected calcium and magnesium. CT head scan and EEG will exclude other underlying causes such as space occupying lesions. Once the diagnosis of idiopathic epilepsy has been made the patient should be advised against driving a motor vehicle and taking part in certain occupations, such as operating machinery or driving public vehicles (e.g. buses). A patient may drive a car if fit free for one year or more, or, if they have only suffered nocturnal seizures for three years. Many of the anticonvulsants used in the treatment of epilepsy have unpleasant side-effects. Patients should be told about the side-effects and then, depending on the frequency of seizures and the effects on the patient's lifestyle, treatment should be commenced.

STATION 1.5

Patient history

I am 24 years old and I have always kept fit and well. About four months ago I began to get increasing weakness of my legs and arms, particularly the arms. It gets worse the more I repeat something, such as chopping or cutting food. I have noticed that my speech is becoming strange, too, as if I had a cold. It is also increasingly difficult to swallow and chew things the longer a meal goes on. The main problem that made me go to the doctor was double vision, which is getting so bad that I can't read the paper, watch television or drive a car. My husband has said that my eyes look droopy.

I don't have any other symptoms. My muscle tone has not changed and I have had no shaking, wasting away or twitching. I can feel things quite normally.

Assessment	Good	Adequate	Poor/not done
1. Polite introduction; establishes rapport	❏	❏	❏
2. Establishes duration of the symptoms	❏	❏	❏
3. Establishes pattern of weakness, i.e. global weakness affecting all 4 limbs (upper more than lower)	❏	❏	❏
4. Characterises the weakness Increases with fatigue	❏	❏	❏
5. Excludes:			
Wasting		❏	❏
Fasciculation		❏	❏
Change in tone of the limbs		❏	❏
6. Establishes associated problems with:			
Swallowing	❏	❏	❏
Eating	❏	❏	❏
Speech	❏	❏	❏
7. Establishes history of visual problems	❏	❏	❏

	Good	Adequate	Poor/not done
8. Excludes sensory symptoms parasthesiae and numbness	❑	❑	❑
9. Excludes other neurological symptoms:			
Fits		❑	❑
Loss of consciousness		❑	❑
Headaches		❑	❑
Tremor		❑	❑
10. Excludes other systemic symptoms	❑	❑	❑
11. Does all in a fluent, professional manner	❑	❑	❑
12. Makes a reasonable attempt at the diagnosis	❑	❑	❑

Diagnosis
Myasthenia gravis

Comment

Myasthenia gravis: this scenario can be difficult for the undergraduate but shows the importance of taking a good history.

Myasthenia is a relatively uncommon autoimmune disorder which affects women slightly more than men. It is due to an autoantibody directed against the postsynaptic part of the acetylcholine receptor and is characterised by fatiguable muscle weakness, that is weakness which worsens with repetition of an action (e.g. chewing of food).

The principal treatments in this disorder are the anticholinesterases, pyridostigmine and neostigmine. In more severe cases, immunosuppression, with prednisolone and azathioprine, is also used. Cyclophosphamide, methotrexate and cyclosporin are used in resistant cases, and where steroids and azathioprine are poorly tolerated.

In young patients with autoantibodies, thymectomy is advocated as up to 60% of these patients have an abnormal thymus gland, including thymoma. Thymectomy in older patients, or those without autoantibodies, has not been shown significantly to change the natural course of their disease.

STATION 1.6

Patient history

I am a 62-year-old retired lorry driver. I am being treated for blood pressure and gout. I was well until about six months ago, since when I have lost 15 kilogrammes and have become increasingly weak. I am right-handed, and my left hand has become shrivelled, as if all the muscles had been sucked out. The right hand is getting weaker and I can't hold a knife or fork in it. My legs are weak but I can still walk about 10 to 20 metres. The weakness seems to spread up the affected limbs. Sometimes I have noticed that the muscles in my arms seem to twitch on their own.

My speech has changed recently and I am finding it increasingly difficult to eat. The food comes back up, often out of my nose, which I find very upsetting. I choke on both solids and liquids and this is not helping my weight loss.

I have not had any visual problems or any headaches, loss of consciousness, fits or other neurological symptoms. My bowels and micturition have been normal and I am relatively well otherwise.

I smoked 20 cigarettes per day until 10 years ago and I drink 20 units of alcohol per week, mainly whisky.

Assessment	Good	Adequate	Poor/not done
1. Polite introduction; establishes rapport	❏	❏	❏
2. Establishes the duration and progression of the illness	❏	❏	❏
3. Establishes character of the weakness	❏	❏	❏
4. Establishes wasting associated with fasciculation	❏	❏	❏
5. Establishes the nature of the swallowing problems and associated speech problems	❏	❏	❏
6. Excludes visual, hearing and comprehension problems	❏	❏	❏

	Good	**Adequate**	**Poor/not done**
7. Excludes other general neurological symptoms:			
Headache		❑	❑
Fits		❑	❑
Loss of consciousness		❑	❑
8. Excludes other systemic illness, in particular ensures normal sphincter control and malignant symptoms:			
Lethargy		❑	❑
Malaise		❑	❑
Loss of appetite		❑	❑
9. Establishes smoking, alcohol and occupation history	❑	❑	❑
10. Does all in a fluent, professional manner	❑	❑	❑
11. Makes a reasonable attempt at the diagnosis	❑	❑	❑

Diagnosis
Motor neurone disease, with both bulbar and corticospinal symptoms.

STATION 1.7

Patient history

I am 24 years old and a professional footballer. I have always been fit and well until about two months ago, when I started getting visual problems and funny feelings in my hands and feet. I had a weird episode six months ago, when I was playing in a match. Suddenly the whole world went hazy and I had to come off the field. The problem had gone by the next day, so I didn't pay much attention to it. Then 6 to 8 weeks ago when I was training, the ball felt spongy on the end of my boot, and I found it difficult to grip my knife and fork. Things have been getting worse ever since. I can't drive the car because I can't feel the pedals or the steering wheel. I haven't been able to train because my feet feel so strange – like cotton wool with pins and needles. My vision has been blurred on and off during the last month, and I've had a dull pain behind my eyes.

In spite of these strange sensations, I have not had any weakness in my arms and legs and there has been no wasting, twitching or shaking. I haven't had any other neurological symptoms. I don't smoke. I drink 5 to 10 units of alcohol a week and don't take any medicines. Apart from these problems I am well, and have never had any serious illnesses.

Assessment	Good	Adequate	Poor/not done
1. Polite introduction; establishes rapport	❑	❑	❑
2. Establishes the duration of the symptoms	❑	❑	❑
3. Establishes distal/glove and stocking distribution of sensory symptoms	❑	❑	❑
4. Excludes associated motor problems:			
Wasting		❑	❑
Fasciculation		❑	❑
Tremor		❑	❑
5. Establishes retro-orbital pain and visual loss	❑	❑	❑

	Good	Adequate	Poor/not done
6. Excludes general neurological symptoms:			
Loss of consciousness		❑	❑
Headaches		❑	❑
Fits		❑	❑
Dizziness		❑	❑
7. Excludes loss of higher functions:			
Swallowing		❑	❑
Speech		❑	❑
Comprehension		❑	❑
Hearing loss		❑	❑
8. Excludes other risk factors for sensory neuropathy:			
Diabetes		❑	❑
Alcohol		❑	❑
Medications		❑	❑
9. Excludes other systemic illness:			
Weight loss		❑	❑
Malaise		❑	❑
GI and GU symptoms	❑	❑	❑
10. Is able to name the three investigations correctly	❑	❑	❑
11. Does all in a fluent, professional manner	❑	❑	❑

Diagnosis

Peripheral sensory neuropathy and visual disturbance secondary to demyelinating disease (principally multiple sclerosis).

Investigations

1. Lumbar puncture to confirm the presence of oligoclonal bands in the CSF.
2. MRI of the brain stem and cervical cord – to establish the presence of areas of demyelination = plaques.
3. Visual evoked responses.
4. Clinical examination should include:
   Fundoscopy to exclude other causes of visual problems and establish the presence of optic atrophy.
   BM stix and urinalysis.

STATION 1.8

Patient history

I am 54 years old and work as an electrician. I have diabetes and high blood pressure. I don't use insulin for my diabetes. Yesterday, while I was out shopping, my left arm and leg went limp and dead, and the left side of my face felt droopy. I had no warning of this, and no headache or blackout. I fell to the floor and had to be helped up. I could understand what people were saying to me but I couldn't talk, even though I knew what I wanted to say. The problems went away after 30 or 40 minutes, and I didn't let the ambulance men take me to hospital because I thought it was a waste of everyone's time. I haven't had any problems overnight, and I feel back to normal today.

I have had high blood pressure for ten years and I've been diabetic for the last five. I've never had a mini stroke or any other stroke, and I've never had any problems with my heart or the circulation in my legs and feet. I had my cholesterol done in the diabetic clinic on my first visit, and they said it was slightly above normal but nothing to worry too much about. My father and brother both died in their 50s of heart and stroke problems.

I've put on a lot of weight since I got divorced three years ago, and I now weigh about 92 kilogrammes. My height is 1.72 metres. I eat all the wrong foods, and I drink 5 or 6 pints of beer a night. I still smoke 30 cigarettes a day. I have missed my last two diabetic clinic appointments and never test my blood or urine. I don't take any exercise, although I was a keen swimmer when young.

Assessment	Good	Adequate	Poor/not done
1. Polite introduction; establishes rapport	❏	❏	❏
2. Establishes the nature of the 'strange turn':			
Global weakness of left upper and lower limbs	❏	❏	❏
Left sided facial palsy	❏	❏	❏
Expressive dysphasia/no receptive problems	❏	❏	❏

	Good	Adequate	Poor/not done
Complete resolution with no recurrence since	❏	❏	❏
Excludes headache, loss of consciousness, fits	❏	❏	❏
Excludes history of similar episodes	❏	❏	❏
3. Establishes the risk factors for transient ischaemic episode:			
Family history of atherosclerotic disease	❏	❏	❏
Previous history of CVA, IHD, PVD	❏	❏	❏
Hyperlipidaemia		❏	❏
Smoking		❏	❏
Hypertension		❏	❏
Alcohol excess		❏	❏
Cardiac arrhythmia and valvular disease		❏	❏
General lifestyle	❏	❏	❏
Exercise			
Diet		❏	❏
Weight and height		❏	❏
4. Explains the diagnosis in a clear, non-jargonistic manner	❏	❏	❏
5. Explains to the patient lifestyle changes that need to be considered	❏	❏	❏
6. Invites patient questions and answers appropriately	❏	❏	❏
7. Does all in a fluent, professional manner	❏	❏	❏

Diagnosis

Transient ischaemic attack (TIA) causing a left hemiparesis, expressive aphasia and a left facial palsy.

Comment

This patient has a very strong family history of premature atherosclerotic related death. He has several primary risk factors for stroke including hypertension, diabetes (which is probably poorly controlled), cigarette smoking and excess alcohol intake. He has a high BMI of 31.1 and a sedentary lifestyle. He has now suffered a TIA.

The following management should be instituted.

- Encouragement to stop smoking, lose weight and start gentle exercise programme.
- Review by dietician – diabetic, low fat, weight-losing diet.
- Ensure blood pressure control.
- Review by hospital diabetologist.
- Addition of aspirin and dipyridamole SR as secondary prophylaxis.
- Review in hospital outpatient department for:
  Duplex USS Carotids
  CXR and ECG
  Echocardiogram
  Possible counselling about divorce and depression.

STATION 1.9

Answers and explanations

1. (C) (d)
This man has developed secondary polycythaemia due to his chronic airways disease with resultant pulmonary hypertension. The polycythaemia causes a procoagulant state which in severe cases leads to thromboembolic disease. Treatment should include treatment of the underlying airways disease and regular venesection, with the aim of reducing the haematocrit (Hct) to 0.50 or less.

2. (E) (c)
This patient demonstrates a pancytopenia secondary to an aplastic anaemia. Thrombocytopenia of less than 10×10^9/litre carries a significant risk of spontaneous bleeding, in this case a spontaneous intracranial haemorrhage. Causes of aplastic anaemia include

- **Congenital**
  Fanconi's anaemia
- **Acquired**
  Idiopathic
  Infection – TB, hepatitis A
  Toxins – chemicals and insecticides; irradiation
  Drugs
    antibiotics
    anti-epileptics
    anti-inflammatories
    antihistamines
    antithyroid
    oral hypoglycaemics
    chemotherapeutic agents.

3. (D) (e)
Primary thrombocythaemia is a relatively uncommon haematological disorder which presents with bleeding (due to abnormal platelet function), bruising and thromboembolic phenomena. It is intimately related to the myeloproliferative disorders, in particular polycythaemia rubra vera.

4.   (A)   (b)

Alcohol excess is shown in the peripheral blood film by macrocytosis and thrombocytopenia. Alcohol abusers are at increased risk of subdural haemorrhage because of increased falls, thrombocytopenia and coagulopathy (causing a raised INR and prolonged APTT) due to the liver's inability to produce clotting factors.

5.   (B)   (a)

This patient has suffered an intracranial haemorrhage due to a grossly elevated INR. This has arisen due to the interaction of erythromycin with warfarin. Caution must be used when prescribing medications for patients on oral anticoagulants and the oral contraceptive pill. (**Warfarin** is an acronym made up of **W**isconsin **A**lumni **R**esearch **F**oundation coum**ARIN**.)

STATION 1.10

Answers

1.	**(D)**	**(e)**
2.	**(E)**	**(d)**
3.	**(F)**	**(a)**
4.	**(A)**	**(f)**
5.	**(C)**	**(b)**
6.	**(B)**	**(c)**

STATION 1.11

Answers and explanations

Sample A = Tuberculosis meningitis (TBM)
Sample B = Viral meningitis
Sample C = Bacterial meningitis

(a)   A and C
Patients with TBM and meningococcal meningitis need all close contacts to be traced, so they may be given prophylactic treatment or screening.

(b)   A and C
Prior to a definitive microbiological diagnosis being made, clinical features or the appearance of the CSF may demand that empirical antibiotic treatment be started. Particularly in patients where a diagnosis of streptococcal or meningococcal meningitis is suspected, any delays in confirming the diagnosis may be fatal.

(c)   A, B and C
All patients with suspected meningitis should be nursed in a quiet, darkened room. They often require intravenous fluids and antiemetic therapy.

(d)   C
Neisseria meningitidis is most commonly associated with DIC but most severe bacterial meningitides may present with multiorgan failure and DIC.

(e)   A
Tuberculosis is more common in the Indian subcontinent but all the meningitides may present in this racial group.

(f)   C
The Anti-Streptolysin O titre (ASOT) is a marker of streptococcal infection.

(g)   A and C
Although there may be significant changes in viral pneumonias, these are rare and the most florid changes occur with tuberculosis and bacterial infections.

(h)   A and C
Hydrocephalus is a relatively rare complication of bacterial and TBM.

(i)   A and B
Bacterial infections are commonly demonstrated by Gram staining; tuberculosis is demonstrated by Ziehl-Neelsen staining; viral infections are demonstrated using viral titres, electronmicroscopy and polymerase chain reaction studies; fungal infections are demonstrated using Indian ink stains.

(j)   A, B and C
Kernig's sign demonstrates meningeal irritation. The sign is elicited by dorsiflexing the foot which will cause pain in the spine, neck and head if positive. All the meningitides may cause a positive Kernig's sign. It may be inappropriate to perform this test in extremely ill patients.

STATION 1.12

Answers and explanations

1.   (F) (d)
Oligoclonal bands, shown by protein electrophoresis, are present in the CSF in over 80% of cases of multiple sclerosis. They are formed by IgG within the CSF but the antigen they are directed against as yet remains unclear. Oligoclonal bands may also be found in the CSF of patients with sarcoidosis, SLE, Behçet's disease, neurosyphilis and viral encephalitis.

2.   (D) (f)
This neonate has *Haemophilus influenzae* meningitis, which is more common in this age group. As with other bacterial meningitides there is a high protein content and a low glucose concentration. A Gram stain gives the microbiological diagnosis.

3.   (E)   (a)
This history is highly suggestive of meningococcal meningitis with secondary DIC. The patient should be treated empirically with high doses of benzylpenicillin and contact tracing should be arranged. All close contacts should receive prophylactic treatment with rifampicin.

4. (A) (e)
This patient gives a classical history of a subdural haemorrhage but over 50% of patients give no history of trauma. Subdural haemorrhages are usually represented by a hyperdense concave rim around the cerebrum on CT head scan. However at 10 days they appear as an isodense rim and therefore may be overlooked.

5. (B) (c)
A sudden severe headache with associated decreased level of consciousness must be treated as a subarachnoid haemorrhage until proven otherwise. The CSF samples are blood stained in the first 24 to 48 hours but samples taken 48 to 72 hours after the onset of symptoms appear discoloured due to altered blood, termed xanthochromia.

6. (C) (b)
Patients presenting with insidious worsening of a dementing type illness should have a dementia screen to exclude treatable causes. This should include VDRL, TPHA and TPA, TFTs and B12. If syphilis serology is positive the patient should have a lumbar puncture to exclude tertiary syphilis. As in this case, the patient should receive a course of benzylpenicillin after 24 hour cover with steroids. This is to reduce the risk of a Jarisch-Herxheimer reaction.

STATION 1.13

Answers 1.13a

A   Parietal bone

B   Frontal bone

C   Supraorbital ridge of frontal bone

D   Zygomatic bone

E   Infraorbital plate of maxilla

F   Nasal septum

G   Mandible

Answers 1.13b

A   Parietal bone

B   Sphenoid temporal bone

C   Pituitary fossa

D   Petrous temporal bone

E   Occipital bone

F   Maxillary air sinus

G   Mandible

STATION 1.14

Answers and explanations

1.   (a) True   (b) True   (c) True   (d) True   (e) True
The skull X-ray shows evidence of intracranial calcification within the right cerebral hemisphere. In this case it is due to Sturge-Weber syndrome. Common causes include:

Intracranial tumours
- Benign – meningioma, pinealoma, neuroma, papilloma, craniopharyngioma, chordoma
- Malignant – oligodendroglioma, metastases

Infection
- Tuberculosis, toxoplasmosis, abscess, hydatid disease, CMV
- Basal meningitis
- Cysticercosis (infestation with tapeworm larvae)

Vascular
- Aneurysm, angioma, atherosclerosis, Sturge-Weber syndrome
- Old infarction, haematoma

Others
- Tuberose sclerosis, hypoparathyroidism, chronic renal failure
- Toxins, lead and carbon monoxide

2.   (a) False   (b) False   (c) False   (d) True   (e) True
This AP skull X-ray shows a compound, depressed left-sided parietal fracture. The patient had been involved in a fight and had been hit over the head with a snooker cue. This type of fracture requires surgical elevation.

3.   (a) True   (b) False   (c) False   (d) True   (e) True
This lateral skull X-ray shows multiple lytic lesions consistent with a 'pepperpot' skull of multiple myeloma. The patient may also have an ESR > 100, paraproteinaemia, hypercalcaemia and Bence-Jones protein (light chains) in the urine. Other associations include renal failure, amyloidosis (which may be responsible for the renal failure), hyper-viscocity and symptoms of pancytopenia.

STATION 1.15

Answers 1.15a

A   Right eye

B   Left optic nerve

C   Nasal septum

D   Zygomatic arch

E   Temporal lobe

F   Sphenoidal air sinus

G   Occipital bone

H   Scalp

I   Left cerebellar hemisphere

J   Left external auditary meatus

Answers 1.15b

A   Frontal bone

B   Falx cerebri

C   Cerebral sulcus

D   Cerebral gyrus

E   Anterior horn of lateral ventricle

F   Septum pellucidum

G   Choroid plexus

H   Posterior horn of lateral ventricle

I   Occipital lobe

J   Occipital bone

STATION 1.16

Answers and explanations

1.   (a) False   (b) False   (c) True   (d) False   (e) True
This CT head scan shows a large left-sided frontal subdural haemotoma. The blood has caused midline shift and obscuration of the left lateral ventricular system. There is no obstruction or hydrocephalus of the contralateral ventricular system. This disorder commonly arises due to trauma, particularly falls, although over 50% of patients with subdural haemorrhage give no such history. It is common in the elderly and in alcohol abusers. Classically, subdurals are represented by a hyperdense concave rim around the brain, as seen in this scan. However, they may be missed if the scan is taken around the tenth day after the initial haemorrhage, as during this period they may appear isodense with the grey matter, which makes them more difficult to define. Extradural haemorrhages classically form a convex interface with the grey matter.

2.   (a) True   (b) False   (c) True   (d) False   (e) True
This CT scan shows intraventricular blood caused by a large subarachnoid haemorrhage. The headache is classically sudden and severe in nature and is associated with a depressed level of consciousness. Patients require supportive therapy with fluids and should be given nimodipine. Patients with a depressed level of consciousness should be electively intubated and ventilated, this helps by reducing intracranial pressure. Neurosurgery should be considered but may not be appropriate in all cases.

3.   (a) False   (b) True   (c) False   (d) False   (e) True
The third scan shows a large right frontal infarct. There is no midline shift or obscuration of the ventricles. Patients with large cerebral infarcts are likely to be hypertensive prior to their stroke, as this is the principal risk factor, and are often hypertensive on admission because of the vascular response to the ischaemic insult. The treatment of the associated hypertension is still unclear and at present hypertension is not treated for 48 to 72 hours post stroke. This may change as thrombolytic therapy in stroke becomes more common practice. All patients should be considered for formal anticoagulation with warfarin, or secondary prophylaxis with aspirin and/or dipyridamole slow release therapy.

STATION 1.17

Answers and explanations

1.   (a) False   (b) False   (c) False   (d) False   (e) False
This CT head scan shows a large intracerebral bleed within the right cerebral hemisphere. Blood appears white on a scan and should not be confused with contrast. There is no evidence of midline shift or hydrocephalus which may occur with such a large bleed. This patient presented with a GCS of 3 which never improved and he died 24 hours after admission. It is important to perform a scan in order to exclude treatable causes of a depressed level of consciousness, and to institute appropriate care, which may include withdrawing 'active' treatment and keeping the patient palliated until death.

2.   (a) False   (b) True   (c) False   (d) False   (e) True
This contrast-enhanced CT head scan shows an enhancing lesion in the right occipital area its appearance being consistent with a meningioma. The patient will not be blind, but will have a left homonymous field defect. The tumour should be excised neurosurgically and if proven to be a malignant meningioma by histology, postoperative radiotherapy should be offered to the patient.

3.   (a) True   (b) False   (c) True   (d) True   (e) False
The first contrast-enhanced CT head scan shows evidence of a ring enhancing lesion with surrounding oedema in the left frontal area. Further views show multiple similar lesions consistent with multiple metastases. The differential cause of a ring enhancing lesion include a cerebral abscess, for example toxoplasmosis, aspergillus and bacterial emboli associated with endocarditis, and malignancy such as cerebral metastases and lymphoma.

STATION 1.18a

Patient history

I am a 23-year-old fashion model who was diagnosed as having epilepsy six months ago. Since diagnosis I have made no changes to my very hectic life and as a consequence the fits have become increasingly more frequent and severe. In the last two weeks I have had several fits, the last at a big fashion show in Milan. It was after this episode that my agent refused to book me for any more work until I 'get sorted out'.

I drink 20–30 units of alcohol per week, mainly in the form of white wine. Occasionally I do drink a lot more at parties. I smoke 10 to 20 cigarettes per day and use occasional recreational drugs including cannabis and cocaine. I am taking no medications other than the oral contraceptive pill and am still driving a car on a regular basis.

No one has ever explained the diagnosis or the precipitating factors of my problems. I am very keen to make lifestyle changes but am very reluctant to start medical treatment.

Assessment	Good	Adequate	Poor/not done
1. Polite introduction; establishes rapport	❑	❑	❑
2. Establishes present level of patient understanding about the diagnosis, complications and treatment	❑	❑	❑
3. Establishes patient understanding of precipitating factors such as alcohol, recreational drugs and flashing lights (relevant to job)	❑	❑	❑
4. Discusses the need to stop/ avoid precipitating factors	❑	❑	❑
5. Discusses the issue of driving - must register with DVLC; can resume driving if fit-free for one year	❑	❑	❑

	Good	Adequate	Poor/not done
6. Discusses the possibility of avoiding drug therapy if precipitating factors are stopped/avoided	❑	❑	❑
7. Discusses the reasons for and against starting drug therapy:			
Will still have to change lifestyle	❑	❑	❑
Will have to take medications regularly	❑	❑	❑
Mentions side-effects	❑	❑	❑
Mentions interactions with the OCP	❑	❑	❑
Emphasises medications may not stop fits	❑	❑	❑
Mentions possibility of combination therapy	❑	❑	❑
8. Invites patient questions and answers appropriately	❑	❑	❑
9. Emphasises that the majority of people diagnosed with epilepsy are fit-free after five years	❑	❑	❑
10. Does all in a fluent, professional manner	❑	❑	❑

Comment

A diagnosis of epilepsy can be quite a shock and depressing for a patient, particularly a young adult. They should be reassured that in the majority of cases a patient is fit-free and off medication within 5 years. There are of course a small minority of difficult, resistant cases.

Initially, if the patient has had only 1 to 2 fits of short duration, a probationary period may be agreed between the neurologist and the patient. Lifestyle changes, for example. excluding alcohol, should be instituted in this period and the patient should be excluded from driving and operating heavy machinery. Epilepsy may stop the patient working and this may need to be discussed with a social worker. If the patient continues to have seizures then drug treatment should be instituted.

In most cases, a single agent should be chosen and this should be tailored to the individual patient, particularly if they are on other medications, (the OCP). The patient should be advised of the possible side-effects, interactions and the regime clearly explained, particularly if loading doses need to be started. Treatment and the seizures should be monitored with easy access clinics and help for the patient.

First-line therapies	Advantages	Side-effects
Sodium valproate	Drug of choice Fewer side-effects No monitoring of levels required	Acute hepatic insufficiency Hair thinning (hair grows back but may be curly!) Weight gain
Carbamazepine	Relatively few side-effects Simple to predict changes in dose as almost linear relation- ship between oral dose and serum levels	Commonly causes a tran- sient erythematous rash Bone marrow suppression (agranulocytosis) Nausea and vomiting Ataxia, blurred vision Cholestatic jaundice
Phenytoin	Effective tonic clonic seizure Drug choice in emergency treatment	Multiple side-effects Particularly 'user unfriendly' in the young adult Narrow therapeutic window
Second-line therapies	**Advantages**	**Side-effects**
Lamotrigine	Add on therapy First-line treatment Reduces seizure in 25% of patients	May exacerbate seizures Skin rashes Sedation Hepatic dysfunction Flu-like symptoms on starting
Vigabatrin	Add on therapy Reduction of seizure frequency in 50% of patients	Sedation Multiple neurological and behavioural problems Confusion/agitation Eye problems

Other drugs which should be considered as 'add on therapies' include primidone, phenobarbitone, clonazepam and clobazam.

STATION 1.19

Answers and explanations

1.   (C)   (f)
Beta interferon remains a controversial treatment for multiple sclerosis. Studies have shown benefits of therapy in patients with relapsing disease with reduction in frequency of acute relapses. However, there has been little proven effect on overall prognosis and disability and some health authorities within the UK have refused to endorse the drug's prescription, due to cost.

2.   (D)   (e)
Anticholinesterases form the main stay of treatment in myasthenia gravis. Immunosuppressants are used in more severe disease and, as in this case, the patient may require thymectomy.

3.   (E)   (a)
Parkinson's disease is treated using L-dopa therapy combined with peripheral decarboxylase inhibitors. Other therapies include dopaminergic agonists such as pergolide and bromocriptine, selegiline and the recent addition of catecholamine-O-methyl transferase (COMT) inhibitors. No therapy has yet been shown to change the insidious progression of the disease.

4.   (A)   (c)
Anticholinesterase inhibitors have recently been shown to slow the progression of Alzheimer's disease. However, as with beta interferon and COMT inhibitors, this therapy has not been shown to change the overall prognosis and therefore it's use has been restricted within the UK.

5.   (F)   (b)
This is a classical history of giant cell arteritis. The patient should be started on high dose steroids immediately and the diagnosis proven by temporal artery biopsy and ESR. There is a 48 hour window between starting treatment and taking a biopsy, after which the diagnostic histological changes disappear.

6.   (B)   (d)
Classical triad of normal pressure hydrocephalus, urinary incontinence, confusion and gait dyspraxia. The treatment of choice is neurosurgical insertion of a ventriculoperitoneal shunt. The title of normal pressure is a misnomer, studies having shown that such patients have fluctuating CSF pressures and that the insertion of the shunt reduces the effects of any rises that may occur.

STATION 1.20

Patient history

I am a second year medical student and was admitted two days ago with a moderately severe headache which came on insidiously over 3 to 4 days. The headache has been poorly relieved despite intravenous fluids and analgesia but the CT head scan performed yesterday was normal. The registrar has explained to me that I need a lumbar puncture but I am not very clear as to what this means. 'Everyone just assumes I understand because I'm a medic'.

Assessment	Good	Adequate	Poor/not done
1. Polite introduction; establishes rapport	❑	❑	❑
2. Establishes present patient understanding of the lumbar puncture	❑	❑	❑
3. Explains the following steps of the procedure: *Position* *patient should be placed on the bed in the left lateral position with the knees tucked up into the chest OR sitting up leaning over the patient table which is topped with pillows*	❑	❑	❑
Patient will feel some pushing on the back and around the tops of the hips as the landmarks are mapped out.	❑	❑	❑
Skin is cleaned with antiseptic, which is cold, and then the lower back is covered with surgical sheets	❑	❑	❑
Local area is then injected with local anaesthetic, which 'stings a little'	❑	❑	❑
Patient will feel some more pushing as the needle is inserted through the skin	❑	❑	❑

	Good	**Adequate**	**Poor/not done**
A small amount of fluid (3mls) is then drained from the spine and this is sent to the laboratory to be looked at under the microscope	❑	❑	❑
The patient will be expected to lie flat for 6 to 8 hours after the procedure and will be given analgesia and fluids	❑	❑	❑
4. Complications: local pain at the puncture site and headache are the primary problems	❑	❑	❑
5. Invites patient questions and answers appropriately	❑	❑	❑
6. Does all in a fluent, professional manner	❑	❑	❑

Comment

What's the definition of a lumbar puncture? Two very frightened people joined by a needle! One should always remember this joke when performing a lumbar puncture. The patient is often very ill and the thought of a doctor putting a needle into their spine makes them even more anxious. The explanation and reassurance prior to the actual procedure is therefore extremely important. The procedure is relatively simple and in experienced hands takes only a few minutes. From a practical point of view the important elements are the positioning of the patient, the drawing out of the landmarks and the insertion of the needle.

Patient position: There are two accepted ways of positioning the patient. (a) The patient is placed in the left lateral position with their lumbar spine parallel to the edge of the bed. They are manoeuvred so their back is on the edge of the bed, or (b) the patient is sat upright leaning over a support, such as the patient's table covered with pillows. Whichever position one uses, always remember to adjust the height of the bed to allow comfort and ease during the procedure.

The landmarks: The ideal interspace to use is the L4/5 space which is conveniently located by drawing a horizontal line between the iliac crests. The vertebral spines should be palpated and the space between them defined. It is important that one can confidently feel this space, otherwise the procedure will be extremely difficult. The space may be marked by using the cap of a biro pen. By pushing gently the cap impression is left in the skin. The advantage of this method is the impression will not be removed by the antiseptic cleaning of the skin.

Insertion of the needle: Once the interspace has been infiltrated with local anaesthetic, one is ready to insert the needle. The needle should be placed at ninety degrees to the skin and inserted through the local anaesthetic needle tracks. In the correct position the needle will pass easily to the spinal ligament, and with a slight 'give' pass into the canal. On withdrawal of the introducer clear CSF should flow back. Commonly one hits bone rather than the ligament. If this occurs, partially withdraw the needle and re-insert at a slightly different angle, using the landmarks for reference.

In acute headache only 3–4 drops of CSF need be collected in each of 3 sterile specimen pots. Two are sent to biochemistry for glucose and protein estimation, the third is sent to microbiology for microscopy and culture. (A simultaneous serum glucose is needed to compare). If viral causes are suspected CSF should be collected for polymerase chain reaction (PCR) studies and viral titres. Always check with the laboratory prior to the procedure what specimens are required for a particular disorder.

STATION 1.21

Patient history

I am 43 years old and have 3 children. Recently, my eldest daughter, aged 14 years old was killed in a hit and run road traffic accident. Prior to the accident I was always quite a happy and carefree person and never thought of myself as unhappy or depressed. Since the accident three months ago, I have not been out of the house more than 4 or 5 times and have lost three stone in weight. I eat very little; surviving on a few cups of tea and occasional snacks which my husband forces me to eat. I have been unable to go back to work and have lost interest in everything around me.

I sleep fitfully through the night and wake at 4.30 or 5 o'clock every morning. I can't accept my daughter's death and have thought several times about ending it all but have never made any plans to carry out any of these thoughts as I must carry on for the sake of my other children. I have no thoughts about the future. My GP placed me on some Valium after the accident but I've refused to see her again. I drink little alcohol, no more than 2 to 3 units a week, but I smoke 30 cigarettes per day. I have no previous history of psychiatric illness but remember my mother was treated for depression when I was a little girl. Do you think I will need to go into hospital?

Assessment	Good	Adequate	Poor/not done
1. Polite introduction; attempts to establish rapport, with realisation that the patient is making poor eye contact and is withdrawn	❏	❏	❏
2. Establishes the preceding life events and duration of the presenting complaint	❏	❏	❏
3. Investigates patient's insight into her illness and reasons for attendance at the clinic	❏	❏	❏
4. Asks about specific symptoms of depression:			
Early morning wakening/sleep disturbance	❏	❏	❏
Loss of appetite and weight	❏	❏	❏
Loss of energy and enthusiasm	❏	❏	❏
View of environment/future	❏	❏	❏
Self harm/suicidal intentions	❏	❏	❏
5. Establishes family/personal history of psychiatric illness	❏	❏	❏
6. Establishes premorbid personality	❏	❏	❏
7. Establishes drug, alcohol and smoking history	❏	❏	❏
8. Does all in a fluent, empathetic, professional manner	❏	❏	❏
9. When asked, decides patient has reactive depression and does not need to be admitted	❏	❏	❏

Diagnosis
Reactive depression secondary to bereavement.

Comment

Management of such a patient should include bereavement counselling, antidepressants (e.g. SSRIs and possible psychoanalysis).

STATION 1.22

Patient history

I am 23 years old and I lost my job as an apprentice car mechanic three months ago. I have always been a bit of a loner and find it difficult to make friends easily. I have had 3 or 4 jobs over the past five years and never seem to be able to settle down to anything for a sustained period. However, I was really enjoying my job in the garage and it was a real shock that I was fired. Since then they have been telling me that the world is against me and that the reason I lost my job was because they are all jealous of me. I killed the dog because they told me that he was an evil force and would kill people very soon if I didn't kill him. My mother and father are plotting with them to keep me away from my work and that's why I had to set the house on fire.

No-one seems to believe me that they are all around and that they are going to take over the world. If they knew I was here they would try to kill me. I was found by a car park attendant at the top of the local multi-storey car park trying to climb over the railings on the top floor because they said they had given me the power to fly. They told me to throw myself off the car park and prove it to the world.

I have never seen them but know they are around. They are always talking about me, and I have heard my name several times on the television recently. I do not drink any alcohol or take recreational drugs but smoke 20 cigarettes per day. I was diagnosed as being depressed six months ago by my GP but only took the tablets for a few months. I don't know if anyone in my family has been mentally ill.

I am not aware that I have been behaving in an abnormal way.

Assessment	Good	Adequate	Poor/not done
1. Polite introduction; tries to establish rapport, appreciating the patient is withdrawn	❑	❑	❑
2. Establishes the nature and duration of the 'strange behaviour'	❑	❑	❑
3. Investigates the patient's insight into his behaviour	❑	❑	❑
4. Establishes/excludes the presence of first rank symptoms of schizophrenia:			
Thought insertion	❑	❑	❑
Thought broadcasting	❑	❑	❑
Thought withdrawal	❑	❑	❑
Somatic passivity	❑	❑	❑
Delusional perception	❑	❑	❑
External control of emotion	❑	❑	❑
5. Establishes alcohol and recreational drug history	❑	❑	❑
6. Establishes/excludes thoughts of deliberate self-harm	❑	❑	❑
7. Establishes personal and family history of psychiatric illness	❑	❑	❑
8. Establishes/excludes precipitating life events	❑	❑	❑
9. Does all in a fluent, empathetic, professional manner	❑	❑	❑

Diagnosis
Acute psychosis secondary to schizophrenia.

STATION 1.23

Patient history

I am 36 years old and work as a prostitute. I recently found out that I am HIV positive. I was diagnosed only two days ago and since then have been working out how to kill myself. Tonight my flatmate told me that she was seeing her new boyfriend and would not be home till tomorrow 'if everything went to plan'. I drank a litre bottle of rum before taking 50 paracetamol tablets, 100 temazepam tablets and 50 Valium tablets which I had acquired on the street this afternoon. Before taking the tablets I wrote three letters, one to my parents, one to my little girl and one to my flatmate, telling them all I was sorry and that I couldn't face life being HIV positive. Unfortunately, I was discovered by my flatmate, who had come home unexpectedly, as her boyfriend had been called out on an emergency job and so couldn't make the date.

I have no good thoughts about the future and I will kill myself as soon as I am out of the hospital.

I took two small overdoses as a teenager, as my father was sexually abusing me. I do not know of anyone else in the family who has attempted or committed suicide. I think I am usually quite a happy-go-lucky person and have never been diagnosed as having a psychiatric illness. I am on no regular medications, I drink 30 to 40 units of alcohol per week (mainly in the form of rum and coke), and occasionally use cocaine and speed. I smoke 20 to 30 cigarettes per day and, occasionally, cannabis.

Do you think I need to be admitted to hospital? If so, why?

Assessment	Good	Adequate	Poor/not done
1. Polite introduction; establishes rapport, acknowledging patient is withdrawn and quiet	❑	❑	❑
2. Establishes events leading up to overdose	❑	❑	❑
3. Establishes timing and method of overdose	❑	❑	❑
4. Establishes suicidal intent:			
Planning	❑	❑	❑
Place	❑	❑	❑
Writing/content of note	❑	❑	❑
Present view of suicide attempt	❑	❑	❑
5. Establishes previous and family history of deliberate self-harm	❑	❑	❑
6. Establishes previous personal and family history of psychiatric illness	❑	❑	❑
7. Establishes alcohol, cigarette and recreational drug history	❑	❑	❑
8. Establishes premorbid personality and view of the future	❑	❑	❑
9. Does all in a fluent, empathetic, professional manner	❑	❑	❑
10. When asked, indicates the patient must be admitted, with logical reasoning	❑	❑	❑

Diagnosis
Serious drug overdose for which the patient needs to be admitted.

STATION 1.24

Patient history from spouse

My husband, who is 28, has been acting very strangely since he lost his job in a city accountancy firm. I am very worried about him and this is why I've come to see the doctor. My husband used to be outgoing and extrovert in nature until six months ago, when he got a promotion, which, I felt, was too much for him. Initially he handled things okay but over several months he began to drink heavily. He seemed to be working almost every night including weekends and became very snappy and withdrawn. The GP saw him, thought he was depressed, and started him on some Prozac. Things improved for a little but two months ago the company was taken over by a larger American company and redundancies were made, including my husband. Over the last month his behaviour has become increasingly bizarre. He has run up large debts with the bank, telling the bank manager and friends that, in fact, he has been promoted to an executive position in the American company and is waiting to go to New York in the spring. He is sleeping less than 2 to 3 hours per night and I have started sleeping in the spare room, as he has become increasingly sexually demanding.

He seems to believe all he is saying and has no regard for me or the children. As far as I know he is not taking any recreational drugs, although he is still drinking a bottle of whisky per day. He has not been taking his antidepressant tablets and is on no other medications. He has no other significant medical or psychiatric history but I know his mother was admitted to a psychiatric hospital when we first started going out, as she had a breakdown and tried to kill herself.

Assessment	Good	Adequate	Poor/not done
1. Polite introduction; establishes rapport with patient and spouse	❏	❏	❏
2. Establishes duration and nature of presenting complaint	❏	❏	❏
3. Establishes premorbid events leading up to illness	❏	❏	❏
3. Establishes symptoms suggestive of mania:			
Increased energy	❏	❏	❏
Disturbed sleep	❏	❏	❏
Increased libido	❏	❏	❏
Grandiose ideas	❏	❏	❏
Delusional ideas	❏	❏	❏
4. Establishes symptoms of depression and patient insight into illness	❏	❏	❏
5. Establishes alcohol, cigarette and recreational drug history	❏	❏	❏
6. Establishes personal and family history of psychiatric illness	❏	❏	❏
7. Establishes premorbid personality	❏	❏	❏
8. Does all in fluent, empathetic, professional manner	❏	❏	❏

Diagnosis

Acute mania (on the background of depression) precipitated by loss of job. This man has a bipolar disorder (i.e. showing symptoms of both mania and depression).

STATION 1.25

Patient history

I am 43 years old and the manager of a semi-professional football team. I need advice about an alcohol withdrawal programme.

I was brought up surrounded by alcohol; my mother and father both drank heavily, my father often becoming violent towards me when drunk. I could have been a professional footballer but my drinking problems stopped me ever progressing from the lower leagues. I have drunk excessively since I was 16 years old, mostly in the form of beer and whisky. Most days I will have a large whisky or two in my breakfast coffee and then have a few whiskies through the morning. At lunch I will have 2 to 3 pints of lager and a couple of whiskies and then in the evening a bottle of whisky, a few beers and occasionally a bottle of wine.

I have lost two jobs in the last five years because of my drinking, and my wife left me two years ago when I lost all our savings through drinking and gambling. I have tried to give up several times and thought I had it under control but I have never tried to dry out formally.

Two weeks ago I got the fright of my life when I was rushed to hospital after vomiting all the blood in my body and nearly dying. The doctors had to look down into my gullet several times to stop the bleeding. The consultant told me that I have severely damaged my liver and that if I don't stop drinking I will almost certainly die in the next year or two. I am determined to put my life back together again and have decided that I must stop drinking. I understand that it will be difficult but I have not had a drink for two days and, although I am a bit shaky, I think I can manage to stop this time.

Assessment	Good	Adequate	Poor/not done
1. Polite introduction; establishes rapport	❑	❑	❑
2. Establishes the duration of patient's alcohol problems	❑	❑	❑
3. Investigates patient's view of his alcohol abuse	❑	❑	❑
4. Establishes drinking patterns: *Drinking alone, drinking in the mornings, drinking to stop symptoms of withdrawal*	❑	❑	❑
5. Establishes quantity of alcohol consumed per 24 hours (divided into wine, spirits and beer)	❑	❑	❑
6. Establishes whether the patient has tried to withdraw from alcohol in the past (formal and informal)	❑	❑	❑
7. Establishes patient's understanding and reasons for detoxification	❑	❑	❑
8. Agrees patient has good motivation and should be placed on the programme	❑	❑	❑
9. Does all in a fluent, empathetic, professional manner	❑	❑	❑

Diagnosis

Long-term alcohol abuser now highly motivated to undergo detoxification after large GI bleed secondary to oesophageal varices.

STATION 1.26

Patient history

I am 27 years old and have always been fit and well. I have come to see you because I just can't stop washing my hands. I've always been very concerned with keeping clean and tidy but recently it has got to the point where I have to wash my hands at least 3 to 4 times an hour. I realise that it's absolutely mad to keep doing it but I just can't help myself. I have now made my hands bleed and they are painful and raw. I have tried to stop but have only managed a few hours and then I feel very anxious that I am getting dirty and have to start again. I have never heard voices telling me to wash my hands. Neither I nor my family have any history of psychiatric illness. There has been no recent upheaval in my life and I am otherwise well. I do not drink any alcohol, smoke cigarettes or take any recreational drugs.

Assessment	Good	Adequate	Poor/not done
1. Polite introduction; establishes rapport	❑	❑	❑
2. Establishes the duration of symptoms and any precipitating life events	❑	❑	❑
3. Establishes frequency of hand washing and events which seem to precipitate need to wash	❑	❑	❑
4. Investigates patient's insight into problem	❑	❑	❑
5. Excludes symptoms of external control and features suggestive of psychosis	❑	❑	❑
6. Excludes symptoms of depression and anxiety	❑	❑	❑
7. Excludes previous personal and family history of psychiatric illness, smoking or recreational drugs	❑	❑	❑
8. Does all in a fluent, professional manner	❑	❑	❑

Diagnosis
Obsessive compulsive disorder.

STATION 1.27

Patient history

I am 72 years old and am usually fit and well. I was admitted 5 days ago with unstable angina. I have been well on the ward until this evening. I am now convinced that the nursing staff and other patients are plotting to kill me and I must be allowed to go home.

I know my name, date of birth and the correct day and month and can count backwards from 20 to 1. I do not know where I am, the correct year, my age or the time of day. I can remember the objects and address at 1 minute but not at 5 minutes. I demand to go home and will not listen to any reasoning by any doctor.

Assessment	Good	Adequate	Poor/not done
1. Polite introduction; establishes patient's identity	❑	❑	❑
2. Establishes why the patient wants to go home	❑	❑	❑
3. Performs a mental test score on the patient, to include:			
Name	❑	❑	❑
Place	❑	❑	❑
Day	❑	❑	❑
Month	❑	❑	❑
Year	❑	❑	❑
Time of day	❑	❑	❑
Date of birth/age	❑	❑	❑
Address or three objects to remember after 1 and 5 minutes	❑	❑	❑
Prime Minister	❑	❑	❑
Monarch	❑	❑	❑
Count backwards from 20	❑	❑	❑

At this point you, acting as the staff nurse on the ward, should ask the doctor if he/she would like to see any of the charts:

	Good	Adequate	Poor/not done
4. Asks for the observation chart to exclude pyrexia, changes in pulse and blood pressure	❑	❑	❑
5. Asks for the drug chart to exclude iatrogenic causes of confusion	❑	❑	❑
6. When asked realises the patient is acutely confused and must stay in hospital	❑	❑	❑
7. Reassures the patient and explains that she must stay in hospital	❑	❑	❑

Diagnosis
Acute confusional state secondary to probable sepsis.

If the doctor asks for the patient's observations:
Pulse 120 regular, BP – 110/80, temperature – 39.5°C.
Drug chart – ISMN 20 mg bd; aspirin 75 mg od; frusemide 40 mg od; perindopril 4 mg od

Comment

When confronted with an acutely confused patient the house officer often forgets to search for a cause and opts to sedate the patient. This is a dangerous course to choose and should be considered only when organic causes of confusion have been excluded.

Sepsis, electrolyte derangement and iatrogenic causes such as drugs should be considered. If sedation is necessary then small doses of haloperidol should be used. In the younger patient up to 10 mg may be necessary but for the elderly 0.5 to 1 mg is often enough.

STATION 1.28

Answers

1.   (C)   (f)
This patient presents with a history of decompensated alcoholic liver disease with resulting encephalopathy. Low Na^+ is caused by secondary hyper-aldosteronism; hypoglycaemia by poor glycogen stores in diseased liver.

2.   (F)   (d)
Carcinoma of the lung may produce several ectopic hormones including parathyroid-like hormone, ACTH and SIADH. A high calcium may also be caused by metastatic bone disease.

3.   (E)   (b)
This young woman presents with a history suggestive of diabetes (poly-uria and polydypsia) associated with an acute chest infection. The infection has caused her diabetes to spiral out of control leading to her hyperglycaemia and precomatose state. To prove the diagnosis of ketoacidosis a bicarbonate and a urinary ketone level are needed but with the information available this is the most appropriate answer.

4.   (A)   (e)
Long-term steroid suppression of the adrenal glands is the most common cause of Addison's disease. Addisonian crisis may be precipitated in such patients when they are unable to take their steroids, for example when vomiting, or when placed under extreme stress such as in an acute, severe illness such as a myocardial infarction. In such circumstances the patient should receive intravenous hydrocortisone until such time as they are well enough to restart their tablets.

5.   (B)   (a)
Uraemia may cause an acute confusional state that may progress to coma. Other biochemical markers of chronic renal impairment include low bicarbonate, indicating metabolic acidosis, low calcium and raised phosphate. Often these patients also have an anaemia of chronic disease.

6.   (D)   (c)
Atypical pneumonias are a common cause of the syndrome of inappropriate ADH secretion. *Legionella* infection causes legionaires' disease, characterised by an acute respiratory tract infection with diarrhoea and confusion. Biochemically there may be low sodium and hypophosphataemia.

STATION 1.29

Answers and explanations

1. (E) (d)
Neuroleptic malignant syndrome is a well recognised phenomenon associated with the initiation and the increase of neuroleptic drugs such as phenothiazines and butyrophenones. The syndrome is characterised by hyperpyrexia, muscle rigidity, tachycardia and impaired consciousness. Treatment should include immediate cessation of the responsible drug and symptomatic treatment with dantrolene which may ease the muscle rigidity.

2. (A) (e)
Brain tumours, including metastases, particularly in the frontal lobes may produce personality changes and aggressive behaviour. This patient may have SIADH secondary to the primary lung tumour or to the secondary brain metastases. The raised calcium may be due to parathryoid-like hormone or bony metastases.

3. (D) (a)
Manic depressives are principally treated with lithium. It has a narrow therapeutic window and commonly causes toxic side-effects. Diabetes insipidus indicated by the polyuria and the raised sodium is a recognised effect.

4. (C) (b)
This patient has several indicators that he is a long-term alcohol abuser, low urea and platelet count with a raised MCV. Alcohol withdrawal *per se* does not cause acute changes in indices.

5. (B) (c)
SSRIs are a relatively new group of antidepressants, they include fluoxetine, paroxetine and sertraline. Hyponatraemia is a relatively common side-effect, particularly in the elderly, and may require cessation of the drug.

STATION 1.30

Answers and explanations

1. (C) (e)
Multi-infarct dementia is often a clinical diagnosis based on a stepwise progressive dementia associated with a previous history of atherosclerotic disease and is confirmed by multiple infarcts seen on CT scan of the head. Alongside Alzheimer's disease it is responsible for 75% of all cases of dementia.

2. (E) (g)
Normal pressure hydrocephalus is diagnosed clinically by the classical triad of confusion, incontinence and gait dyspraxia. It is confirmed by CT head scan and lumbar puncture which show dilated ventricles and a normal opening pressure of 10–15 cm of CSF. Normal pressure is perhaps a misnomer as studies have shown that these patients have episodic rises in their CSF pressure which is thought to be responsible for the confusion.

3. (A) (f)
Hypothyroidism is a reversible cause of dementia and all patients with a diagnosis of dementia should have a thyroid function test. If found to be hypothyroid thyroxine should be introduced at a low dose of 25 microgrammes daily for a week or two, then increased slowly over several weeks until the TSH is suppressed and the free thyroxine increased into the normal physiological range.

4. (G) (b)
Tertiary syphilis may produce a dementing type illness associated with cranial and peripheral nerve lesions. This syndrome is known as general paralysis of the insane (GPI) and causes mixed upper and lower motor neurone signs in the lower limbs (i.e. areflexia and extensor plantars). Neurosyphilis is confirmed when the CSF is positive for VDRL, TPHA and FTA.

It is treated with intravenous penicillin with steroid cover for 24 hours prior to the antibiotics to prevent the Jarisch-Herxheimer reaction.

5. (F) (c)
This patient has B12 deficiency which may cause a dementing illness associated with anaemia, and subacute combined degeneration of the spinal cord (SACD) which causes a peripheral neuropathy associated with progressive lower limb weakness and ataxia. The patient should be treated with intramuscular B12 injections.

6. (D) (a)
Creutzfeldt-Jakob disease has two forms, a genetic disease and an acquired form. It presents with a rapid dementia associated with variable progressive neurological signs and symptoms. The diagnosis may be confirmed by EEG, CSF prion proteins and brain biopsy, although the latter is now not recommended.

7. (B) (d)
Hypoparathyroidism is a relatively rare cause of dementia. It presents with hypocalcaemia which if severe enough causes seizures and tetany. It may produce ectopic calcification in the cornea and the central nervous system. The treatment should include intravenous calcium supplementation, if tetany is apparent, add oral 1-hydroxychole-calciferol.

STATION 1.31a

Patient history

I am a 23-year-old schizophrenic, diagnosed two and a half years ago. After an initial period when I was quite ill and required a lot of inpatient care, I am now relatively well controlled and, after discussion with my CPN and the registrar, I would like to know more about depot injections. Although I have had several talks with the CPN I am not sure about the timing of the injections, what the injections consist of, at what sites I'll be injected and how this will improve things for me.

I'm a bit scared of needles as they remind me of when I was really sick. I am hoping to go to university and am very keen to try the treatment if I am suitable.

Assessment	Good	Adequate	Poor/not done
1. Polite introduction; establishes patient identity and reason for attending the clinic	❏	❏	❏
2. Establishes present understanding of the treatment	❏	❏	❏
3. Establishes present method of treatment and control	❏	❏	❏
4. Explains advantages of depot injections	❏	❏	❏
5. Explains method and timing of depot injections:			
Initial need for test dose	❏	❏	❏
Injections initially given with slow reduction of tablets	❏	❏	❏
Injection made up of 2 to 3 ml oily solution	❏	❏	❏
Injection sites rotated to avoid local complications	❏	❏	❏
Need to titrate dose to suit individual, which may take several months	❏	❏	❏

	Good	Adequate	Poor/not done
Once suitable dose is found injections are given every 2 to 4 weeks	❏	❏	❏
6. Explains local and systemic side-effects	❏	❏	❏
7. Invites patient questions and answers appropriately	❏	❏	❏
8. Does all in a fluent, professional manner	❏	❏	❏

STATION 1.32

Answers

The major antipsychotic and antidepressive medications have numerous side-effects which often overlap. The most appropriate drug combination and dosage must be tailored for the individual.

1. (E) (g)
Lithium has a narrow therapeutic range and its plasma levels should be closely monitored. The normal lithium therapeutic range to aim for is between 0.4 to 1 mmol^{-1}. Toxicity occurs at levels of 1.5 mmol^{-1} and severe, life-threatening toxicity occurs at 2 mmol^{-1}. Lithium has many side-effects and the decision to use it should be taken by an expert with plasma monitoring facilities available. All patients on lithium should be issued with a lithium card

Regular side-effects of lithium (1.5–2.0 mmol^{-1})
Early changes are non-specific and include agitation and apathy which may be confused with signs of worsening of the underlying condition.
- Nephrogenic diabetes insipidus (polyuria/polydypsia)
- Neurological: fine tremor (may become coarse), decreasing level of consciousness, confusion, dysarthria, dizziness
- Gastrointestinal disturbances: vomiting, diarrhoea, anorexia, weight gain and oedema.

Severe side-effects of lithium (> 2 mmol^{-1})
- Neurological: hyperextension of limbs, hyper-reflexia, seizures
- Psychiatric: confusion, toxic psychoses
- Circulatory collapse: shock
- Hypothyroidism ± goitre
- Raised ADH
- Hypokalaemia with associated ECG changes
- Renal failure

Toxicity should be treated by withdrawal of the drug and, if renal impairment is associated, haemodialysis should be considered. Hypovolaemia, circulatory collapse and electrolyte imbalance should be corrected. Diabetes insipidus and hypothyroidism should be treated in the usual ways.

2. (F) (c)
SSRIs such as fluoxetine, paroxetine, sertraline and citalopram are antidepressants. They have less sedative effect and are less cardiotoxic than the tricyclic antidepressants and are therefore particularly useful in the elderly. The mechanism of hyponatraemia is unclear but is thought to be due to SIADH. It is one of the commonest reasons to stop their use in elderly patients who often have concurrent diuretic therapy which also causes hyponatraemia.

3. (A) (d)
Amitriptyline is a tricyclic antidepressant used in depressive conditions particularly where sedation is required. It has several side-effects including anticholinergic, cardiovascular, haematological and psychiatric effects. It may cause agranulocytosis, thrombocytopenia and eosinophilia, as well as hyponatraemia and derangement of the LFTs.

4. (B) (f)
The neuroleptic malignant syndrome may arise with phenothiazines (e.g. chlorpromazine), butyrophenones (e.g. haloperidol) and rarely with tricyclic antidepressants. It is characterised by a high fever, fluctuating level of consciousness, muscle rigidity and autonomic dysfunction such as urinary incontinence and resting tachycardia. The diagnosis should be suspected from the history and confirmed by grossly elevated CK levels and negative sepsis screen (the principal differential). Treatment should include withdrawal of the drug and supportive measures, including nutrition, intravenous fluids and urinary catheterisation.

5. (G) (b)
The phenothiazines are principally used in the treatment of schizophrenia and other psychoses. They have multiple side-effects including extrapyramidal movement disorders, for which procyclidine is given, anticholinergic effects, cardiovascular, endocrine and haematological effects. They may also cause derangement of the LFTs and cholestatic jaundice.

6. (C) (e)
Phenelzine is a MAOI. Their use is restricted because of the interactions they have with food substances such as cheese and yeast extracts, alcoholic drinks, and other drugs, particularly indirect acting sympathomimetics such as nasal decongestants and cough mixtures. They should not be given with the other classes of antidepressants as this too may lead to sympathomimetic effects. These interactions may precipitate dangerous rises in blood pressure, usually signalled by a severe, throbbing headache. All patients on MAOIs should be issued with a warning card explaining these interactions.

A less common side-effect includes peripheral neuropathy, similar to that caused by isoniazid.

7. (D) (a)
Flupenthixol is principally used in depot injections for the long-term control of schizophrenia. As with chlorpromazine it has multiple side-effects and may cause endocrine effects including hyperprolactinaemia, galactorrhoea and menstrual irregularity.

STATION 2.1

Patient history

I woke up on Monday morning (four days ago) with a very itchy right eye. I kept rubbing it and the next day my left eye was red and felt gritty and was watering. I tried washing my eyes under the tap but it didn't help much.

Two boys from my scout troop also had red eyes when we returned from a weekend 'outward bound' trip. We had spent two days camping in the forest and swam in the stream. My mother thinks I may have picked up a bug in camp.

I had a squint when I was young and had to wear glasses with a black patch on one side for a long time. My eyes are alright now.

Assessment	Good	Adequate	Poor/not asked
1. Polite introduction; establishes rapport	❑	❑	❑
2. Establishes severity and duration of symptoms	❑	❑	❑
3. Symptom progression and/or complications	❑	❑	❑
4. Enquiry into causative or associated factors	❑	❑	❑
5. Relieving factors or remedial measures	❑	❑	❑
6. Past medical history	❑	❑	❑
7. Makes reasonable attempt at a working diagnosis	❑	❑	❑
8. Performs all in a fluent, professional manner	❑	❑	❑

Comment

Four main causes of painful, red eyes are:
- Conjunctivitis
- Blepharitis (inflammation of lid margins with secondary ocular irritation)
- Allergic reactions
- Dysthyroid eye disease.

The relevant questions are:

Is there a discharge? Mucopurulent discharge is associated with bacterial conjunctivitis.

Is the patient atopic? He may be prone to allergic reactions in response to pollen, house dust or animal hair.

Is the patient hyperthyroid?

In conjunctivitis, the conjunctiva is usually diffusely red and haemorrhages may be present. The inflammation usually starts in one eye before infecting the other. The discharge may be purulent in bacterial infection and watery in viral infection or in atopic allergies. Pain is unusual whilst discomfort and irritation are common.

STATION 2.2

Answers and explanations

1. (D) (e) (H)
Keratoconjunctivitis sicca is part of the 'dry' sicca syndrome asociated with lacrymal and salivary gland infiltration by lymphocytes. The dry eye should be protected with hypromellose eye drops, which act as artificial tears, lubricating the cornea.

2. (E) (d) (J)
Anterior uveitis or iritis is associated with several systemic disorders including ankylosing spondylitis, Reiter's syndrome, Behçet's disease and sarcoidosis. It may be associated with pupillary constriction.

3.   (A)   (c)   (G)
Bacterial conjunctivitis is commonly caused by *Staphylococcus aureus,*
Haemophilus influenzae and *Streptococcus pneumoniae.* Less common
infections include gonococcus, trachoma, toxoplasmosis, and adeno
and herpes viruses.

4.   (B)   (a)   (I)
Scleritis and episcleritis are associated with rheumatoid arthritis and
Wegener's granulomatosis. It may lead to scleromalacia and perforation
if left untreated.

5.   (C)   (b)   (F)
HSV-1 and HSV-2 may both cause eye infection, although HSV-1 is
predominantly responsible. The infection should be treated with topical
acyclovir or vidarabine.

Comment

> Acute glaucoma is one of the most serious and sinister causes of red
> eye. The eye is often very painful and feels hard and uncomfortable.
> If glaucoma is suspected, an ophthalmology opinion should be
> sought.

STATION 2.3

Patient history

> I grind and polish gem stones and work on an electric lathe. My left
> eye became sore a couple of days ago and the pain is getting worse.
> My sight in that eye has become blurred and I find that the glare
> hurts the eye. I wear a magnifying eye-piece on my right eye when
> at work. My eyesight has been excellent and I do not wear
> spectacles. My general health is good except for a long-standing
> stomach ulcer for which I am on ranitidine. There is a history of
> glaucoma in the family. My mother and an older sister have this
> condition.

Assessment	Good	Adequate	Poor/not done
1. Polite introduction; establishes rapport	❑	❑	❑
2. Establishes severity and duration of symptoms	❑	❑	❑
3. Symptom progression and/or complications	❑	❑	❑
4. Enquiry into causative/ associated factors	❑	❑	❑
5. Relieving factors or remedial measures	❑	❑	❑
6. Past medical history	❑	❑	❑
7. Makes a reasonable attempt at a working diagnosis	❑	❑	❑
8. Performs all in a fluent, professional manner	❑	❑	❑

Comment

Questions to ask are:

1. Was the patient involved in activity associated with a high risk of corneal foreign body?
2. Is there a history of trauma to the eye?
3. Is looking at bright light painful?
4. Is vision blurred? (This is common in the painful red eye due to excess watering or a central corneal abrasion. Acute glaucoma causes corneal clouding and is a frequent cause in the elderly.)
5. Does the patient wear contact lenses? (Overworn or poorly cleaned contact lenses may induce corneal abrasion or ulcers.)
6. Has the patient had iritis (eye inflammation) in the past?
7. Has the patient had an eye operation recently? (Irritation to corneal sutures following cataract or squint surgery may produce a red, painful eye.)

STATION 2.4

Answers

1. Figure 2.4a   Hyphaema
    Figure 2.4b   Iridocyclitis
    Figure 2.4c   Retinal oedema and haemorrhage
    Figure 2.4d   Papilloedema

2. Traumatic iritis
    Glaucoma
    Dislocated lens or cataract
    Vitreous haemorrhage
    Retinal tear leading to retinal detachment
    Choroidal rupture
    Scleral rupture
    Optic nerve injury

3. **True:**   a, c, d
    False: b, e

Comment

Blunt injury to the eyeball causes compression of the iris by aqueous humour, causing a hyphaema or pressure increase in the posterior chamber, producing vitreous haemorrhage, retinal tear or scleral rupture. A 'blow out' fracture is when the compression force also causes the orbital floor to fracture. Initial treatment is to apply eye patches to both eyes to decrease eye movement, and the administration of diuretics and/or steroids to decrease intraocular pressure.

STATION 2.5

Answers

Figure 2.5a: Convergent squint (left eye). Refractory correction

Figure 2.5b: Acute conjunctivitis
Wash the eyes with normal saline or tap water

Figure 2.5c: Dysthyroid eye disease
Exposure keratitis (diplopia, cranial nerve palsies
III, IV VI, secondary glaucoma)

Figure 2.5d: Retinoblastoma
Pupillary white reflex

Comment

Retinoblastoma is usually detected during the first year of life. The patient is brought to the clinic on account of the peculiar white or yellow reflex 'amaurotic cat's eye'. The tumour is multicentric, affecting the other eye in a quarter of the patients. Extension along the optic nerve to the brain is common. Treatment is removal of the eye with a long length of the optic nerve. Exenteration of the orbit is required in locally advanced tumours. The prognosis is usually dismal.

STATION 2.6

Answers

1. Grave's orbitopathy

2. Exophthalmos or dysthyroid eye disease

3. Double vision
   Exposure keratitis
   Retinal or optic neuronal vascular impairment and secondary glaucoma

4. High doses of steroids with/without immunosuppressive agents
   Ensure lid closure at night by lid taping
   May require tarsorrhaphy or orbital decompression

Comment

Exophthalmos in Grave's disease is caused by exophthalmos-producing factor secreted by the hypothalamus. The condition does not always regress with control of the hyperthyroid state. When ophthalmoplegia or chemosis threatens vision, orbital decompression may be required. Systemic corticosteroids are often beneficial in reducing orbital oedema. In severe cases local radiotherapy to the orbit is required.

STATION 2.7

Answers

1. Chalazion (meibomian or tarsal cyst).

   A. Chalazion clamp   C. Curette
   B. Scalpel   D. Fine scissors

3. Equipment layout: chalazion clamp, chalazion curette, fine scissors and forceps, scalpel (No 11 and 15 blades), anaesthetic eye drops (amethocaine 1% of oxynuprocaine 0.4%), local anaesthetic for injection (0.5% Marcain or 1% lignocaine), antibiotic eye ointment, eyepad.

   Anaesthetise conjunctiva with drops.
   Local infiltration of anaesthetic agent (1– 2ml) around swelling
   Apply clamp so that cyst protrudes on conjunctival surface
   Vertical conjunctival incision into cyst
   Curette contents
   Instil antibiotic ointment
   Apply eyepad over closed eye and apply pressure for 10 minutes.
   Postoperative care: bathe eye daily and instil ointment twice daily for 3 days.

Comment

Inflammation of the glands of the eyelid results in a chalazion (meibomian cyst). They present as an acute or chronic swelling of the lid; spontaneous resolution is rare. Treatment is surgical; the conjunctival sac is well anaesthetised along with the lid. The latter is everted and a vertical incision is made at the point of greatest discoloration. The cavity is evacuated and curetted. The procedure is repeated if granulation tissue develops in the wound. A stye is an infection of an eyelash follicle.

STATION 2.8

Answers

1. Cataract

2. Congenital: infantile, Down's syndrome, dystrophic myotonia
   Metabolic: diabetes, galactosaemia, hypocalcaemia
   Steroid induced
   Physical causes (e.g. injury)
   Secondary to other eye disease
   Skin diseases: atopic dermatitis
   Senility

3. Maturity of a cataract

4. Surgical extraction of cataract, with intraocular lens implant.

Comment

No medical measures are useful in the treatment of cataract once eye opacities have developed. In acquired cataract a metabolic cause such as diabetes mellitus must be looked for and treated. Surgical removal is indicated when the cataract is mature. In the meantime, the refraction should be corrected at frequent intervals as it deteriorates. Advice should be given on adequate illumination for reading.

A secondary cataract is when the opacity returns following lens extraction. This is due to part of the lens cortex sticking to the capsule and subsequently proliferating, especially when the cataract is not mature. Further surgery is usually indicated.

STATION 2.9

Assessment	Good	Adequate	Poor/not done
1. Demonstration of visual acuity (6/6 normal) of each eye using the Snellen chart	❏	❏	❏
2. Test of peripheral vision of each eye, comparing with your own (Figure 2.9a)	❏	❏	❏
3. Test for hemianopia (homonomous defect) (figure 2.9a)	❏	❏	❏

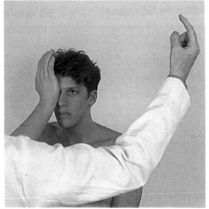

Fig. 2.9a

Comment

Examination of the central vision is tested by using the letter sets on a Snellen chart at a distance of six metres. Vision is expressed as a fraction of the normal – the latter being 6/6, if the patient only sees the letter twice its size, visual acuity is 6/12. (These figures are written on each line of the chart.)

The visual fields can be quickly assessed by the confrontation test, in which the patient closes one eye, looking straight with the other eye into the corresponding eye of the doctor. The doctor's moving finger is introduced in turn from the periphery in the four diagonal positions, and the patient indicates once the movement is seen. A more precise test is carried out by perimetry, where the visual fields are mapped.

STATION 2.10

Answers and explanations

1. (D) (g)
Wilson's disease is due to an abnormality of copper metabolism, centred in the biliary tree, leading to ectopic deposition within the viscera. The common sites include the liver, eye, basal ganglia, myocardium and kidneys.

The Kayser–Fleischer rings are pathognomonic and appear as grey corneal rings in dark eyes and brown rings in light-coloured eyes.

2. (H) (e)
Down's syndrome (trisomy 21) is associated with several eye abnormalities, including epicanthic folds, keratoconus, brushfield spots and infantile cataracts.

3. (A) (f)
Marfan's syndrome is an autosomal dominant disorder due to abnormalities within the fibrillin gene on chromosome 15. Fibrillin is an important component of several connective tissues, including the suspensory ligament of the lens. The abnormality classically causes superior dislocation of the lens, unlike homocystinuria, a similar clinical condition, which causes downward dislocation. The unsupported iris wobbles with movement, termed 'iridodonesis'.

4. (G) (a)
Pingueculae are subconjunctival areas of yellowish brown. These are raised, yellowish-white areas that occur, usually nasally around the limbus of the eye. They are often bilateral and predominantly occur in middle to old age. They are usually benign but may be associated with Gaucher's disease, in which they may have a more brown pigmentation.

5. (B) (d)
Tuberous sclerosis is an autosomal dominant disorder but commonly arises through spontaneous mutation. It is associated with the classical triad of adenoma sebaceum, epilepsy and severe mental retardation. Retinal phacomas are glial masses seen on retinoscopy. Other common lesions include shagreen patches and ash leaf spots.

6.   (C)   (b)
Angioid streaks are irregular grey lines radiating out from the optic disc. They may occur in pseudoxanthoma elasticum, Paget's disease of the bone, sickle cell disease and Ehlers–Danlos syndrome. They may be associated with blue sclera in pseudoxanthoma.

7.   (F)   (h)
Cherry red spots occur in several of the sphingolipidoses, including Neimann–Pick and Tay–Sachs disease. They arise due to the abnormal sphingolipid accumulation within the ganglion cells centred within the macula.

8.   (E)   (c)
Blue or pigmented sclera arise in several disorders, including osteogenesis imperfecta, pseudoxanthoma elasticum and alkaptonuria.

This list, and the answers to the 'red eye' in station 2.2 emphasise the importance of the clinical examination of the eye. For diagnosing common conditions, such as anaemia and jaundice, to hereditary disorders, the eye should not be overlooked.

STATION 2.11

Patient history

I am 65 years old and a retired car salesman. I had a heart attack 12 years ago and have long-standing diabetes mellitus, which is controlled with diet and tablets. I also have high blood pressure.

In the last six months I have had four or five episodes of dizziness associated with vomiting. The last episode was 2 weeks ago. I attended the Accident and Emergency Department and they referred me to this clinic.

The episodes come on suddenly with no obvious cause. The last one started while I was just sitting and reading the newspaper. It's as if the whole world is spinning round, like being drunk. It doesn't get any better if I stand up or lie down, or if I move my head, although this makes me feel more nauseated. I have been sick a few times. I have no other neurological symptoms and haven't had any tinnitus or deafness. The episodes last five to six hours and then just go away.

I am taking atenolol for my blood pressure and heart problem. I stopped taking aspirin tablets about a year ago because I felt I did not need them any more.

Assessment	Good	Adequate	Poor/not done
1. Polite introduction; establishes rapport	❏	❏	❏
2. Establishes duration of presenting complaint	❏	❏	❏
3. Establishes what the patient means by dizziness (i.e. vertigo)	❏	❏	❏

	Good	Adequate	Poor/not done
4. Establishes/excludes the characteristics of vertigo:			
Onset – acute or insidious	❏	❏	❏
Pattern – continuous or episodic	❏	❏	❏
Duration of episodes	❏	❏	❏
Relieving factors	❏	❏	❏
Exacerbating factors	❏	❏	❏
Associated auditory problems (i.e. deafness, tinnitus)	❏	❏	❏
Other neurological symptoms *(i.e. diplopia, dysarthria, ataxia)*	❏	❏	❏
Associated nausea and *vomiting*	❏	❏	❏
5. Establishes previous medical history, i.e. hypertension, CVA, IHD, DM	❏	❏	❏
6. Establishes treatment history (i.e. excludes drugs causing postural hypotension)	❏	❏	❏
7. Makes a reasonable attempt at a diagnosis	❏	❏	❏
8. Does all in a fluent, professional manner	❏	❏	❏

Diagnosis
Vertebrobasilar transient ischaemic attacks.

STATION 2.12

Patient history

I am married and work as a medical secretary at a private clinic in town. I woke up this morning bleeding from the nose with blood all over the pillow and the bed-sheet. I could not stop the bleeding with finger pressure over the bridge of the nose. I have had nose bleeds in childhood and early teens but had grown out of it. At the time my doctors could not find a cause for it.

I have always been in excellent health except during my two pregnancies four and six years ago when I developed pre-eclampsia and was put on tablets to control my blood pressure. I stopped taking these two to three months after the birth of my children. When I was pregnant I had kidney and bladder infections which cleared on antibiotics. I am presently not on any medications.

Assessment	Good	Adequate	Poor/not done
1. Polite introduction; establishes rapport	❏	❏	❏
2. Establishes severity and duration of symptoms	❏	❏	❏
3. Symptom progression and/or complications	❏	❏	❏
4. Enquiry into causative/associated factors	❏	❏	❏
5. Relieving factors or remedial measures	❏	❏	❏
6. Past medical history	❏	❏	❏
7. Makes a reasonable attempt at a working diagnosis	❏	❏	❏
8. Performs all in a fluent, professional manner	❏	❏	❏

Comment

Nose bleeds may be due to local or systemic causes. Patients who are hypertensive do not bleed more often but when epistaxis occurs it may be more severe and may require admission. Bleeding uncontrolled by external pressure requires gauze packing or balloon compression for 24–48 hours with bed rest and sedation.

In the young patient bleeding is usually from the anterior aspect of the nasal septum (Little's area) and the bleeding area moves posteriorly with age. Other systemic causes are familial telangiectasia (Osler's disease), blood dyscrasias and anti-coagulant therapy.

STATION 2.13

History from parent

We are staying at a holiday camp and Susie became listless three days ago and then started running a fever, developed a sore throat and has become hoarse and is losing her voice. I have been giving her two teaspoonfuls of Calpol every few hours but last night she became hot, flushed and breathless and I am very worried that she is now catching her breath and coughing hurts her throat.

Susie has had chest infections in the past when she had the 'flu but she has never had problems with her breathing. She has always been an active child and her health has been very good on the whole. She was a premature baby and was nursed in an incubator for nearly a month when she was born.

Assessment	Good	Adequate	Poor/not done
1. Polite introduction; establishes rapport with parent and child	❏	❏	❏
2. Establishes severity and duration of symptoms	❏	❏	❏
3. Symptom progression and/or complications	❏	❏	❏
4. Enquiry into causative/associated factors	❏	❏	❏
5. Relieving factors or remedial measures	❏	❏	❏
6. Past medical history	❏	❏	❏
7. Makes a reasonable attempt at a working diagnosis	❏	❏	❏
8. Performs all in a fluent, professional manner	❏	❏	❏

Comment

Acute tonsillitis is a pyogenic infection of the tonsillar lymph nodes caused usually by group A haemolytic *Streptococcus* spp. It is characterised by sore throat, hoarseness, dysphagia and fever. There may be cervical lymphadenopathy (jugulo-digastric nodes). White pustules may be visible on the surface of the palatine tonsils.

Recurrent infection, particularly if this is over an 18–24 month period, is an indication for tonsillectomy.

Surgery is also indicated for airway obstruction, peritonsillar abscess and the sleep apnoea syndrome. There is no evidence of long-term immunological sequelae following tonsillectomy.

STATION 2.14

Answers

A.

1. Right sided LMN facial nerve palsy

2. Ask the patient to whistle, smile and frown or grimace
   Attempt to open the eyelids against resistance

B. All are **True**

Comment

In upper motor neurone lesions of the facial nerve the lower part of the face is more severely affected. Recovery is usual and precedes that of the limbs on the affected side. In lower motor neurone lesions the weakness is to the same extent in both upper and lower halves of the face. Paralysis is often severe, causing facial asymmetry at rest. Tears and saliva may drip down that side. Bell's palsy is unilateral and is of sudden onset and presumed to be an immune response, producing facial nerve swelling and resultant compression in the narrow confines of the temporal bone. Complete or partial recovery is usual. Steroid therapy is indicated within the first 48 hours of onset.

STATION 2.15

Answers

1. Pleomorphic adenoma of the parotid gland, mixed cellular histological pattern

2. Conservative, superficial parotidectomy

3. Facial palsy; identify and preserve the facial nerve trunk and its branches during surgery

4. Carcinoma of the parotid gland

Comment

A swelling of the parotid gland must be distinguished from other swellings in the cheek and anterior triangle of the neck, the most common being enlarged lymph nodes. Pleomorphic adenomas are benign but may become malignant after a period of many years. Fine needle aspiration cytology of the lesion is to be avoided, due to the risk of tumour implantation in the subcutaneous tissue. Enucleation of the tumour from its false capsule results in recurrence, and treatment is by parotidectomy; the facial nerve and its branches that are present within the gland must be identified and preserved. Most parotid tumours lie superficial to the facial nerve branches and a superficial conservative parotidectomy is performed. When the deep part of the gland is involved, great care must be taken to preserve the overlying nerves when resecting the tumour.

STATION 2.16

History from carer

Timmy has been irritable for the past four days and has been off his food. He was running a fever yesterday and was violently sick this morning. He keeps holding his left ear and crying. He wouldn't let me get near his ear and he goes into tantrums. I am at my wits' end coping with him and he refuses to take his Calpol syrup.

I have had him for a little over a year and he has had the odd cold and 'flu and tummy upset. His mother told me that he was a well baby and has had all his vaccinations. She didn't say anything about having ear problems.

Assessment	Good	Adequate	Poor/not done
1. Polite introduction; establishes rapport with patient and carer	❏	❏	❏
2. Establishes severity and duration of symptoms	❏	❏	❏
3. Symptom progression and/or complications	❏	❏	❏
4. Enquiry into causative/ associated factors	❏	❏	❏
5. Relieving factors or remedial measures	❏	❏	❏
6. Past medical history	❏	❏	❏
7. Makes a reasonable attempt at a working diagnosis	❏	❏	❏
8. Performs all in a fluent, professional manner	❏	❏	❏

Comment

Acute suppurative otitis media (middle ear infection) in children usually follows a recurrent upper respiratory tract infection. Initially there is an inflammation of the Eustachian tube progressing to inflammation of the tympanic membrane. Otoscopy reveals a red, lustreless bulging drum. Untreated, the infection may lead to perforation of the drum or spread to the air cells in the mastoid or petrous temporal bone.

A persisting discharge indicates chronicity (glue ear) and may present with hearing loss, recurrent ear infections, developmental or behavioural problems.

STATION 2.17

Assessment	Good	Adequate	Poor/not done
1. Auroscopic examination			
(a) Polite introduction; establishes rapport and explains the examination	❏	❏	❏
(b) Technique of examination			
Positions patient appropriately	❏	❏	❏
Inserts auroscope confidently and safely	❏	❏	❏
Retracts pinna	❏	❏	❏
Visualisation of structures	❏	❏	❏

2. Otitis externa
   Otitis media
   Infectious (bullous) myringitis
   Perforation of the drum

Comment

The positioning of the auroscope and technique of examination are important as injury to the external meatus and the drum may be caused by injudicious movement (figure 2.17a). Children may require sedation.

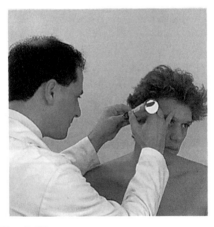

Fig. 2.17a

STATION 3.1

Patient history

I am 43 years old and have had non insulin dependent diabetes for the past 4 years. I have had raised blood pressure for the last 3 years. About 6 months ago I began to experience a dull aching in the front of my chest, particularly when running or 'overstraining'. The pains last from 3 to 5 minutes but then settle down. In the last month the pain has been coming on more regularly and I have had two episodes of pain while at rest.

This episode of pain began 6 to 8 hours ago while I was watching television. It is the worst pain I've ever had, like someone sitting on my chest. The pain is across the front of my chest and radiates to my jaw and left arm. The pain is not related to position or breathing. It was eased with oxygen in the ambulance and with some spray under my tongue in the Accident and Emergency Department.

My father died aged 62 of heart problems. My older brother also has ischaemic heart disease (angina).

I have smoked about 10–20 cigarettes a day since I was 17 and drink 2–3 whiskies at night. I do not know my 'cholesterol' level, but am otherwise well.

Assessment	Good	Adequate	Poor/not done
1. Polite introduction; establishes rapport	❏	❏	❏
2. Establishes previous history of similar chest pain	❏	❏	❏
3. Establishes onset of current chest pain	❏	❏	❏
4. Establishes character of pain	❏	❏	❏
5. Establishes site of the pain	❏	❏	❏
6. Establishes sites of radiation of the pain	❏	❏	❏
7. Establishes relieving factors	❏	❏	❏
8. Establishes exacerbating factors	❏	❏	❏

	Good	Adequate	Poor/not done
9. Establishes associated factors (e.g. palpitations, sweating, nausea, dyspnoea)	❑	❑	❑
10. Establishes associated risk factors of ischaemic disease:			
Smoking		❑	❑
Hypertension		❑	❑
Diabetes		❑	❑
History of IHD, PVD, CVA	❑	❑	❑
Family history of IHD, CVA		❑	❑
Alcohol excess		❑	❑
Hyperlipidaemia		❑	❑
11. Does all in a fluent, professional manner	❑	❑	❑
12. Makes the correct diagnosis	❑	❑	❑

Diagnosis
Ischaemic cardiac chest pain – unstable angina/myocardial infarction.

STATION 3.2

Patient history

> I am 29 years old and a policeman. I am normally fit and well and have no significant illnesses of note. I do not smoke or drink alcohol. Over the last week I thought I had flu, with worsening lethargy, muscle pain and a sore throat. In the last 2 days I have also had a fever and chest pain.
>
> The pain is sharp, in the middle of my chest and it radiates to my shoulders and the left side of my chest. The pain seems to be worse when I am lying down but seems better when I lean forward. It is also eased with paracetamol or aspirin.

Assessment	Good	Adequate	Poor/not done
1. Polite introduction; establishes rapport	❏	❏	❏
2. Establishes any previous similar episodes of pain	❏	❏	❏
3. Establishes onset of the chest pain	❏	❏	❏
4. Establishes character of the chest pain	❏	❏	❏
5. Establishes site of the pain	❏	❏	❏
6. Establishes radiation of the pain	❏	❏	❏
7. Establishes exacerbating factors (e.g. position)	❏	❏	❏
8. Establishes relieving factors	❏	❏	❏
9. Establishes associated symptoms (e.g. fever, pharyngitis, myalgia)	❏	❏	❏
10. Excludes risk factors of ischaemic heart disease	❏	❏	❏
11. Makes a reasonable attempt at the diagnosis	❏	❏	❏
12. Does all in a fluent, professional manner	❏	❏	❏

Diagnosis
Acute viral pericarditis

Comment

Acute pericarditis is inflammation of the pericardium. It is characterized clinically by a sharp anterior chest pain, eased with leaning forward and NSAIDs, and exacerbated by lying down, movement and inspiration. The pain may radiate to the shoulders, neck and back.

Principal causes:

- **Bacterial**: *Streptococcus, Staphylococcus, Haemophilus,* tuberculosis
- **Viral**: this is a common cause; Coxsackie may occur in epidemics
- **Metabolic**: uraemia
- **Malignancy**: bronchial, breast, leukaemia, myeloma, Hodgkin's disease
- **Postmyocardial infarction**: common after anterior MIs
- **Dressler's syndrome**: occurs 1 month to 1 year after an acute MI. It is an autoimmune disorder characterized by fever, pericarditis and pericardial effusion.

STATION 3.3a

Patient history

I am 33 years old and have previously been fit and well. My father died unexpectedly 6 weeks ago of a heart attack. In the last 3 to 4 weeks I have been experiencing left-sided chest pains and I am worried that these might be angina.

The pain is just below my nipple and is sharp in nature. It seems to go through to my back and is made worse when I press on the area where the pain is. The pain lasts a few seconds at a time and then stops. There is no association with exertion and I have no other symptoms with it. I have never suffered similar pains in the past.

I have smoked 15 to 20 cigarettes a day for 10 years and drink 20 to 30 units of alcohol per week, mainly in the form of beer. I am not diabetic and I have not had any heart problems, a stroke or blood vessel disease. There is no other family history of heart disease, diabetes or stroke. At school I was a keen sportsman but have let myself go recently. I now do little exercise. I am not taking any medications.

I am very concerned about the pains and think I may be in danger of having a heart attack, like my father. I think perhaps I should consider changing my lifestyle.

Assessment	Good	Adequate	Poor/not done
1. Polite introduction; establishes rapport	❑	❑	❑
2. Establishes chest pains only started after father's death	❑	❑	❑
3. Establishes characteristics of the pain:			
Site		❑	❑
Character		❑	❑
Duration		❑	❑
Radiation		❑	❑
Relieving factors		❑	❑
Exacerbating factors		❑	❑
Associated symptoms		❑	❑
4. Establishes patient's risk factors for ischaemic heart disease:			
Smoking	❑	❑	❑
Alcohol intake	❑	❑	❑
Lipids	❑	❑	❑
Family history of IHD, CVA, PVD	❑	❑	❑
Previous medical history, e.g. diabetes, PVD, IHD, CVA	❑	❑	❑
5. Reassures patient of benign nature of chest pain	❑	❑	❑
6. Addresses patient's concerns in an empathetic manner	❑	❑	❑
7. Addresses risk factors and lifestyle changes (i.e. stopping smoking, exercise, weight loss)	❑	❑	❑
8. Does all in a fluent and organised manner	❑	❑	❑

Diagnosis

Non-ischaemic chest pain probably of musculo-skeletal origin.

STATION 3.4

Patient history

I am 67 years old and I have had angina for 8 years. I have not had a heart attack. In the last 2 to 3 months I have been getting fast, irregular palpitations. I am not aware of anything that specifically brings them on. When I get them, I also feel a tightness across my chest, not unlike my normal angina, with dizziness, sweating, nausea and a feeling that I am going to pass out. I have never lost consciousness. The palpitations last between 30 seconds and 5 minutes and have, on occasion, woken me up.

I am known to have heart problems but have no diabetes, blood vessel disease in my legs or feet and have not had a stroke. I gave up smoking 6 years ago and drink 5 to 6 gin and tonics per week. I am on aspirin and GTN spray.

Assessment	Good	Adequate	Poor/not done
1. Polite introduction; establishes rapport	❏	❏	❏
2. Establishes duration of the symptoms	❏	❏	❏
3. Establishes character of the palpitations (i.e. rate and rhythm)	❏	❏	❏
4. Establishes onset and duration of the palpitations	❏	❏	❏
5. Establishes/excludes associated symptoms:			
Sweating		❏	❏
Fainting feeling		❏	❏
Dizziness		❏	❏
Loss of consciousness		❏	❏
Chest pain		❏	❏
Nausea		❏	❏

		Good	Adequate	Poor/not done
6.	Establishes risk factors for cardiac disease and palpitations			
	Smoking		❏	❏
	Alcohol excess		❏	❏
	IHD, CVA, PVD		❏	❏
	Diabetes		❏	❏
	Hypertension		❏	❏
7.	Establishes present medications: Aspirin and GTN spray	❏	❏	❏
9.	Does all in a fluent, professional manner	❏	❏	❏
10	Makes a reasonable attempt at the diagnosis	❏	❏	❏

Diagnosis
Paroxysmal fast irregular palpitations – differential includes paroxysmal atrial fibrillation or ventricular tachyarrhythmia.

STATION 3.5

Patient history

I am a retired chartered surveyor, aged 63. I was well until 8 months ago, when I started to experience shortness of breath when walking. Initially it didn't worry me too much, and I could still walk 3 to 4 miles on the flat. However, in the last few months this has progressively worsened and now I can only manage 400 to 500 metres, and less on hills. I am forced to stop because of the breathlessness. In the last 3 to 4 weeks my ankles have been swelling to the point where I can no longer put on my shoes. During this time I have had to sleep with 3 pillows. In the last few weeks I have woken several times with breathlessness, which has resolved about 10 minutes after I have got out of bed.

I have not had any palpitations, chest pain, cough, sputum, coughing up of blood or wheeziness.

I have never previously been ill, in particular I have never had any form of heart disease, a stroke, diabetes or blood vessel disease in my legs or feet. I gave up smoking 15 years ago, and drink only 1 to 2 pints of beer per week. I am not on any medications at present.

Assessment	Good	Adequate	Poor/not done
1. Polite introduction; establishes rapport	❑	❑	❑
2. Establishes the duration of symptoms	❑	❑	❑
3. Establishes previous and present exercise tolerance	❑	❑	❑
4. Establishes presence of peripheral oedema	❑	❑	❑
5. Establishes 3 pillow orthopnoea and episodes of paroxysmal nocturnal dyspnoea	❑	❑	❑
6. Excludes other cardiac symptoms (e.g. palpitations, angina)	❑	❑	❑

	Good	Adequate	Poor/not done
7. Excludes respiratory symptoms, e.g. cough, sputum, wheeze, haemoptysis	❑	❑	❑
8. Excludes common precipitating causes and risk factors for heart failure:			
Ischaemic heart disease		❑	❑
Hypertension		❑	❑
Alcohol excess		❑	❑
Smoking		❑	❑
Valvular heart disease		❑	❑
Current medications		❑	❑
Known diabetes, stroke or peripheral vascular disease		❑	❑
9. Does all in a fluent, professional manner	❑	❑	❑

Diagnosis
Idiopathic cardiac failure

STATION 3.6

Assessment	Good	Adequate	Poor/not done
1. Polite introduction; establishes rapport	❑	❑	❑
Colour, skin nutrition and warmth. Muscle bulk	❑	❑	❑
Technique of palpation and description of peripheral pulses (i.e. femoral, popliteal, posterior tibial, dorsalis pedis, peroneal)	❑	❑	❑
2. Measurement of brachial systolic pressure	❑	❑	❑
Measurement of ankle systolic pressure	❑	❑	❑
Calculation of the pressure index	❑	❑	❑
3. Does all in a fluent professional manner	❑	❑	❑

Comment

Chronic lower limb ischaemia clinically manifests as trophic skin change and reduction in muscle bulk. Reduced or abnormal femoral pulses suggest aorto-iliac disease; the abdomen should be palpated to exclude an aneurysm.

Ankle: brachial pressure index is a sensitive measure of foot perfusion. The post-exercise index is measured after 1 to 5 minutes exercising on a treadmill. It indicates the extent of collateral circulation and the degree of occlusive disease. In significant disease the index falls following exercise.

STATION 3.7

Answers

1.	I normal	II normal	III normal	IV C
2.	I normal	II normal	III raised	IV A
3.	I raised	II raised	III raised	IV F
4.	I raised	II raised	III raised	IV B
5.	I normal	II raised	III raised	IV E
6.	I normal	II raised	III raised	IV D

Comment

Acute bleeding disorders encountered during surgery or in its immediate aftermath are due to haemodilution from IV fluids or large volume banked blood transfusions. Other causes are hypoxia, intravascular haemolysis, infection and thrombosis. Abruptio placentae, amniotic fluid embolus and retained products of conception produce bleeding disorders in obstetric practice.

The investigation of a suspected bleeding tendency begins with the bleeding history, this may suggest an acquired or congenital disorder of primary or secondary haemostasis. Clinical evaluation of the patient's history, family history, details of site, frequency and character of haemorrhagic manifestations (e.g. purpura, bruising, haematoma, haemarthrosis) may suggest the diagnosis, this is confirmed by screening tests and, if necessary, by specific investigations.

STATION 3.8

Answers and explanations

1. (C) (d)
G6PD deficiency is an X-linked disorder which has several recognized variants. The variant suffered by black Africans and black African Americans (G6PD GdA-) has a self-limiting haemolytic anaemia as the bone marrow is able to compensate by increasing red cell production. However, in the Mediterranean variant (G6PD Gd Med) following an oxidant insult (e.g. sepsis, myocardial infarction or diabetic coma) gross haemolysis occurs and will be fatal unless the cause is treated and the patient is transfused. Classically this reaction may be seen after the ingestion of fava beans. Heinz bodies are seen in the blood film (hence the expression, 'Beans means Heinz'!).

2. (D) (e)
This patient presents with the classical symptoms of a mycoplasma pneumonia. This is associated with a cold antibody (IgM) Coomb's positive autoimmune haemolytic anaemia. A Coomb's test is performed using a combination of the patient's serum and Coomb's serum. Coomb's serum is an antihuman serum and causes agglutination of the patient's red cells if certain antibodies are present on their surface. The temperature at which these antibodies attach themselves to the red cells characterize the haemolysis into cold (37 °C) and warm (40 °C) types.

3. (B) (c)
This patient has β-thalassaemia which is a common haemolytic disorder especially found around the Mediterranean, the Middle East and the Indian sub-continent. The patients with severe disease, thalassaemia major, present in the first few years of life with recurrent infections, severe anaemia and extramedullary haemopoiesis. These patients require regular transfusion and often develop transfusion siderosis. This is countered by using the chelating agent desferrioxamine.

4. (E) (a)
SLE is associated with a warm (IgG) Coomb's positive autoimmune haemolytic anaemia. Other causes include carcinoma, haematological malignancy (e.g. CLL and lymphoma) and drugs, the most common being methyl dopa.

5. (A) (b)

Sickle cell disease is a common haemolytic disorder in black races particularly those from Africa, the Caribbean and in African Americans. It also occurs in the Indian sub-continent and the Middle East. The haemolysis is often mild in heterozygotes and may remain undiscovered until a severe insult, such as sepsis or general anaesthesia. Homozygotes present in childhood and suffer a debilitating multisystem disorder. Complications include bone pain, bone necrosis, including avascular necrosis of the femoral head, and rarely *Salmonella* osteomyelitis; cerebral infarcts and epilepsy, acute papillary necrosis and tubulo-interstitial nephritis causing renal failure and pneumonitis leading to respiratory failure.

Treatment of an acute sickle cell crisis should include treatment of the precipitating cause, maintenance of hydration with intravenous fluids, oxygen via face mask and analgesia, usually with opiates.

STATION 3.9

Answers

(A)	3		(D)	6
(B)	5		(E)	1
(C)	2		(F)	4

Comment

Warfarin is a coumarin anticoagulant which exerts its effects by acting as a vitamin K antagonist, inhibiting factors II, VII, IX and X of the clotting cascade. Warfarin therapy should aim to maintain the INR between 2–3 for thromboembolic disease and between 3–4 for prosthetic heart valves. One should never reverse the effects of warfarin with a full dose of vitamin K (10 mg) unless instructed to do so by a haematologist or senior medical opinion. If a full dose is given the patient cannot be anticoagulated with warfarin for 3 months and the patient therefore requires subcutaneous heparin. If the patient is actively bleeding the anticoagulant effect can be reversed using FFP and small doses of vitamin K, 1–4 mg.

When faced with a patient with liver disease who has a raised INR, vitamin K should be administered carefully by intravenous injection. These patients should not receive intramuscular injections as this causes severe intramuscular haematomas and necrosis.

STATION 3.10

Answers and explanations

Blood test	Blood bottle
(a) Check Hb post transfusion	A
(b) Blood glucose	B or F
(c) Serum lipids	B
(d) Cross match	D
(e) Serum potassium	B
(f) Auto antibody screen	B
(g) Malaria screen	A
(h) Atypical pneumonia screen	B
(i) Thyroid function tests	B
(j) Platelet count – thrombocytopenia	A
(k) INR	C
(l) Amylase	B
(m) FDPs (fibrinogen degradation products)	C
(n) Serum osmolality	B
(o) ESR	A or E

Bottle

A – 4.5 ml bottle containing EDTA. Traditionally has purple top. Principally used for FBC; Glycosylated HB [HBAlc], Blood film and T-cell and B-cell markers. It is now used for the ESR.

B – This is a 7 ml bottle containing a clot activating agent [gel] in its base. It is used for U+Es, serum glucose, amylase, LFTs, TFTs, Lipids, Cardiac Enzymes, autoantibodies and osmolality. It ma have an orange or an orange and black speckled top.

C – This is a 4.5ml bottle containing Sodium Citrate. It is used for coagulation tests including INR, APTT, TT, FDPs and D-Dimer. It has a light blue top.

D – This is a 7.0 ml bottle with a pink top which is solely used for cross match samples. It has to be completed including a signature.

E – This black topped bottle is used for an ESR but has been largely replaced by the FBC bottle.

F – This grey topped bottle is used solely for measurement of serum glucose. Its use has been made redundant in both hospitals by the ability of the new machines to analyse glucose from bottle B.

STATION 3.11

Answers

1.	(D)		5.	(A)
2.	(G)		6.	(C)
3.	(F)		7.	(E)
4.	(B)			

Comment

Creatine phosphokinase (CPK) or creatine kinase has several isoenzymes and is found primarily in voluntary muscle, myocardium and brain tissue. Medical students are often only aware that a raised CPK or CK is caused by an acute myocardial infarction. However, strokes, recurrent falls, non-accidental injury and myositis are all common causes and need to be taken into consideration in a differential diagnosis. Patients should not be given thrombolytic therapy solely on the basis of a raised CPK.

STATION 3.12

Answers

1. For limb leads see Figure 3A, page 62; for chest leads V1–V6 see Figure 3.12ai

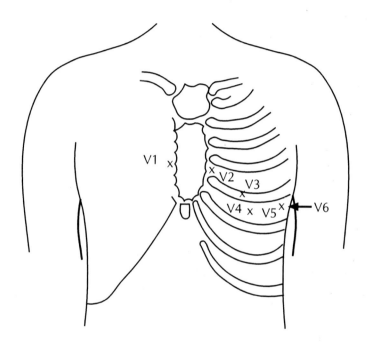

Fig. 3.12ai

2. (a) Sinus bradycardia, 56 bpm
   (b) Sinus rhythm
   (c) Normal axis
   (d) No the P wave is broadened and notched suggesting P mitrale
   (e) Yes
   (f) Yes
   (g) ST elevation: leads STII, III and a aVF
   ST depression: leads V3–6, I and aVL
   This is consistent with an acute inferior MI with widespread septolateral ischaemia.

STATION 3.13

Answers

1. **(a) True** **(b) True** **(c) False** **(d) False** **(e) False**
This ECG shows a right bundle branch block pattern with first degree heart block and left axis deviation. This combination is termed trifascicular block. The rate is approximately 100 bpm. This pattern may lead to complete heart block and the patient should have a 24-hour tape to exclude prolonged episodes of heart block. Such patients need a permanent pacemaker.

2. **(a) True** **(b) True** **(c) False** **(d) True** **(e) False**
This is a left bundle branch block pattern. There is a sinus tachycardia with P pulmonale. The axis is normal. Left bundle branch block is a pathological pattern whereas right bundle branch block occurs in approximately 3% of the healthy population.

3. **(a) True** **(b) False** **(c) False** **(d) True** **(e) True**
This patient is in atrial fibrillation. Rate = 100–150; axis normal; voltage criteria of left ventricular hypertrophy – the S wave in V2 + the R wave in V5 > 40 mm. (In this case the SV1 + RV5 = 25 + 27 = 52 mm)

4. **(a) True** **(b) True** **(c) False** **(d) True** **(e) True**
The ECG shows an acute inferoposterior MI with lateral ischaemia. There is evidence of first degree heart block and such ischaemia predisposes to various degrees of atrioventricular nodal block. The patient should be treated with aspirin and, if no contraindications, thrombolysis.

5. **(a) True** **(b) False** **(c) False** **(d) False** **(e) True**
This ECG was taken from a patient with a large pulmonary embolism. There is a sinus tachycardia with the axis deviating toward the right. There is a right bundle branch block pattern and the rarely seen S1,Q3,T3 pattern (i.e. a deep S wave in lead I, and a Q wave and inverted T wave in lead III).

STATION 3.14

Answers and explanations

1. (a) False (b) False (c) True (d) False (e) True
This is a portable erect (AP) CXR showing diffuse interstitial shadowing consistent with pulmonary oedema. The patient should initially be treated sitting upright with oxygen and intravenous diuretics.

2. (a) True (b) False (c) False (d) False (e) False
This chest X-ray shows evidence of chronic biventricular cardiac failure. The 6 signs of cardiac failure on a CXR are cardiomegaly, pleural effusions, fluid in the horizontal fissure, upper lobe blood diversion, Kerley B lines and interstitial oedema (classically giving the fluffy 'bat winging' appearance). Kerley B lines are small horizontal straight lines at the bases of lung fields and represent fluid between the interlobular septa and lymphatics (not present on this X-ray).

3. (a) False (b) False (c) True (d) True (e) True
This X-ray shows 'mitralisation' of the left heart border. There is cardiomegaly and loss of the left atrial appendage leading to a straight left heart border. Associated radiographic signs include enlarged pulmonary arteries and 'pruning' of the peripheral pulmonary markings, consistent with secondary pulmonary hypertension. The mitral valve may also be calcified.

4. (a)True (b) False (c) True (d) False (e) False
This X-ray shows a large globular heart consistent with a pericardial effusion. As an effusion enlarges it may constrict the heart to the point where it is unable to contract. This is termed cardiac tamponade. Clinical signs associated with tamponade, or a large effusion, include low volume pulse, hypotension, pulsus paradoxus and Kussmaul's sign. The ECG shows small, low voltage complexes.

STATION 3.15

Answers

(A) Left main stem
(B) Right coronary artery
(C) Marginal branch of the right coronary artery
(D) Left anterior interventricular artery
(E) Apex of the left ventricle
(F) Stenosis in right coronary artery

1. Inferior leads II, III and aVF

2. Typically – sinus bradycardia and varying degrees of heart block including complete heart block. This may require insertion of a temporary pacemaker.

3. In symptomatic single vessel disease, balloon angioplasty is often recommended.

STATION 3.16

Answers

A. 1. Carotid arteriogram/angiogram

    2. A - Common carotid artery
       B - Internal carotid artery
       C - External carotid artery

    3. Tight stenosis of the origin of the internal carotid artery

    4. Non-critical stenosis: aspirin or persantin therapy to reduce rouleaux formation and 3 to 6-monthly duplex scan surveillance
       Critical stenosis: balloon angioplasty or carotid endarterectomy

B. 1.   (a) no   (b) no   (c) yes   (d) no
    2.   (a) yes   (b) no   (c) no   (d) yes
    3.   (a) no   (b) yes   (c) yes   (d) yes
    4.   (a) yes   (b) yes   (c) yes   (d) no

Comment

Atheromatous plaques in the intima may produce luminal narrowing or may ulcerate, producing atheromatous emboli, leading to a stroke. Critical stenosis (narrowing > 70%) or ulceration on angiography with TIAs requires revascularisation to restore normal blood flow to the cerebral hemisphere.

STATION 3.17

Answers

1. (a) Femoral angiogram (arteriogram)
   (b) Stenosis of the iliac arteries
   (c) Smoking, hypercholesterolaemia, diabetes mellitus, hypertension, family history of arterial disease
   (d) Claudication, rest pain, peripheral gangrene

2. (a) False   (b) True   (c) False   (d) False

Comment

Claudication is the main symptom of PVD, with rest pain and gangrene being the end result of disease progression. Angiography is indicated for progressive disease to ascertain suitability for vascular reconstruction. Long-term graft patency is also dependent on controlling or eliminating predisposing factors, such as diabetes, hypercholesterolaemia and smoking.

STATION 3.18

Patient history

I am 47 years old and unemployed. I was admitted 5 days ago with newly diagnosed unstable angina and diabetes. I don't really understand what is going on despite the educational sessions from the specialist cardiac and diabetes nurses. I am particularly concerned about:
(i) When to take the spray?
(ii) Will the spray fit in my hand bag?
(iii) Will my angina stop me going to my keep fit classes?

Assessment	Good	Adequate	Poor/not done
1. Polite introduction; establishes rapport	❑	❑	❑
2. Establishes patient understanding of GTN's use	❑	❑	❑
3. Explains situations in which to use the spray: *Whenever angina pain comes on Prophylactically when you know pain may come on (e.g. before strenuous exertion)*	❑	❑	❑
4. Explains in a clear, simple manner how to use the spray. Mentions the need to: *Stop whatever you are doing and to sit down*		❑	❑
Shake the spray and then remove the top		❑	❑
Give 2 sprays under the tongue		❑	❑
If pain is unrelieved after 5–10 minutes, give 2 further sprays		❑	❑
5. Warns that if pain is poorly relieved or unrelieved after 15–20 minutes take 300 mg of aspirin and call an ambulance	❑	❑	❑
6. Explains common side-effects (e.g. headache, dizziness and postural hypotension)	❑	❑	❑
7. Invites questions and addresses patient's anxieties	❑	❑	❑
8. Does all in a fluent, professional manner	❑	❑	❑

STATION 3.19

Answers

1.

(A) Efferent arteriole
(B) Afferent arteriole
(C) Bowman's capsule
(D) Glomerulus
(E) Cortex
(F) Medulla
(G) Descending limb of the loop of Henlé

(H) Loop of Henlé
(I) Ascending limb of the loop of Henlé
(J) Distal convoluted tubule
(K) Collecting duct

2.

a) 4
b) 1
c) 2

d) 3
e) 2
f) 1

Explanations

Site 1: ascending limb of the loop of Henlé. This is the site of action of loop diuretics, which inhibit resorption. They are extremely potent diuretics and cause hypokalaemia, hyponatraemia, hypomagnesaemia and postural hypotension.

Site 2: the proximal area of the distal convoluted tubule. This is the site of action of the thiazide diuretics Bendrofluazide and Metolazone. They inhibit sodium resorption and commonly cause hyponatraemia, hypokalaemia and hypomagnesaemia.

Site 3: the distal convoluted tubule. This is the site of action of potassium sparing diuretics such as amiloride and triamterene. These are weak diuretics but are used in combination with thiazides and loop diuretics.

Site 4: the collecting ducts. This is the site of action of the aldosterone antagonist spironolactone. This diuretic is principally used in the secondary hyperaldosteronism that occurs with cardiac, renal and hepatic failure.

STATION 3.20

Answers

1. (D) (e)
This patient describes two of the classical side-effects of amiodarone. This drug is useful in both supraventricular and ventricular arrhythmia but unfortunately has many side-effects. Patients should always be warned about the side-effects of the drug and this should be recorded in their notes. Common side-effects include: pulmonary fibrosis; photo-sensitive rash; slate grey pigmentation of the skin; derangement of the liver function tests; derangement of thyroid activity causing both hypo and hyperthyroidism; microcorneal deposits.

2. (E) (a)
The patient describes a rare side-effect of digoxin; xanthopsia or the visual field turning yellow. Digoxin has a narrow therapeutic window and is a common cause of drug-induced side-effects, particularly in patients with impaired renal function. It commonly presents with bradycardia and nausea. It may cause both supraventricular and ventricular arrhythmias and, in high toxic levels, may require treatment with 'Digibind' which is a Fab fragment which binds to digoxin and makes it inert in the plasma.

3. (A) (f)
Shortness of breath post myocardial infarction may have many causes. Beta blockers have become established as one of the principal treatments during the initial 48 hours post-acute infarct but contraindications must be excluded viz asthma and moderate to severe heart failure.

4. (B) (c)
Calcium channel blockers are a common treatment for essential hypertension. The side-effects of flushing and headaches are due to vasodilatation. The other side-effect of fluid retention may cause worsening cardiac failure but may occur in isolation. Remember all ankle oedema is not due to cardiac failure!

5. (F) (b)
The medical treatment of Wolff-Parkinson-White includes flecainide and amiodarone which have a very similar side-effect profile. As when amiodarone is prescribed, the patient should be made aware of the common side-effects and this should be recorded in the notes.

6. (C) (d)
Sotalol is a class III anti-arrhythmic with partial beta blocker effect. It is a useful drug in the treatment of atrial fibrillation but cannot be used in patients with cardiac failure.

STATION 3.21

Patient history

I am 46 years old and a fireman. I have been transferred from the Accident and Emergency Department for a 'clot busting' treatment. I have not been told anything more than this.

I have been treated for high blood pressure and NIDDM for the past seven years but have been otherwise well. I go to see the doctor in the diabetic clinic twice a year and have a few changes in the back of my eyes, which have remained unchanged in the past few years.

I have never suffered with any bleeding problems or indigestion and have never been told that I have an ulcer. I have no other contra-indications for thrombolysis treatment. I am a bit concerned when told about the risk of bleeding into the brain, but will have the treatment if you explain things carefully, but will not accept the therapy if I am not satisfied with your explanation.

Assessment	Good	Adequate	Poor/not done
1. Polite introduction; establish patient identity	❏	❏	❏
2. Establish present patient understanding of treatment	❏	❏	❏
3. Explains the treatment in a clear, non-jargonistic manner	❏	❏	❏
4. Mentions the common side-effects – flushing, warm feeling as the thrombolysis is given; dizziness; nausea and vomiting	❏	❏	❏
5. Mentions the uncommon side-effects: haemorrhagic stroke; gastrointestinal and general bleeding; severe allergic reaction: shortness of breath, wheeze and cardiovascular collapse	❏	❏	❏
6. Excludes absolute contra-indications:			
Active bleeding problems (e.g. peptic ulceration)	❏	❏	❏
Streptokinase in the previous two years	❏	❏	❏
Major surgery within the last ten days	❏	❏	❏
Recent major trauma	❏	❏	❏
Any previous history of intracranial haemorrhage	❏	❏	❏
Uncontrolled hypertension	❏	❏	❏
7. Discusses relative contra-indications (e.g. diabetic retinopathy)	❏	❏	❏
8. Invites questions and addresses patient's concerns	❏	❏	❏
9. Does all in a fluent, professional manner	❏	❏	❏

STATION 3.22

Comment

It is essential to make sure that when cross matching blood for a patient all the details are filled in correctly and as comprehensively as possible. Most mistakes related to blood transfusions are caused by bureaucratic error. The units of blood are collected from the blood bank with the lower part of the original request form, shown below. When putting up a new unit of blood, the unit details should be checked by two people, against the patient's details, and the details on the form below.

Fig. 3.22ai

HEALTH AUTHORITY				**24 HOUR INTRAVENOUS FLUID PRESCRIPTION CHART**						

DATE XX – MONTH – YEAR **FOR PATIENTS WITH MORE THAN ONE INTRAVENOUS LINE**

CONSULTANT DR LITTLE	WARD FLEMMING	Use computer label if available Unit No. 123432
HOUSE OFFICER	HOSPITAL ST PETER'S	Surname THOMAS / Forenames DEBRA
DRUG IDIOSYNCRASY — NIL —		Address / Sex M/F / D of B 13/09/19 / Weight

TYPE OF IV FLUID	VOLUME	INFUSION RATE	TIME STARTED	NURSES SIGNATURE	PRESCRIPTION FOR DRUGS TO BE ADDED TO FULL BOTTLE					
					DRUG ADDED AND SOLVENT	DOSE OF DRUG	H.O.'s SIG	ADDITION TIME	ADDED BY	PHARM.

INTRAVENOUS LINE 1 ; SPECIFY TYPE (eg CVP, Peripheral)   LABEL LINE

TYPE OF IV FLUID	VOLUME	INFUSION RATE								
DATE Normal Saline	100ml	30mins								
Blood	1 UNIT	4 Hourly								
Blood	1 UNIT	4 Hourly								
Frusemide 40mg (PO) after 2nd unit										
Blood	1 UNIT	4 Hourly								
Blood	1 UNIT	4 Hourly								
Normal Saline	100ml	30mins								
Frusemide 40mg (PO) after Normal Saline										

Signature

INTRAVENOUS LINE 2 ; SPECIFY TYPE (eg CVP, Peripheral)   LABEL LINE

INTRAVENOUS LINE 3 ; SPECIFY TYPE (eg CVP, Peripheral)   LABEL LINE

INTRAVENOUS FLUID THERAPY SHOULD BE REVIEWED EVERY 24 HOURS AND ALL PREVIOUS REGIMENS CANCELLED

NOTE: THE PRESCRIPTIONS FOR INTRAVENOUS FEEDING MUST BE COMPLETED BY NOON TO ALLOW PHARMACY TO PREPARE THE PRODUCT.

Fig. 3.22bi

STATION 3.23

Assessment	Good	Adequate	Poor/not done
1. Polite introduction; requests the notes and establishes the patient identity	❏	❏	❏
2. Stops the present unit of blood, checks from the notes the patient and unit details; rechecks the unit and the cross match form	❏	❏	❏
3. Examines the patient to exclude focal signs of sepsis and allergic phenomena (e.g. wheeze, rashes)	❏	❏	❏
4. Takes blood for:			
Full blood count		❏	❏
Clotting		❏	❏
Re-cross match		❏	❏
Antibody screen		❏	❏
Blood cultures		❏	❏
5. Informs the laboratory that new cross match is required	❏	❏	❏
6. Further sepsis screen: MSU; wound swabs; CXR	❏	❏	❏
7. Asks nursing staff to continue doing observations of temperature, pulse, blood pressure and respiratory rate every 30 minutes for next few hours	❏	❏	❏
8. If transfusion is essential the new unit must be sited as soon as possible	❏	❏	❏
9. Does all the in a fluent, professional manner	❏	❏	❏

STATION 3.24

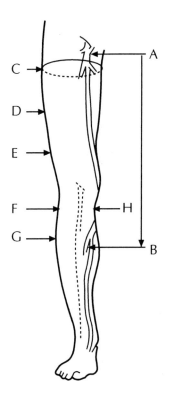

Fig. 3.24a

Assessment	Good	Adequate	Poor/not done
1. Describes the distribution of the varicose veins (long and/or short saphenous, upper and/or lower leg)	❏	❏	❏
2. Describes the status of skin around the gaiter area, looking for eczema, pigmentation, loss of subcutaneous tissue, scarring and ulceration	❏	❏	❏
3. Palpates for a cough impulse over the saphenofemoral and saphenopopliteal junctions, and main perforator sites in the thigh	❏	❏	❏

	Good	Adequate	Poor/not done
4. Uses the tap test appropriately	❑	❑	❑
5. Uses the tourniquet test appropriately	❑	❑	❑
6. Uses Perthes' test appropriately	❑	❑	❑
7. Comments on the use of the colour or hand-held doppler as a valuable addition in detecting retrograde flow in perforating veins and in planning any necessary surgery	❑	❑	❑

Comment

Cough impulse palpable at point A labelled on Figure 3.24a
Tap test: palpable retrograde venous impulse, on tapping proximally, veins or varices at B (i.e. A → B)
Use of tourniquet: the venous tourniquet is placed around the upper thigh (C) after raising the leg to empty the venous system, then stand the patient and time refilling. Normal filling takes 25 seconds or more: varices fill within a few seconds when incompetent perforators are sited below the level of the tourniquet. The tourniquet is placed at successively lower levels (D–G) to localise the level of the incompetence.

Perthes' test: the venous tourniquet is placed below the knee (H) followed by 10 tip-toes. The activity of the muscle pump should empty the deep system and blood should, therefore, empty from the varices into deep veins. If the varices become more tense, it implies deep venous occlusive disease with associated incompetence.

STATION 3.25

Assessment	Good	Adequate	Poor/not done
1. Ulcer: establishes: *Site, size* *Flat/sloping edge* *Slough-covered base with no granulation* *No deep penetration* *Surrounding induration and pigmentation*		❏	❏
2. Additional history: *Pain and disability* *Varicose veins* *Previous DVT and trauma* *Peripheral vascular disease and diabetes*		❏	❏
3. Additional examination:			
Extent of induration		❏	❏
Fixation of ulcer		❏	❏
Ankle mobility		❏	❏
Inguinal lymphadenopathy		❏	❏
Venous incompetence		❏	❏
Pulses and sensation in the leg		❏	❏
Abnormality of other leg		❏	❏
4. Carries out all in a fluent, professional manner	❏	❏	❏

Comment

Venous ulceration is a late sequelae of the postphlebitic limb. The ulceration is sited just above the medial and, to a lesser extent, the lateral malleolus. It can be large but rarely penetrates the deep tissues. Although it can be healed by elevation and reduction of swelling, it frequently persists, causing chronic discomfort and severe pain, particularly if accompanied by secondary infection. Recurrence frequently follows minor trauma. Venous bleeding can occasionally be quite severe, but is readily controlled by elevation and a firm dressing.

Other common causes of leg ulceration include trauma and chronic ischaemia. In the latter the ulceration occurs over and between the toes, and over pressure sites, particularly the heel and malleoli. The condition may co-exist with venous problems, and pulses must always be checked.

Diabetic ulcers may be ischaemic but an associated peripheral neuropathy places the foot at risk of ulceration, particularly over weight-bearing areas, such as the heads of the metatarsals. The problem is accentuated by the predisposition to infection. With all lower limb ulcers, carefully examine and monitor progress of the skin edge for evidence of malignancy. Malignant change in a pre-existing ulcer, or primary malignancy can be easily missed when sited over classical sites for other pathology.

STATION 3.26a

Patient history

I am a 23-year-old bus driver who was admitted for a clot in my right leg, due to being on the pill, no-one has explained the warfarin therapy and I am anxious to learn all about the treatment. I do not have a regular partner and need advice on alternative contraception. I am not allergic to any medications and am not on any regular medicines.

I drink 6–8 whisky and sodas on a Saturday night, but cannot drink at other times because of my job. I do not smoke.

I would like to know:

a) How long will I be on the treatment?
b) What happens if I get sick and can't take the tablets?

Assessment	Good	Adequate	Poor/not done
1. Polite introduction; establishes rapport	❏	❏	❏
2. Establishes patient's present understanding of treatment	❏	❏	❏
3. Explains therapy in a clear, non-jargonistic manner	❏	❏	❏
4. Mentions the following points regarding therapy:			
Why patient is taking treatment	❏	❏	❏
Duration of therapy	❏	❏	❏
Importance of compliance	❏	❏	❏
Side-effects principally haemorrhage	❏	❏	❏
What to do in case of haemorrhage	❏	❏	❏
Need for blood monitoring in anticoagulation clinic	❏	❏	❏
Need to carry anticoagulation book	❏	❏	❏
Need for alternative contraception	❏	❏	❏
Interaction with other medications/alcohol	❏	❏	❏
Need to tell dentist or other doctors about treatment	❏	❏	❏
5. Invites patient's questions and answers appropriately	❏	❏	❏
6. Does all in a fluent, professional manner	❏	❏	❏

STATION 4.1

Patient history

I am 23 years old and asthmatic. My asthma is not well controlled. I was first diagnosed aged 14, and have had at least 1 to 2 admissions a year since then. The last admission was 3 months ago and I was ventilated in intensive care. I have been previously ventilated 3 times. I continue to smoke 5 to 10 cigarettes a day and have to use my inhalers 3 to 4 times per day. I am at present on salbutamol, Atrovent and Becloforte inhalers and have been on prednisolone 30 mg for the past 4 days. My normal PEFR when well is 550 l/min.

The present illness started 5 days ago with a slight head cold but I am now coughing up thick green sputum and am short of breath and wheezy, particularly at night. I am sleeping very badly and feel exhausted, like before I was ventilated the last time. I have had a fever but have not noticed any blood being coughed up or chest pain.

I have no pets and do not know of anything specifically that exacerbates my asthma. I did not have hayfever or eczema as a child and I don't know any other family members who have eczema, asthma or hayfever.

Will I need to be admitted, or will I be able to go home?

Assessment	Good	Adequate	Poor/not done
1. Polite introduction; establishes rapport	❑	❑	❑
2. Establishes duration/initial diagnosis of asthma	❑	❑	❑
3. Establishes normal asthma control, i.e. medications and the frequency of use; normal PEFR	❑	❑	❑
4. Establishes previous hospital admissions	❑	❑	❑
5. Establishes if the patient has been ventilated in the past	❑	❑	❑
6. Establishes duration and nature of the present illness	❑	❑	❑
7. Establishes/excludes the following symptoms:			
Cough – nocturnal; daytime	❑	❑	❑
Sputum – volume; colour; consistency	❑	❑	❑
Haemoptysis		❑	❑
Worsening wheeze		❑	❑
Fever		❑	❑
Chest pain-pleuritic		❑	❑
Disturbance of sleep		❑	❑
8. Establishes whether patient is a smoker	❑	❑	❑
9. Asks about precipitating factors, (e.g. pets, allergens, occupation)	❑	❑	❑
11. When asked, appreciates patient must be admitted	❑	❑	❑
10. Does all in a fluent, professional manner	❑	❑	❑

Diagnosis
Poorly controlled asthmatic now needing admission due to acute infective exacerbation.

STATION 4.2

Patient history

I am 49 years old and have had a cough for the past 10 days. The cough is generally dry, with occasional clear sputum but no blood. I have been slightly short of breath around the house and have felt dreadful for the past 4 days, like I've had flu. I have not noticed any wheezing. I have been very feverish in bed at night with drenching sweats. I have not had any other systemic upset. I smoke 20 cigarettes a day and work in the accounts department of a high street bank. I have not been on any foreign travel recently and have not been in contact with anyone else with similar symptoms. I am not on any regular medications and am otherwise well.

Only if asked
I have noticed that two of my prize budgerigars have been very sick recently, in fact one died 3 days ago.

Assessment	Good	Adequate	Poor/not done
1. Polite introduction; establishes rapport	❑	❑	❑
2. Establishes duration of presenting complaint	❑	❑	❑
3. Establishes/excludes the following symptoms:			
Cough		❑	❑
Sputum		❑	❑
Haemoptysis		❑	❑
Dyspnoea		❑	❑
Wheeze		❑	❑
Fever		❑	❑
4. Establishes smoking history	❑	❑	❑
5. Establishes risk factors of atypical pneumonia: pets, occupation, foreign travel, contacts	❑	❑	❑
6. Excludes underlying cardiac and respiratory disorders	❑	❑	❑
7. Excludes other systemic upset, (e.g. diarrhoea, confusion, rashes, arthralgia, myalgia)	❑	❑	❑
8. Does all in a fluent, professional manner	❑	❑	❑

Diagnosis

Atypical pneumonia – probably *Chlamydia psittaci*.

STATION 4.3

Patient history

I am 61 years old and a retired car factory worker. I am a lifelong smoker, smoking 30 cigarettes a day. I have been getting progressively unwell over the last 2 to 3 years. Every winter for the last 8 to 9 years I have had a severe cough with thick green sputum. This has worsened and now seems to happen all the year round. I can only walk about 50 to 60 metres on the flat without stopping, due to breathlessness and wheeze. I have a near-constant cough and have to sleep with 3 pillows otherwise I am more breathless. I have never noticed any blood in my sputum and have not been feverish in the past few months. I do not suffer with any chest pains, swelling of the ankles or episodes of breathlessness at night.

My GP recently started me on some inhalers but I rarely use them as they seem to do little good. I take no other regular medications and I am otherwise fit and well, with no other systemic symptoms.

Assessment	Good	Adequate	Poor/not done
1. Polite introduction; establishes rapport	❑	❑	❑
2. Establishes duration of presenting complaint	❑	❑	❑
3. Establishes/excludes the following symptoms:			
Cough		❑	❑
Sputum		❑	❑
Haemoptysis		❑	❑
Dyspnoea		❑	❑
Wheeze		❑	❑
Orthopnoea		❑	❑
Exercise tolerance	❑	❑	❑
Sleep disturbance		❑	❑
Fever		❑	❑
4. Excludes cardiac symptoms (e.g. angina, oedema)	❑	❑	❑
5. Establishes occupational and smoking history	❑	❑	❑
6. Establishes medication and allergy history	❑	❑	❑
7. Excludes any other systemic symptoms	❑	❑	❑
8. Does all in a fluent, professional manner	❑	❑	❑

Diagnosis

Chronic airflow limitation – by definition this patient has chronic bronchitis.

STATION 4.4

Patient history

I am 63 years old and a retired plumber. I am a lifelong smoker. I was admitted from the outpatient clinic because of a 3 month history of weight loss and coughing up blood. Initially the blood was brownish clots mixed in with clear sputum but now there is fresh blood and it occurs 4 to 5 times per day. I have developed a dry irritating cough with breathlessness on exertion. My exercise tolerance is about 500 to 1000 metres on the flat but I have noticed that I am short of breath at the top of the 14 stairs in my home. I have no history of fever, chest pain, wheeze, difficulty in breathing when lying down or palpitations. I have lost about 2 stone in weight in the last 3 months and have felt increasingly lethargic over this time. I do not feel like eating anything at the moment and have no energy or enthusiasm. In the last few weeks my voice has become hoarse.

I have smoked 20 cigarettes a day for the last 35 years, and drink 5 to 10 pints of beer per week. I may have been exposed to asbestos in the past but I'm not sure.

When asked

I am very concerned that I may have cancer and don't want my wife to find out if it is, as I think she would go to pieces. Her father has just died of cancer of the prostate.

Assessment	Good	Adequate	Poor/not done
1. Polite introduction; establishes rapport	❑	❑	❑
2. Establishes duration of the presenting complaint	❑	❑	❑
3. Characterises the haemoptysis (e.g. volume, frequency, altered or fresh blood)	❑	❑	❑
4. Establishes associated respiratory symptoms – cough and dyspnoea	❑	❑	❑
5. Excludes other respiratory symptoms – chest pain, sputum and fever	❑	❑	❑
6. Establishes associated symptoms – hoarseness of voice	❑	❑	❑
7. Establishes systemic symptoms of neoplasia – lethargy, malaise, loss of weight and appetite	❑	❑	❑
8. Establishes smoking and occupational history	❑	❑	❑
9. Addresses the patient's anxieties in an empathetic manner	❑	❑	❑
10. Does all in a fluent, professional manner	❑	❑	❑

Diagnosis
Carcinoma of the lung.

STATION 4.5

Patient history

I am 18 years old and am normally fit and well. Currently I am studying for my A levels. Last night I developed a sharp pain just under my left breast. The pain has no radiation and has gradually worsened in intensity overnight with no relief from paracetamol. The pain is much worse when I move around, and when I take a deep breath it takes my breath away. I have coughed up 2 clots of fresh blood this morning but have had no other cough, sputum, or fever. I have become increasingly anxious and breathless over this period.

Risk factors for a pulmonary embolism (only when asked do you admit to these problems).
I recently started on the oral contraceptive pill; I smoke 10 cigarettes a day. My brother died of a clot to the lung suddenly 2 years ago. I came back on a 23 hour coach journey from Germany 2 days ago.

I have never had problems with blood clots, thrombosis in my legs, or a clot in my lungs.

I have had no injuries recently, and no fractures or operations; I have never been pregnant.

Assessment	Good	Adequate	Poor/not done
1. Polite introduction; establishes rapport	❑	❑	❑
2. Establishes duration of the symptoms	❑	❑	❑
3. Establishes characteristics of the chest pain – sharp, pleuritic, left midzone, worse on movement, no relief	❑	❑	❑
4. Excludes other respiratory and cardiac symptoms: cough, sputum, wheeze, oedema	❑	❑	❑
5. Establishes history of acute haemoptysis	❑	❑	❑
6. Establishes/excludes risk factors for pulmonary embolism:			
Oral contraceptive pill		❑	❑
Long distance journey		❑	❑
Smoking		❑	❑
Recent major operation		❑	❑
Recent major fracture		❑	❑
Pregnancy		❑	❑
Previous history of PE or DVT		❑	❑
Family history of PE or DVT		❑	❑
History of coagulopathy		❑	❑
7. Establishes no other systemic upset	❑	❑	❑
8. Does all in a fluent, professional manner	❑	❑	❑
9. Establishes the correct diagnosis of pulmonary embolism	❑	❑	❑

Diagnosis
Left sided pulmonary embolism with multiple risk factors.

STATION 4.6

Patient history

I am 16 years old, and I am studying for GCSE exams. Over the last 3 to 4 months I have become increasingly short of breath, particularly when playing sport. The breathlessness initially started during the winter, and was particularly bad when I was playing football in the cold wind. My breathing has slowly worsened and I am now finding it hard to do even short periods of exercise.

I have been sleeping badly because of a persistent cough and wheezing during the night, and I am now having to sleep with 3 pillows. I have not had any sputum, fever, coughing up of blood or swelling of my ankles.

I smoke 2 to 3 cigarettes at weekends but recently have had to stop because it makes me very wheezy. I have some goldfish but no other pets, and have never had eczema, hayfever or asthma. My brother and my mother both have eczema and my sister has asthma.

Assessment	Good	Adequate	Poor/not done
1. Polite introduction; establishes rapport	❑	❑	❑
2. Establishes duration of present illness	❑	❑	❑
3. Establishes exacerbating factors of breathlessness	❑	❑	❑
4. Establishes associated symptoms – nocturnal cough, wheeze, orthopnoea	❑	❑	❑
5. Excludes other respiratory symptoms – sputum, haemoptysis, fever and chest pain	❑	❑	❑
6. Establishes lack of sleep due to cough and wheeze	❑	❑	❑
7. Establishes/excludes associated risk factors – smoking, pets, pollen and dust	❑	❑	❑
8. Establishes history of atopy	❑	❑	❑
9. Establishes family history of asthma and atopy	❑	❑	❑
10. Does all in a fluent, professional manner	❑	❑	❑
11. Makes a reasonable attempt at the diagnosis	❑	❑	❑

Diagnosis
New onset of asthma.

STATION 4.7

Answers and explanations

1. (E) (c)
This man has chronic respiratory failure causing pulmonary hypertension, right sided heart failure and polycythaemia. Management may include regular venesection with an aim to reduce the haematocrit (Hct) to less than 0.50.

2. (C) (d)
The patient has a microcytic anaemia secondary to gastrointestinal blood loss due to her NSAID treatment. Chronic rheumatoid arthritis may also cause a microcytic anaemia through the anaemia of chronic disease.

3. (A) (b)
This patient is suffering from a grossly raised platelet count or thrombocytosis. This is an uncommon cause of thrombo-embolic disease leading to deep vein thrombosis (DVT) and myocardial infarction, CVAs and limb ischaemia.

4. (B) (e)
Mycoplasma pneumonia causes several haematological problems including haemolytic anaemia, a depressed white cell count with a relative lymphopenia and thrombocytopenia. The haemolysis is confirmed by the reticulocytosis causing the raised MCV.

5. (D) (a)
Sickle cell disease is one of the most common haemoglobinopathies, being particularly prevalent amongst Afro-caribbean races. It often presents as an acute sickle crisis due to infection, drugs or metabolic disturbance. Acute sickle crises are characterised by bony pain, pneumonitis, splenic pain and infarction, and acute haemolysis.

STATION 4.8

Answers and explanations

1.   (C)   (e)
The carcinoid syndrome is more commonly associated with gastro-intestinal tumours but is well recognised with pulmonary lesions. The tumours produce 5HT which is responsible for the wheeze and diarrhoea. The flushing is caused by various mediators including substance P, kallikrein and bradykinins.

2.   (D)   (c)
Hypercalcaemia associated with lung tumours may be caused by ectopic parathormone, bony metastases, cyclic-AMP-stimulating factor or a prostaglandin. Ectopic parathormone is most commonly expressed by squamous cell carcinoma. Initial therapy should include intravenous rehydration and hydrocortisone but the use of intravenous bisphosphonates, followed by oral maintenance therapy, has now become the standard treatment.

3.   (E)   (d)
The SIADH in this case may be caused by a primary lung tumour or cerebral metastases. Both may be responsible for these symptoms and, after correction of the hyponatraemia, a CT head scan should be performed. SIADH is proven by a paired urinary and plasma osmolality, where the urinary osmolality is raised relative to the plasma osmolality. The urinary sodium may be normal or raised but the plasma sodium is always low. Other criteria for diagnosing SIADH include normal renal and adrenal function and the absence of hypotension, hypovolaemia and oedema.

4.   (B)   (a)
Lung tumours metastasise to cervical, supraclavicular and contralateral hilar lymph nodes, the brain, liver and bone. The enlarged liver feels hard and 'craggy' and may present with jaundice or deranged LFTs.

5.   (A)   (b)
Small cell tumours and bronchial carcinoid may both produce ectopic ACTH. The patient presents with the familiar clinical features of Cushing's syndrome but is characterised by severe malaise and hypokalaemic alkalosis. Metyrapone and, more rarely, ketoconazole, are used to block the synthesis of cortisol but tumour excision remains the best treatment.

STATION 4.9

Answers and explanations

1. (F) (g)
Sarcoidosis is now thought to be due to an, as yet undefined, allergen causing an abnormal T helper cell response. It causes bilateral hilar lymphadenopathy and mid and upper zone pulmonary fibrosis.

2. (E) (f)
Wegener's granulomatosis is made up of a classical triad of upper and lower respiratory tract symptoms and renal failure. The disease is characterised by the presence of the cANCA antibody, in particular the antiproteinase 3 antibody, which is directly involved in the pathogenesis of the disorder.

3. (B) (a)
Churg-Strauss is a variant of polyarteritis nodosa (PAN). It presents in young adults with asthma, peripheral eosinophilia, subcutaneous lesions, peripheral neuropathy and vasculitis. Unlike PAN it rarely involves the kidneys. The non-specific pANCA (anti-myeloperoxidase antibody), has been identified in this disorder but cannot be used to characterise it, as it is found in many other immune based diseases including inflammatory bowel disease and autoimmune hepatitis.

4. (C) (e)
Goodpasture's syndrome is the association of pulmonary haemorrhage and an acute glomerulonephritis. It has now been renamed anti-glomerular basement membrane disease. The autoantibody is directed against type IV collagen, which is common to the basement membrane in both the glomeruli and the alveoli.

5. (G) (c)
Rheumatoid arthritis commonly affects the lungs. The principal respiratory presentations include pleurisy and exudative pleural effusions. Pulmonary fibrosis, similar to cryptogenic fibrosing alveolitis, pulmonary nodules and 'honeycombing', may also occur.

6. (A) (d)
Systemic lupus erythematosus does not affect the lungs as commonly as rheumatoid arthritis. It may produce an exudative effusion and rarely pulmonary fibrosis.

7.   (D) (b)
Progressive systemic sclerosis is characterised by the antiSCL 70 antibody. The lungs are commonly affected by fibrosis which may become generalised with 'honeycombing' and pulmonary hypertension.

STATION 4.10

Answers and explanations

1.   (D) (c)
This patient has Guillain-Barré syndrome with both motor and sensory neuropathy, the blood gas results infer type II respiratory failure, the pH is normal. The HCO_3^- is normal which shows this patient does not normally retain CO_2. The patient is young and this set of blood gases infer he is tiring with poor respiratory effort, a similar picture may be found in severe asthma. The treatment of choice is ventilation and plasmapheresis.

2.   (E) (d)
This man has acute pulmonary oedema which causes a type I respiratory failure. He also has a metabolic acidosis shown by the low pH and HCO_3^-, this is probably due to a lactic acidosis caused by poor tissue oxygenation.

3.   (B) (e)
These results are consistent with type II respiratory failure, a respiratory acidosis and compensatory metabolic alkalosis. This combination is seen in chronic CO_2 retainers where the respiratory acidosis is caused by the retention of CO_2 and the metabolic alkalosis by the retention of HCO_3^-. These patients should be given 24% (28% maximum) O_2 therapy.

4.   (C) (a)
This patient has had a PE and demonstrates type I respiratory failure with a respiratory alkalosis. She is hypoxic which is important to note as occasionally such patients are diagnosed as 'hysterical' and are given a paper bag to rebreathe into! Type I failure in this age group is always pathological and should be taken seriously.

5.   (A) (b)
This patient has a respiratory alkalosis but has no respiratory failure. She has been hyperventilating and this is shown by the supersaturated high levels of oxygen with low CO_2. This patient should be treated with a re-breathing bag and reassurance.

STATION 4.11

Answers

1.	A	6.	C
2.	B and C	7.	B
3.	A +/- B	8.	A
4.	B and C	9.	A, B and C
5.	B	10.	A and C

Comment

Patient (A) – demonstrates a restrictive lung defect with resting hypoxia and reduced transfer coefficient. In view of the history of rheumatoid arthritis this picture would fit with fibrosing alveolitis. These patients have type I respiratory failure and classically the hypoxia worsens with exercise.

Patient (B) – the history and lung function tests suggest underlying obstructive airways disease. The reduced transfer coefficient suggests probable emphysema and excludes late onset asthma. The data do not indicate whether there is any reversibility. This is demonstrated by repeating the FEV_1 and FVC tests pre- and post-nebuliser. Demonstration of reversibility is important as it indicates whether inhaled steroid therapy may be useful.

Patient (C) – this history is suggestive of myasthenia gravis. These patients get an obstructive lung defect as they are unable to move their chest wall due to the neuromuscular defect. The transfer coefficient is normal as there is no alveolar problem.

STATION 4.12

Answers and explanations

(A) Trachea
(B) Right 5th rib (anterior aspect)
(C) Left 7th rib (posterior aspect)
(D) Aortic knuckle
(E) Left heart border (left ventricle)
(F) Right pulmonary artery
(G) Right costodiaphragmatic angle
(H) Left dome of diaphragm
(I) Right heart border (right atrium)
(J) ECG sticker

1.	True	6.	True
2.	True	7.	True
3.	False	8.	False
4.	False	9.	False
5.	False	10.	False

This is a well-centred PA chest radiograph of an elderly woman. The cardiothoracic ratio is normal. There is calcification within the aortic knuckle probably due to atherosclerotic degeneration. There is no evidence of soft tissue abnormalities, cardiac failure, perforated viscus or fractures. The bones are relatively osteopenic but there is little evidence of arthritic degeneration. There are 8 anterior ribs visible and flattening of the diaphragm which indicates a degree of hyperexpansion.

STATION 4.13

Answers and explanations

(a) 1. True   2. False   3. False   4. True   5. True
This is a PA poorly penetrated CXR showing hyperexpanded lung fields and flattened diaphragms. There is marked pulmonary apical fibrosis resulting in the hilar being pulled upwards towards the apices. The fibrosis was secondary to tuberculosis in this patient, other causes include pneumoconiosis, ankylosing spondylitis, rheumatoid arthritis and malignancy.

(b) 1. False   2. False   3. True   4. True   5. False
This is a well-penetrated, well-centred PA chest X-ray showing a cavitating area in the left apex. The commonest cause of this appearance is tuberculosis. Other causes of cavitation include *Staphylococcus, Klebsiella, Pseudomonas*, fungal infection and malignancy.

(c) 1. True   2. False   3. False   4. False   5. False
This is a well-penetrated, slightly rotated chest X-ray showing a right middle lobe pneumonia, with loss of definition of the right heart border. The lateral view clearly shows the consolidated lobe. The heart and left lung are normal.

(d) 1. True   2. True   3. True   4. True   5. False
This is quite a complicated X-ray to interpret correctly. There is loss of the right costodiaphragmatic angle, with multiple fluid levels above it. There is a 10%, by area, pneumothorax clearly seen in the right upper/mid zone. There is also blunting of the left costodiaphragmatic angle. This represents a right hydropneumothorax with adhesions causing the fluid levels and a small left pleural effusion. This patient had tuberculosis. Causes of pleural effusions should be divided by their protein content, into transudates (< 30g/l) and exudates (> 30g/l).

(e) 1. True   2. False   3. False   4. True   5. False
This is an AP chest X-ray showing a near 100% by area right sided pneumothorax. There is a chest drain in situ (just), with a kink seen at the skin entry site, possibly explaining why there has been no re-expansion of the lung. When describing a pneumothorax one should describe the size, by the area of the lung field occupied by the air within the hemithorax. The costodiaphragmatic angles have been missed on this X-ray and a repeat film should be requested to comment fully on the chest.

(f) **1. True**   **2. False**   **3. True**   **4. True**   **5. False**
This a well-centred PA chest X-ray showing a large round mass in the right mid/lower zone. The most likely cause of this appearance is a bronchogenic carcinoma; this was confirmed on sputum cytology. The lung fields are hyperexpanded with flattened hemidiaphragms indicating probable chronic airways disease, most likely caused by cigarette smoking. There are no bone metastases seen.

STATION 4.14

Answers and explanations

(a) **1. False**   **2. False**   **3. False**   **4. True**   **5. False**
This is a poorly penetrated PA chest X-ray showing multiple round lesions in both lung fields. These are consistent with 'cannonball' metastases, which commonly arise from breast, testicular, thyroid, renal or gastrointestinal primaries and in malignant trophoblastic disease. In children they may arise from Ewing's sarcoma and osteogenicsarcoma. Multiple round lesions may also be produced by infections, e.g. abscesses, coccidioidomycosis, histoplasmosis and hydatid disease, Wegener's and Caplan's syndrome.

(b) **1. True**   **2. False**   **3. True**   **4. False**   **5. True**
This is a PA chest X-ray showing bilateral hilar lymphadenopathy (BHL). The differential diagnosis includes sarcoidosis, lymphoma, tuberculosis and bronchial carcinoma. The bones are normal and there is no evidence of myeloma.

(c) **1. True**   **2. False**   **3. True**   **4. False**   **5. True**
This X-ray shows evidence of peribronchial thickening and basal cystic changes consistent with bronchiectasis. This may be caused by childhood infections, e.g. whooping cough and measles, aspiration of a foreign body and proximal obstruction due to mucus plugging or hilar masses, e.g. tuberculosis or malignancy. The commonest inherited cause is cystic fibrosis; other rare disorders include Kartagener's syndrome, Williams-Campbell syndrome and immunodeficiencies such as hypogammaglobulinaemia and Chediak-Higashi syndrome.

(d) **1. False**   **2. False**   **3. True**   **4. False**   **5. True**
This X-ray shows evidence of collapse/consolidation of the right upper lobe. The horizontal fissure is elevated due to loss of volume. Lobar collapse is principally caused by proximal obstruction of the bronchus. In this case there was a central obstructing carcinoma.

(e) 1. False   2. False   3. False   4. True   5. True
This X-ray shows a retrocardiac shadow causing a 'double' left heart border. This is due to left lower collapse which may be easily overlooked.

STATION 4.15

Answers

(a)		(b)	
(A)	Trachea	(A)	Left main bronchus
(B)	Sternum	(B)	Oesophagus
(C)	Left sternoclavicular joint	(C)	Right main bronchus
(D)	Thoracic vertebra	(D)	Descending thoracic aorta
(E)	Ribs	(E)	Termination of the SVC
(F)	Right scapula	(F)	Right scapula
(G)	Left lung	(G)	Thoracic vertebra (T6)
(H)	SVC	(H)	Ascending thoracic aorta
(I)	Oesophagus	(I)	Pulmonary trunk division

STATION 4.16

Answers and explanations

1. This is an AP chest X-ray showing a grossly enlarged aortic knuckle, consistent with a thoracic aortic aneurysm. There is evidence of calcification about 1cm from the edge of the dilated area suggesting dissection away from the true wall of the aorta, (marked by the calcification).

2. The CT scan of the thorax confirms the presence of a dissecting thoracic aortic aneurysm. The structures labelled are:
(A) Sternum
(B) Ascending thoracic aorta
(C) Trachea
(D) Dissecting aneurysm of the descending thoracic aorta
(E) Superior vena cava

3. This is a venogram of the left lower limb showing a filling defect in the superficial femoral and calf veins. This is consistent with a DVT and requires anticoagulation. With the introduction of low molecular weight/fractionated heparins, patient can now receive a standard, once-daily subcutaneous heparin injection, the dose being calculated by their weight. Patients with proven DVT should be anticoagulated with heparin and then started on warfarin for at least 3 months. Underlying risk factors such as the use of the OCP should be removed, and patients with no obvious cause investigated for possible coagulopathies. A coagulopathy screen should be performed prior to anticoagulation and should include: INR, APPT, Factor V Leiden, anticardiolipin antibody and proteins C and S levels. Venography is relatively expensive and technically difficult in a swollen limb; it is being superceded by colour doppler ultrasound of the veins.

STATION 4.17

Answers and explanations

(a) This is a radiolabelled ventilation (V)/perfusion (Q) scan showing a mismatched defect in the right lower lobe. The patient is asked to inhale a radiolabelled gas and is then injected with a contrast medium. 3 outcomes are possible.
  (1) A normal scan – all areas are ventilated and perfused
  (2) Matched defects – areas of the lungs have both poor ventilation and perfusion. This arises in patients with pre-existing lung disease, e.g. fibrosis, bronchiectasis and chronic airways disease. V/Q scans in such patients are often difficult to interpret and other modes of investigation should be employed.
  (3) Mismatched defects – as in the scan shown there are areas of normal ventilation with poor/no perfusion. This implies pulmonary embolism.

  Patients with mismatched defects should be formally anti-coagulated with heparin (this should have already been started) and then warfarin. They should receive warfarin for at least 6 months and any underlying risk factors, such as being on the OCP, should be addressed.

(b) This patient has had pulmonary angiography showing a massive pulmonary embolism cutting off the blood supply to the right lower lobe and most of the left lung. This represents a 'saddle' embolism which sits across the pulmonary arteries. The longer of the 2 radio-opaque tubes represents the Swan-Gantz catheter through which the contrast medium has been delivered. The other more centrally located tube is an endotracheal tube. Treatment of such massive emboli is still extremely difficult and the prognosis remains very poor. One treatment which has been tried is violent thrusting of the Swan-Gantz catheter in and out of the pulmonary artery while injecting streptokinase through it. Surgical evacuation of the embolus under extracorporeal circulatory bypass is successful in selected patients.

STATION 4.18

Patient history

I am 22 years old and have been recently diagnosed as asthmatic. I am unemployed at present but am hoping to get a job in retailing. I was meant to see the respiratory specialist nurse yesterday about how to use my inhalers but she was away sick. I have very little idea of how to use them but have watched the other patients on the ward using theirs. I am a non-smoker. I am not very good at understanding exactly what doctors tell me so I would like a very clear and simple explanation. I would like to know whether I should use the inhaler before vigorous exercise like sex.

Assessment	Good	Adequate	Poor/not done
1. Polite introduction; establishes rapport	❏	❏	❏
2. Establishes patient's present understanding of the treatment	❏	❏	❏
3. Explains use of the inhaler, covering the following points:			
Shake the inhaler with the cap on	❏	❏	❏
Remove the cap from the mouthpiece	❏	❏	❏
Take breath in and then fully exhale	❏	❏	❏
Place mouthpiece into mouth	❏	❏	❏
synchronously take a deep breath in as you press the top of the inhaler down	❏	❏	❏
Repeat from step (3) to step (5)	❏	❏	❏
4. Explains about gargling/rinsing out mouth after using steroid inhaler	❏	❏	❏
5. Establishes patient understanding allowing him to demonstrate technique	❏	❏	❏
6. Explains to patient correct situations to use inhalers, i.e. prophylactic and regular use	❏	❏	❏
7. Invites patient to ask questions, and answers appropriately	❏	❏	❏
8. Does all in a fluent, nonjargonistic, professional manner	❏	❏	❏

STATION 4.19

Patient history

I am 31 years old and I have asthma, which is not well controlled. I have been ventilated twice in the last year and the consultant has decided that I need to be put on steroids for the foreseeable future. I am very anxious, as I have heard that steroids can make you very fat and give you terrible acne. I am reluctant to take the tablets and since discharge from the hospital I have missed several doses. I am also worried about my diabetes which, up till now, has been quite well controlled.

Assessment	Good	Adequate	Poor/not done
1. Polite introduction; establishes rapport	❑	❑	❑
2. Establishes patient's understanding and anxieties about steroid therapy	❑	❑	❑
3. Explains the need for the addition of the steroids	❑	❑	❑
4. Explains the following about the steroid therapy:			
Must never miss a dose		❑	❑
If too sick to take the tablets, should seek medical help	❑	❑	❑
Check patient has a steroid card		❑	❑
5. Explains long-term side-effects of the steroids:			
Thinning and bruising of the skin		❑	❑
Cushing's and Addison's syndromes	❑	❑	❑
Hypertension		❑	❑
Acne and weight gain (reversible)	❑	❑	❑
6. Explains the effects on diabetes and the need to closely monitor control. Probable need to increase insulin	❑	❑	❑

		Good	Adequate	Poor/not done
7.	Invites patient questions, and answers appropriately	❏	❏	❏
8.	Does all in a fluent, professional manner	❏	❏	❏

STATION 4.20

Patient history

I am 64 years old and have been diagnosed with chronic airways limitation. I have had several admissions to hospital in the last year with chest problems and nearly died on this admission. The doctors want to put me on oxygen treatment at home but I am not very keen. I have just given up smoking in the last 3 months but occasionally sneak a puff from my husband, who continues to smoke. I don't think he will give it up for anything! I do not think any new treatment will help me, and I am resigned to dying in the next few months.

However, now you have told me the oxygen may help my illness and actually decrease my likelihood of dying I should like to give it a chance.

Assessment	Good	Adequate	Poor/not done
1. Polite introduction; establishes rapport	❏	❏	❏
2. Explores patient's understanding of the oxygen therapy and her anxieties about the treatment	❏	❏	❏
3. Ensures patient has stopped smoking and understands the dangers of smoking around oxygen	❏	❏	❏
4. Explains wearing oxygen for over 15 hours per day will decrease periods of illness and, over longer periods (19+ hours per day), may increase life expectancy	❏	❏	❏
5. Invites patient questions and answers appropriately	❏	❏	❏
6. Does all in a fluent, nonjargonistic professional manner	❏	❏	❏

Comment

To qualify for home oxygen therapy a patient must have a resting $PaO_2 < 7.3$ KPa; $PaCO_2 > 6.0$ KPa; $FEV_1 < 1.5$ litres, FVC < 2.0 litres. They must have stopped smoking and the dangers of smoking with oxygen therapy must be explained clearly. Studies have shown that maintaining these patients on oxygen for 15+ hours a day decreases their morbidity and for 19+ hours a day decreases their mortality.

Two oxygen points are set up around the house, usually in the sitting room and the bedroom. Patients do not have to pay for their therapy, which is often a major concern. The oxygen must be prescribed by their GP and must, therefore, be agreed with them before therapy can be instituted.

STATION 4.21a

Patient history

I am 53 years old and have come to the day-care centre for a bronchoscopy. I have been told by the registrar in the outpatient clinic that I have a 'shadow' on the chest X-ray, which needs to be looked at. I am unsure about the procedure and am quite anxious about it. I have been told a camera is passed into the lung but I am very confused by this.

At the end of the consultation you should ask the doctor – 'Do you think that the shadow on the chest X-ray is cancer?'

Assessment	Good	Adequate	Poor/not done
1. Polite introduction; establishes rapport	❏	❏	❏
2. Establishes identity of patient and reason for attendance	❏	❏	❏
3. Establishes present understanding of the procedure	❏	❏	❏
4. Explains the procedure in a clear, nonjargonistic manner	❏	❏	❏
5. Explains the common complications post procedure:			
Sore throat	❏	❏	❏
Drowsiness	❏	❏	❏
Chest discomfort	❏	❏	❏
6. Explains the uncommon complications of the procedure:			
Surgical emphysema	❏	❏	❏
Pneumothorax	❏	❏	❏
Pneumomediastinum	❏	❏	❏
7. Invites questions, and answers appropriately	❏	❏	❏
8. Deals with the issue of the mass on the CXR in sympathetic, sensitive manner	❏	❏	❏
9. Does all in a fluent, professional manner	❏	❏	❏

STATION 5.1

Patient history

I have been suffering from a bad back for the past four years, and it is getting worse. It comes on when I lift patients or wheel heavy trolleys at work. The pain first started when I tried to stop a patient falling off a trolley and badly strained my back. It is now in the middle of my back and moves round to my hips. I am prevented from doing work in the house and was advised to lie on a firm mattress, which I do.

I have had physiotherapy to my back, which helps only for a while. The pain is getting worse, and I think my back is permanently damaged and I should claim compensation.

Assessment	Good	Adequate	Poor/not done
1. Polite introduction; establishes rapport	❑	❑	❑
2. Enquires into presenting symptom (i.e. site, duration and radiation)	❑	❑	❑
3. Precipitating/aggravating/relieving factors	❑	❑	❑
4. Past treatment and results	❑	❑	❑
5. Associated health factors; work-related stress; social/economic factors	❑	❑	❑
6. Does all in a fluent, professional manner	❑	❑	❑
7. Makes a reasonable attempt at the diagnosis	❑	❑	❑

Diagnosis
Lumbar spondylosis

Comment

In patients over 40 years of age with long-standing back pain that is related to activity or posture, the most likely diagnoses are osteoarthritis and lumbar spondylosis. The latter is the result of disc degeneration (following recurrent prolapse) with displacement of the posterior facet joints. The unsupported movement in flexion and extension produces a form of segmental instability and may result in disabling symptoms. There may be neurological signs of an old disc prolapse (e.g. an absent knee or ankle jerk). Radiological features are characteristic of 'spondylosis'. Conservative measures, with management of pain, are sufficient for the majority of sufferers who are prepared to live with their problem. If, however, activity is severely restricted, surgical decompression should be considered. This may be combined with spinal fusion.

STATION 5.2

Patient history

I am a 38-year-old medical secretary and have been having attacks of severe pain and stiffness in my neck. I cannot think of anything specific that brings it on, except occasionally sudden movements or lying on one side. When I have the pain I am unable to hold my head up, and the pain moves to my neck muscles and goes down to my shoulder.

The pain started about six months ago but I cannot remember hurting or straining my neck at the time. When the neck pain comes on I have recently felt tingling and pins and needles in my right hand, which slowly passes off after a few hours. My neck generally feels stiff and I cannot look behind me without the risk of bringing on the pain. It is affecting my work, as I have to lie down to relieve the symptoms.

Assessment	Good	Adequate	Poor/not done
1. Polite introduction; establishes rapport	❏	❏	❏
2. Establishes presenting symptom – site, duration and radiation	❏	❏	❏
3. Establishes precipitating/ aggravating/relieving factors	❏	❏	❏
4. Symptoms radiating to adjacent/ related sites (i.e. upper limb and back)	❏	❏	❏
5. Associated health factors: work-related stress, social/ economic factors	❏	❏	❏
6. Does all in a fluent, professional manner	❏	❏	❏
7. Makes a reasonable attempt at the diagnosis	❏	❏	❏

Diagnosis
Cervical spondylosis

STATION 5.3

Assessment	Good	Adequate	Poor/not done
1. Polite introduction; establishes rapport	❑	❑	❑
2. Inspection: presence of deformity or muscle wasting; wry neck/ neck stiffness	❑	❑	❑
3. Palpation: tender areas and muscle spasm; cervical nodes, thyroid and trachea	❑	❑	❑
4. Movement: active range of movements	❑	❑	❑
5. Upper limbs: sensation, power, reflexes. Radial pulse at rest and in downward traction	❑	❑	❑
6. Does all in a fluent, professional manner	❑	❑	❑

Comment

The two common symptoms in the neck are pain and stiffness. Deformity usually appears as a wry neck; occasionally the neck is fixed in flexion. Numbness, tingling and weakness in the upper limb is due to nerve root or brachial plexus pressure, the former from a prolapsed intervertebral disc and the latter from a cervical rib.

Cervical spondylosis (degeneration and flattening of the inter-vertebral disc) and disc prolapse (with nerve root compression) are the two common conditions affecting adults. Analgesia, heat treatment and rest (in a collar) are usually adequate for the majority. Traction in disc prolapse and physiotherapy in disc degeneration are effective in relieving more severe symptoms. Surgical fusion following evacuation of the disc space is seldom indicated in either condition.

STATION 5.4

This is a Colles' fracture.

Assessment	Good	Adequate	Poor/not done
1. Technique for infiltration of local anaesthetic	❑	❑	❑
2. Technique of traction, disimpaction and reduction	❑	❑	❑
3. Maintenance of reduction and application of a plaster cast	❑	❑	❑
4. Post-reduction instructions to patient	❑	❑	❑

Comment

Although resuscitation and pain relief in multiple injuries take precedence over treatment of fractures/dislocations, there must be no undue delay in attending to the latter, as the swelling and inflammation that rapidly set in make reduction increasingly difficult.

Closed reduction: under appropriate anaesthetic and muscle relaxation, the fracture is reduced by a three-fold manoeuvre:
(i)   pull distal part in line with the shaft of bone
(ii) re-position distal part as the fragments disengage
(iii) adjust alignment in each plane. Alignment of the fragments is more important than exact opposition, except when the fracture involves an articular surface, when internal fixation may be required.

STATION 5.5

Answers

1.   Glasgow Coma Scale

2.   Pupillary size and reflexes
     Limb tone (and clonus)
     Limb reflexes

Comment

Unconsciousness following head trauma may indicate bilateral injury to the cerebral cortices, injury to the reticular activating system of the brain stem or increased intracranial pressure and decreased cerebral perfusion due to an expanding intracranial haematoma. Severe head injuries are usually admitted unconscious with a Glasgow Coma Scale score of 8 or less and require urgent assessment of the following:

A.   Airway – must be secured by a naso-laryngeal or oropharyngeal intubation. The cervical spine must be maintained in alignment until fractures have been excluded.

B.   Breathing – oxygen exchange is monitored and optimum ventilation with oxygenation is instituted to prevent hypoxic injury to the brain.

C.   Circulation – sources of extracranial bleeding are identified and controlled with volume replacement. Circulatory status is monitored by pulse, BP and CVP measurements.

D.   Neurological disability – presence of pupillary reflex, alteration in resting muscle tone, presence of abdominal, cremasteric and limb reflexes, Babinski response.

STATION 5.6

Answers

1.
Patient	A	RTS	6
Patient	B	RTS	10
Patient	C	RTS	12
Patient	D	RTS	8

2. Treatment priority in the following order:
    patient A, patient D, patient B, patient C.

Comment

Patients A and D are in severe respiratory distress and are both hypovolaemic. They require airway maintenance with cervical spine, ventilatory and circulatory support. Patient A, in addition, requires urgent head injury assessment. Patient B is moderately breathless and may have sustained a head injury. She requires a clear airway and oxygenated inspired air via a reservoir face mask. She requires further assessment for a head injury. Patient C is physiologically stable but not necessarily physiologically normal. An occult chest or abdominal injury, or even a head injury, may be present and she must, therefore, be observed overnight.

STATION 5.7

Answers

1. Extensive bruising over the lower back, extending to the right flank and abdomen.

2. Severe blunt impact to the side of trunk.

3. Injury to right kidney
    IVU
    CT scan (contrast enhanced of both kidneys)

4. Thoraco-lumbar spine
    Pancreas
    Liver
    Adrenal glands

Comment

Severe trauma may result in capsular tears or fragmentation of the kidney, and little if any bleeding is present per urethrum. Instead, severe haemorrhage occurs into the retro-peritoneal space. Hypovolaemic shock is imminent, and the circulatory volume must be replenished. Continuing haemorrhage may necessitate surgical repair or nephrectomy performed as an emergency. Injuries that do not disrupt the pelvi-calyceal system, and in the absence of significant extra-capsular bleeding, may be managed conservatively; kidney function must be closely monitored.

The patient is transported from the scene of the accident in a supine position, strapped to a long spine board with head and neck support. Following the ABCs of primary assessment, the patient is log-rolled to her left side, which is co-ordinated by four members of the resuscitation team. The back is examined for bruising and tenderness or numbness and muscle spasm. Radiology of the dorsal spine follows if indicated. Immobilisation is maintained until spinal injury is ruled out. Fluid resuscitation must be initiated when early signs and symptoms of blood loss are apparent or suspected. CVP measurement prevents over-transfusion.

STATION 5.8

Assessment	Good	Adequate	Poor/not done
1. Polite introduction; establishes rapport	❏	❏	❏
2. Asks the patient to point out the site of the pain and any radiation	❏	❏	❏
3. Inspection:			
standing – stability (Trendelenburg test)	❏	❏	❏
Walking – poise and gait	❏	❏	❏
Lying – shortening or rotation; muscle bulk or wasting	❏	❏	❏
4. Palpation/measurement:			
Limb shortening ?real or apparent	❏	❏	❏
Limb circumference	❏	❏	❏
5. Movement: fix normal hip on performing active/passive movements (Thomas' test)	❏	❏	❏
6. Power: ROM against resistance	❏	❏	❏
7. Does all in a fluent, professional manner	❏	❏	❏

Comment

Hip disorders are characterised into well-defined age groups, with the age of onset serving as a guide to the probable diagnosis.

Age of onset	Probable diagnosis
0–5 years	Congenital dislocation
5–10 years	Perthes' disease
10–18 years	Slipped epiphysis
Adult	Avascular necrosis
	Rheumatoid arthritis
	Osteoarthritis

A limp may be due to pain, shortening or abductor weakness of the hip. The Trendelenburg test assesses stability and is positive in dislocation/subluxation, shortening of the femoral neck or osteoarthritis.

Lumbar lordosis masking a fixed flexion deformity is eliminated by flexing both hips together, followed by extending the joint in question, whilst keeping the other flexed.

When measuring limb length, the pelvis must be at right angles to the spine to eliminate apparent shortening. True shortening is assessed by measuring from the anterior superior iliac spine to the medial malleolus of each limb. When real shortening is present, flexing the knees with the heels together determines whether the shortening is above or below the knee.

STATION 5.9

Assessment	Good	Adequate	Poor/not done
1. Polite introduction; establishes rapport	❑	❑	❑
2. Establishes site of pain and radiation	❑	❑	❑
3. Inspection (from front and behind) comparing both sides	❑	❑	❑
4. Palpation: confirm normal joint anatomy	❑	❑	❑
5. Movement:			
Active – ROM	❑	❑	❑
Comment on scapular rotation	❑	❑	❑
Passive – ROM with and without scapular fixation	❑	❑	❑
Power – deltoid: abduct against resistance	❑	❑	❑
Serratus anterior: push against a wall	❑	❑	❑
Pectoralis major: push hands on hips	❑	❑	❑
Trapezius: shrug shoulders	❑	❑	❑
6. Does all in a fluent and professional manner	❑	❑	❑

Comment

Subluxation/dislocation of the shoulder joint or fracture of the proximal humerus are confirmed following AP and lateral radiographs.

The rotator cuff is a sheet of tendons of surrounding muscles closely applied over the top and sides of the shoulder capsule and inserted into the greater and lesser tuberosities of the humerus. Arching over the cuff is a fibro-osseous hood, the coracoacromial arch, with the subacromial bursa intervening. The rotator cuff syndrome is a painful condition caused by the impingement of the tendons with the arch, due to inflammation, causing swelling of the cuff, the tendons or the subacromial bursa. Other causes are calcification or tears of the supraspinatus tendon, osteophyte formation and osteoarthritis of the acromioclavicular joint.

Closed reduction is used for all minimally displaced fractures and those that are stable following reduction, and for treating most fractures in children.

STATION 5.10

Assessment	Good	Adequate	Poor/not done
1. Sandbags and tape; collar	❏	❏	❏
2. Application of a semi-rigid collar in neutral position	❏	❏	❏
Sandbag supports to head and taped support to chin	❏	❏	❏
3. Inspection of neck for swellings, bruising and wounds:			
Gentle palpation for tenderness	❏	❏	❏
Spinal cord integrity:			
Test for motor power on same side (corticospinal tract)	❏	❏	❏
Test for pain and temperature sensation on opposite side (spinothalamic tract)	❏	❏	❏
Test for position and vibration sense on same side (posterior column)	❏	❏	❏
Spinal vertebral integrity:			
Lateral and AP cervical spine radiographs	❏	❏	❏

Comment

Patients with spinal injuries are often erroneously regarded as a 'specialist problem' and any deterioration activates urgent transfer procedures to a specialist centre without actively correcting spinal hypoxia and hypoperfusion.

During the primary survey the signs and symptoms of shock should not be assumed to be due to the spinal injury. Even when a spinal cord injury exists, adequate perfusion must be maintained with oxygen delivery to the lungs to limit secondary neurological damage.

Bradycardia with hypotension is not found in hypovolaemic shock and may indicate a cervical spinal injury in an unconscious patient; care should be taken to prevent overhydration and pulmonary oedema by CVP monitoring.

STATION 5.11

Answers	Good	Adequate	Poor/not done
1. Objectives: to identify and commence immediate treatment of limb-threatening conditions	❏	❏	❏
Group & crossmatch for blood transfusion	❏	❏	❏
Set up IV infusion	❏	❏	❏
Administer systemic analgesia (narcotic)	❏	❏	❏
Immobilisation: application of traction splintage	❏	❏	❏
Confirm neurovascular limb viability post-reduction (i.e. skin sensation, colour, pulses)	❏	❏	❏

2. **False**

3. **True**   a, c and d
   False b

4. **True**   a, c, d, e and f
   False b

Comment

Multiply-injured patients do not do well if non-surgical management of fractures involves prolonged periods of traction and bed rest. Early surgical fixation of fractures reduces pain and blood loss, and the incidence of pulmonary embolism and sepsis. Early mobilisation improves pulmonary function, promotes faster union and reduces infection. Trauma patients with limb injuries often have other major injuries that may require transportation to specialist centres. Traction splints may not fit some ambulances or helicopters, and the logistics of urgently transporting these patients must be worked out in advance.

STATION 5.12

Answers

1. Tibia and fibula; plate and screws

2. Internal fixation of tibia and fibula

3. a, b, c, and d but not e are appropriately treated with this technique

Comment

In internal fixation a fracture is held reduced with transfixing screws or tension wires, which pass through the bone above and below the fracture and are firmly fixed to a closely-applied plate. Complications of internal fixation are due to poor technique, poor operating conditions or poor equipment. They are:

*   Iatrogenic infection which may lead to chronic osteomyelitis.
*   Non-union if the bony ends are fixed too far apart (e.g. in the forearm and leg when one bone is fractured and the other remains intact).
*   Implant failure, resulting in metal fracture when stressed across the fracture line.
*   Re-fracture of the bone which may occur if the implant is removed too soon. Following removal the bone is weak and initially requires protection.

STATION 5.13

Answers

1.   Tibia and fibula
       External fixator and screws

2.   External fixation

3.   **True**   a, b, d and e
       False   c

Comment

In external fixation a compound fracture is held reduced with transfixing screws or tension wires, which pass through the bone above and below the fracture and are firmly fixed to an external frame. This procedure is used for fractures associated with extensive soft tissue injury requiring the wound to be left open for regular toilet and/or debridement, inspection or skin grafting.

Most complications associated with internal fixation also occur in external fixation. More sophisticated external frames incorporate a system of hoops and tension wires to immobilise fractures, correct deformities, lengthen bones and transpose segments of bone.

STATION 5.14

Answers

1.   Figure 5.14a: Fractured ribs and pneumothorax
2.   Figure 5.14b: Disruption of the pelvic ring denoting a crush injury
     Figure 5.14c: Free gas in the upper abdomen indicating ruptured
                   hollow viscus
3.   **True**: c, d, f, g
     False: a, b, e, h

Comment

In the severely injured patient, treatment priorities must be established based on overall assessment. Immediate measures must consist of rapid primary evaluation, resuscitation of vital functions and then a more detailed secondary assessment and the initiation of definitive care.

The initial process is regarded as the A B C D and E of trauma care and identifies immediately life-threatening conditions as shown:

A   Airway maintenance with cervical spine control
B   Breathing and the need for assisted ventilation
C   Circulation with haemorrhage control
D   Disability indicating neurological deficit
E   Exposure requires completely undressing but preventing hypothermia

STATION 5.15

Answers

1. (a)   Scoliosis of the dorsal spine
    (b)   Primary lateral curvature – Cobb's angle
    (c)   Idiopathic in the vast majority of teenagers
           Neuromuscular lesions in children
           Osteosclerosis of the spine in the elderly
    (d)   Functional bracing with rigid pelvic and chin
           supports
           Surgical correction with rods and wires

2. **True**   a
    False   b, c and d

Comment

The most common group is adolescent idiopathic scoliosis and it is usually found in girls. Lateral primary curves < 20 degrees either resolve or remain unchanged. Curves > 30 degrees are conspicuous and require correction or would otherwise progress. In this patient the lateral curve is about 30 degrees and requires functional bracing with a Milwaukee or Boston brace. Patients should be encouraged to wear it most of their waking and sleeping hours. Progress must be assessed four-monthly. Surgical treatment is reserved for failure of conservative measures or for severe deformities.

STATION 5.16

Answers and explanations

1. **(a) False** **(b) False** **(c) False** **(d) True** **(e) True**
This CT head scan shows evidence of cerebral oedema. There is loss of sulci and the 'ground glass' appearance of oedema. The patient would benefit from an intravenous mannitol infusion which would reduce cerebral oedema.

2. **(a) False** **(b) False** **(c) True** **(d) True** **(e) True**
This CT head scan shows a large right sided extradural haemorrhage. The extradural haemorrhage is produced by rupture of a meningeal vessel, such as in a boxing injury. Classically, the patient has a period of lucidity prior to becoming increasingly drowsy. The treatment is a burr hole through the skull to reduce the pressure and evacuate the clot. As shown an extra dural haemorrhage produces a convex interface with the cerebral hemisphere.

3. **(a) False** **(b) False** **(c) False** **(d) False** **(e) True**
This scan shows bilateral frontal, intracerebral blood. Surgical exploration and evacuation of the blood clot is indicated in this patient due to the extensive nature of the frontal lobe laceration and deterioration of cerebral function.

4. **(a) False** **(b) True** **(c) True** **(d) False** **(e) False**
This is a lateral skull X-ray showing a large fronto-parietal fracture CT scan and is a better modality for imaging bone, MRI is better for soft tissue. This injury is consistent with blunt rather than sharp trauma.

5. **(a) False** **(b) True** **(c) True** **(d) True** **(e) False**
This scan shows midline shift towards the right with areas (white) of intracerebral blood. The patient should be treated with mannitol. Surgical intervention is not indicated immediately but may be required for obstructing hydrocephalus.

STATION 5.17

Assessment	Good	Adequate	Poor/not done
Skin preparation and draping	❑	❑	❑
Injection of local anaesthetic into surrounding tissue	❑	❑	❑
Wound cleaning, irrigation and debridement	❑	❑	❑
Skin suturing technique	❑	❑	❑
Wound dressing technique	❑	❑	❑

2. **True:**   b, c, e, h, i and j

     False: a, d, f and g

Comment

Wound management is aimed at optimal healing with minimal scarring and maximal recovery of tensile strength of injured tissues, with restoration of function. Adequate wound debridement cannot be achieved without preliminary infiltration with a local anaesthetic agent. However, heavily contaminated wounds requiring extensive cleaning or debridement require a general anaesthetic and are managed by secondary closure a few days later.

STATION 5.18

Assessment	Good	Adequate	Poor/not done
1. Identification of site of chest drain (i.e. 5th interspace, mid-axillary line)	❑	❑	❑
Skin prep and draping	❑	❑	❑
Infiltration of local anaesthetic	❑	❑	❑
Skin incision, insertion of chest drain and securing it with a suture tie	❑	❑	❑
Connection to water seal drainage bottle	❑	❑	❑
Suture of chest wound and application of sterile dressing	❑	❑	❑

2.	A	Pneumothorax
	B	Right main bronchus
	C	Collapsed lung

Comment

Placement of a chest drain is an emergency procedure when an injured lung is being progressively compressed by air and/or blood entering the pleural cavity. The presence of haemopneumothorax rarely requires the placement of both apical and basal drains, as a single, correctly-sited drain is adequate to drain both the air and the blood. Bleeding from a chest drain that initially drains 1500 ml or exceeds 750 ml in two hours usually indicates a significant vascular injury and requires thoracotomy for control.

A tension pneumothorax presenting as an acute emergency may be immediately relieved by introducing a wide bore cannula into the pleural cavity.

STATION 5.19

Answers

1.	A	Local anaesthetic, syringe and needle
	B	Central venous catheter set
	C	Giving set attached to IV fluid bag
	D	CVP manometer with 3-way connector

Assessment	Good	Adequate	Poor/not done
2. a. Supine positioning of manikin Introduction of needle 1 cm below mid-point of the clavicle and advanced towards the suprasternal notch, thereby cannulating the subclavian vein	❑	❑	❑
alternatively Head down positioning of manikin Introduction of needle close to the medial edge of the sternomastoid muscle and advance towards suprasternal notch thereby cannulating the internal jugular vein	❑	❑	❑
b. Withdrawal of venous blood into the syringe, removal of the latter, introduction of guide wire through the needle into the vein and removal of the needle	❑	❑	❑
c. Venous catheter introduction over the guide wire into the vein and removal of the wire	❑	❑	❑
d. Aspirate to confirm catheter in the vein by withdrawal of venous blood into the syringe	❑	❑	❑

	Good	Adequate	Poor/not done
e. Secure the catheter to the skin with an op-site dressing; chest radiograph to confirm correct positioning and to exclude lung complications	❑	❑	❑

Comment

Shock is defined as an abnormality of the circulation that results in inadequate delivery of oxygen to vital tissues. Haemorrhage is the most frequent cause of shock after injury. The earliest signs of shock are tachycardia and cutaneous vasoconstriction. Thus an injured patient who is cold and clammy and tachycardic is in shock unless proven otherwise. Aggressive fluid resuscitation must be initiated when early signs and symptoms of blood loss are apparent or suspected. CVP monitoring prevents over-transfusion. The return of normal blood pressure, pulse pressure and pulse rate indicate restoration of the circulatory volume and the return of a normal urine output (30 to 50 ml/hr in an adult) indicates restoration of normal organ perfusion.

STATION 5.20

Answers

1. **True** a and d
   False b and c

2. A   Litre of warmed saline
   B   1% lignocaine with adrenaline
   C   Peritoneal dialysis catheter
   D   Scalpel
   E   Suture material

3. The catheter is inserted into the midline, close to the umbilicus (point X in Figure 5.20bi)

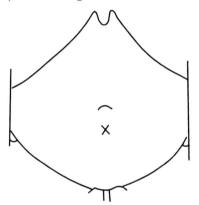

Fig. 5.20bi

Comment

Diagnostic peritoneal lavage (DPL) is indicated in assessing abdominal visceral injury when clinical examination is unreliable, for example in head injuries with altered level of consciousness, injuries to the chest or pelvis, and with spinal cord injuries.

Prior to introducing a DPL catheter, the stomach and urinary bladder should be emptied by nasogastric tube and urinary catheter to prevent injury to these structures. Following instillation of a litre of warmed, normal saline, more than half the instilled volume should be recovered in the ensuing hour. Failure to do so suggests a diaphragmatic or bladder injury or, rarely, intravasation into a loop of bowel through a tear therein.

STATION 6.1

Assessment	Good	Adequate	Poor/not done
1. Ascertains the time and size of the overdose	❑	❑	❑
2. Ascertains what the house officer and A&E staff have already done (i.e. information given to patient)	❑	❑	❑
3. Establishes any clear reason(s) for the patient to refuse treatment	❑	❑	❑
4. Explains to the house officer what can be done: *If the patient is rational, one cannot force treatment on her*	❑	❑	❑
Needs to explain clearly and simply the effects of the paracetamol overdose, (i.e. liver poisoning)	❑	❑	❑
Explain clearly and simply the treatment (i.e. intravenous parvolex or oral N-acetyl cysteine)	❑	❑	❑

Comment

In this case the initial suicide attempt and the refusal of treatment in itself shows serious suicidal intent. The patient is placing her life at risk and may have an underlying depressive illness for which psychiatric care should be provided immediately. The implications of having or not having the treatment should be fully and clearly explained and the patients' understanding assessed.

The Court of Appeal has ruled that a patient lacks capacity only if impairment of her mind renders her unable to decide whether to consent or refuse treatment, and that if she lacks capacity seeking consent is futile. Treatment may be provided in these circumstances under the common law justification of necessity.

The House of Lords has stated that a competent patient on reaching a balanced judgement on adequate information received may choose to reject medical advice for any or no reason. Her unequivocal assurance that her refusal is an informed decision should be documented. Such a patient may sue for battery and false imprisonment if treated against her will and when her refusal is respected there is no prospect of her (or her estate, if she dies) suing for negligence or negligent advice.

STATION 6.2a

Patient history

I am 56 years old and I have two daughters. I found out recently that the reason for my father's suicide was that he had just been diagnosed as having Huntington's chorea. I know very little about the disorder except that sufferers become demented and usually die prematurely. I understand that it is passed on through the genes, and this is why I asked for the test, which the other doctor organized.

I don't want to tell my relatives, as I am frightened for myself and for their well-being. I could not face my daughters knowing that I might have given them a fatal illness, as I am sure they would never forgive me. I love my three brothers and two daughters, and would not want any harm to come to any of them.

(When the doctor has clarified the situation): I feel much more reassured now and will agree to allow you to tell the rest of the family.

Assessment	Good	Adequate	Poor/not done
1. Polite introduction; establishesrapport	❏	❏	❏
2. Establishes patient's understanding of Huntington's chorea	❏	❏	❏
3. Establishes patient's understanding about the inheritance/genetics of the disease	❏	❏	❏
4. Tries to elicit reasons why the patient does not want the family to know:			
Embarrassment – self/family	❏	❏	❏
Shame – self/family	❏	❏	❏
Protection – self/family	❏	❏	❏
Disclosure of father's/ grandfather's illness	❏	❏	❏
Investigates family dynamics – possible conflicts between siblings/daughters and patient	❏	❏	❏

	Good	Adequate	Poor/not done
Tries to reason with the patient; clarifies genetics and effects of disorder; patient's obligations	❑	❑	❑
Explains duties to patient – respect of patient's wishes, confidentiality	❑	❑	❑
Explains that he is obliged and able to inform the other family members without mentioning or involving the patient	❑	❑	❑
5. Does all in a fluent, professional manner.	❑	❑	❑

Comment

The BMA's code of practice on genetic counselling would argue that the patient's daughter, because she may be affected, is entitled to the information despite the patient's wishes. The Court of Appeal has held that information obtained in a confidential relationship may be disclosed if in the public interest. It would seem that a possibility of preventing the birth of a child with the disorder may be considered sufficient to merit disclosure. Further, the patient's daughter may, in the course of time, bring a case of negligence against you for failing in your duty to warn her of a foreseeable risk.

STATION 6.3a

Relative's history

I am the daughter of the patient, Mr Jones. My brother does not really know what is going on and is unable to attend. I am the patient's primary carer. In the last few months I have had to do all his cleaning, washing, bathing and shopping. My father has become increasingly confused and is incontinent of urine all the time. He is often found on the floor, and in the last few weeks has been wandering outside. He leaves the gas on and often mistakes the oven for the fridge. (Maggots were found in the oven.) I can't cope with him any more and don't see why everyone else is trying to let him go home, where he is plainly unsafe. My daughter has been ill over the last week, so I have been unable to come to the hospital and see my father.

Assessment	Good	Adequate	Poor/not done
1. Polite introduction to relatives; introduces/invites other members of health care team to introduce themselves	❏	❏	❏
2. Establishes ground rules of the meeting: chairperson, time limits of the meeting, when questions should be asked	❏	❏	❏
3. Establishes reasons for the meeting	❏	❏	❏
4. Establishes patient's case from the medical notes	❏	❏	❏
5. Presents other health care members' reports/invites them to report	❏	❏	❏
6. Invites relatives to air their concerns	❏	❏	❏
7. Addresses patient's concerns in a logical manner (e.g. gas being capped off, cognitive function much improved)	❏	❏	❏
8. Invites patient to air his views	❏	❏	❏

	Good	**Adequate**	**Poor/not done**
9. Agrees/establishes compromise situation	❏	❏	❏
10. Ensures all parties are in agreement and understand the situation	❏	❏	❏
11. Does all in a fluent, professional manner	❏	❏	❏

Comment

This situation has arisen because of an organic illness. The urinary tract infection has caused the insidious worsening of his general state and has led the daughter to feel that her father is no longer coping, becoming too difficult for her to manage. Through medical treatment and good rehabilitation, the patient is now much improved. Simple communication between the relatives and staff, and demonstration of the 'new, improved' Mr Jones, would probably have obviated the need for the care-planning meeting.

In such cases the staff must assess the patient when at his/her best. Therapies must have been allowed to take effect prior to a home visit or ward assessment.

If the patient is considered of 'reasonable cognitive ability' every avenue must be explored in order to allow the patient to go home. All safety precautions must be implemented, the patient fully briefed and a 'trial of failure' initiated (that is, where everyone but the patient is convinced he/she will probably fail at home). Through maximising home support and helping relatives cope, this trial of failure is often successful for relatively lengthy periods.

STATION 6.4a

Comment

This situation encompasses a very important principle, that of appropriateness of care. Although increasing age is often quoted as a negative prognostic factor, it is usually the only factor considered in such situations. In this situation the patient with the worst prognosis is, in fact, the young 24-year-old man. The appropriateness of treating a man with AIDS and multi-organ failure is not the question, but the appropriateness of treating him at the expense of one of the other patients is. If the consultant in charge of the AIDS patient's case decides that his ventilation should be continued, this patient should not be moved, as he is the most unwell and the least likely to survive transfer. The 83-year-old man is also unlikely to survive a prolonged transfer, so it is one of the other patients who should be moved to another hospital.

STATION 6.5

Patient history

I am a 30-year-old university graduate and couldn't get any job at all until 6 months ago. I have been driving a mini-cab for a local firm and have been earning good money. Although I know it is totally illegal, I haven't informed the DVLC or my employer that I am epileptic.

I was diagnosed as having epilepsy 5 years ago, and haven't had a seizure for the last 10 months. This must mean that I am cured! I understand that I should be able to drive again but not for another year or so. I can't give up my job, as my wife is expecting our second child in 3 months.

Assessment	Good	Adequate	Poor/not done
1. Polite introduction; establishes rapport	❑	❑	❑
2. Establishes why the patient is attending	❑	❑	❑
3. Establishes the patient's control of seizures and compliance with treatment	❑	❑	❑
4. Establishes patient's understanding of the law regarding epilepsy and driving	❑	❑	❑
5. Establishes why the patient continues to drive	❑	❑	❑
6. Looks for possible areas of compromise (e.g. 6 weeks' sick leave/holidays; explanation to employer with GP support; social services support)	❑	❑	❑
7. Raises issues of family and social obligations	❑	❑	❑
8. Informs the patient of the legal obligation for the doctor to inform the DVLC	❑	❑	❑
9. Agrees on a compromise with the patient	❑	❑	❑
10. Does all in a fluent, professional manner	❑	❑	❑

Comment

The BMA code of practice states that when there is a conflict between a doctor's duty to society and patient confidentiality, the doctor should seek to persuade the patient to disclose the information, or to give permission for the doctor to disclose it. The prevention of potential harm to society should supersede the duty of confidentiality. In this case the patient is wrong. The law states that a patient must be fit free for one year, or have had only nocturnal seizures for three or more years to be able to drive. Since the patient has been fit free for 10 months, he could negotiate with his employer, with the GP's help, in order to keep his job. In two months, if still fit free, he would be able to drive again legally.

STATION 6.6a

Patient history

I am a 52-year-old schoolteacher. My husband died in a road traffic accident 5 years ago, and I have been drowning my sorrows ever since. My GP performed some routine blood tests on me about 3 months ago, and I was sent to see the liver specialist and told to cut down on my drinking. I am a little nervous but otherwise have no problems with the biopsy. The consultant told me it was a small cut on the right side of my tummy to get a small piece of liver.

Assessment	Good	Adequate	Poor/not done
1. Polite introduction; establishes rapport	❑	❑	❑
2. Establishes patient identity and reason for admission	❑	❑	❑
3. Establishes patient's present understanding of the procedure	❑	❑	❑
4. Explains the procedure in a clear, non-jargonistic manner	❑	❑	❑
5. Mentions the need for:			
Patient to lie flat on the bed	❑	❑	❑
Duration of the procedure	❑	❑	❑
Patient able to hold a deep breath for 10 seconds	❑	❑	❑
Procedure performed under local anaesthetic	❑	❑	❑
Skin cleaned and infiltrated with local anaesthetic	❑	❑	❑
Small incision made over lateral aspect of the right upper quadrant	❑	❑	❑
Needle passed into the liver and a small amount removed	❑	❑	❑
6. Common side-effects explained	❑	❑	❑
7. Uncommon side-effects explained	❑	❑	❑
8. Post procedure period explained	❑	❑	❑

	Good	Adequate	Poor/not done
9. Invites patient questions, and answers appropriately	❏	❏	❏
10. When asked, states that the procedure cannot be performed until FBC and INR are known	❏	❏	❏
11. Asks patient to sign consent form	❏	❏	❏
12. Does all in a fluent, professional manner	❏	❏	❏

Comment

Contraindications to this procedure include:

a. Patient unable to lie flat or take deep inspiration
b. Local infection of skin
c. Ascites
d. Intra-abdominal sepsis
e. Deranged clotting (INR >1.4)
f. Platelets <80

STATION 6.7a

Patient history

I am 43 years old and have received a letter from the hospital asking me to attend today for endoscopy. No one has explained anything to me, and I have no idea what this is all about. I would like the situation clearly explained. My doctor did mention that I am anaemic and that this may need looking into.

Assessment	Good	Adequate	Poor/not done
1. Polite introduction; establishes rapport	❑	❑	❑
2. Establishes patient identity and reason for procedure	❑	❑	❑
3. Explains the procedure in a clear, non-jargonistic manner	❑	❑	❑
4. Explains the following elements of the procedure:			
Performed normally with local anaesthetic spray	❑	❑	❑
Can be given sedation but not a general anaesthetic	❑	❑	❑
Endoscope (telescope/instrument) is about 1cm in diameter passed down into stomach	❑	❑	❑
Look down into oesophagus (gullet), stomach and first part of bowel	❑	❑	❑
Can take small pieces of the lining (biopsies) to look at under microscope	❑	❑	❑
Uncomfortable but no pain during procedure	❑	❑	❑
Mentions common side-effects – sore throat and gullet	❑	❑	❑
Mentions rare side-effects –			
Oesophageal tear	❑	❑	❑
Mediastinitis	❑	❑	❑
Pneumomediastinum	❑	❑	❑

5. Invites patient questions, and
    answers appropriately   ❑   ❑   ❑
6. Does all in a fluent,
    professional manner   ❑   ❑   ❑

Comment

Indications for upper GI endoscopy:

Acute –   Upper GI bleed/haematemesis or melaena
             Acute oesophageal obstruction.
Chronic –   Investigation of dysphagia, hypochromic microcytic
             anaemia, weight loss, vomiting, dyspepsia, coeliac
             disease/malabsorption.

STATION 6.8a

Patient history

I am 62 years old and a retired school teacher. I am being investigated for constipation and weight loss. I am very concerned that I may have cancer of the bowel, because this is what my sister died of. My GP described the colonoscopy to me briefly and said the doctors would pass a camera into my bowel. I am not sure what this means.

Assessment	Good	Adequate	Poor/not done
1. Polite introduction; establishes rapport	❏	❏	❏
2. Establishes patient identity and reason for attendance	❏	❏	❏
3. Establishes patient's present understanding of the procedure	❏	❏	❏
4. Explains the procedure in a clear, non-jargonistic manner	❏	❏	❏
5. Explains the elements of the procedure:			
Procedure performed using intravenous sedation	❏	❏	❏
Endoscope passed in through anus up into the bowel	❏	❏	❏
Endoscope is about 1cm in diameter, flexible, and carries a fibre optic light allowing the operator to see inside the bowel	❏	❏	❏
Allows biopsies to be taken	❏	❏	❏
6. Mentions common side-effects – PR bleeding; discomfort during procedure	❏	❏	❏
7. Mentions uncommon side-effects – small tears of bowel treated conservatively; larger tears of bowel requiring operation	❏	❏	❏

	Good	Adequate	Poor/not done
8. Invites patient questions and addresses anxieties	❏	❏	❏
9. Does all the above in a fluent, professional manner	❏	❏	❏

Comment

Indications for colonoscopy:

Acute –   Bleeding from the lower bowel.

Chronic – Investigation of weight loss, change in bowel habit, bleeding or mucus PR, hypochromic microcytic anaemia.

STATION 6.9a

Patient history

> I am 36 years old and work in a factory. I have been getting pain in the top right part of my tummy for the last 6 to 8 months. The pain is particularly bad after fried foods. The pain was so bad 3 days ago that I called out my GP and I was admitted to hospital. Yesterday I had a scan, which showed that a gallstone was blocking up my liver. I have been told that I need a special test which allows the doctors to look inside my bowel, near the liver, and remove the stone. I am happy to have this procedure but I do not understand any of the anatomy, or how they will manage to get the gallstone out without opening me up.

Assessment	Good	Adequate	Poor/not done
1. Polite introduction; establishes rapport	❏	❏	❏
2. Establishes the patient's identity and reason for the ERCP	❏	❏	❏
3. Establishes patient's present understanding of ERCP	❏	❏	❏
4. Explains ERCP in clear, non-jargonistic terms	❏	❏	❏
5. Explains the following elements of the procedure: *Procedure is performed under intravenous sedation, not general anaesthetic*	❏	❏	❏
Endoscope is about 1 cm in diameter. It is flexible and carries a fibre optic light which allows the operator to see inside the bowel	❏	❏	❏
Endoscope is passed down through the gullet into the first part of the bowel	❏	❏	❏
The sphincter of Oddi is identified and cut, using instrument passed down the endoscope	❏	❏	❏

	Good	Adequate	Poor/not done
Metal cage/basket is passed up into the biliary tree	❑	❑	❑
Gallstone is removed using the cage	❑	❑	❑
If the procedure is unsuccessful, further attempts may be undertaken	❑	❑	❑
Patient may require surgical intervention	❑	❑	❑
6. Invites patient questions, and answers appropriately	❑	❑	❑
7. Does all in a fluent, professional manner	❑	❑	❑

Comment

The use of ERCP is quite specific. Most patients having an ERCP will also have to give consent for the use of contrast media being injected through the sphincter of Oddi and X-ray images being taken of the resulting patterns through the biliary tree and pancreatic ducts. Consent must be obtained for sphincterotomy which frequently accompanies ERCP.

One specific use of ERCP is the insertion of stents to keep open biliary ducts in benign and malignant conditions.

All patients for ERCP receive prophylactic anitbiotics for 24 hours pre- and post-procedure, and should have nil by mouth for 8 hours pre-procedure.

It is often difficult for patients to conceptualise the anatomy and how stents/wire baskets may be sited using an endoscope. ERCP is often best explained using a diagram.

STATION 6.10a

Patient history

> I am 43 years old and was admitted to hospital 2 days ago with a fever, exertional dyspnoea and lethargy. I have been told I have a new heart murmur and it is suspected I have an infection on the heart valve. I know this procedure is to look at the heart valves and to try to see if they are damaged but I have not been told anything else. I am a little anxious about the whole thing and wondered if it is possible to be put to sleep for the procedure.

Assessment	Good	Adequate	Poor/not done
1. Polite introduction; establishes patient identity	❑	❑	❑
2. Establishes present understanding of the procedure	❑	❑	❑
3. Explains the procedure in a clear, non-jargonistic manner	❑	❑	❑
4. Mentions the following information:			
Procedure performed with patient conscious	❑	❑	❑
Patient can be given injection to make them sleepy	❑	❑	❑
Instrument is about 3-4 cm at its thickest	❑	❑	❑
The procedure should be no more than uncomfortable	❑	❑	❑
5. Mentions the common complications – sore throat and oesophagus	❑	❑	❑
6. Mentions the uncommon complications – oesophagus rupture; Mediastinal sepsis; death	❑	❑	❑
7. Re-establishes patient understanding of procedure	❑	❑	❑

	Good	Adequate	Poor/not done
8. Invites questions and answers appropriately	❏	❏	❏
9. Does all the above in a fluent, professional manner	❏	❏	❏

Comment

Transoesophageal echocardiogram requires the placement of the echo probe in the gullet adjacent to the heart and moved to obtain adequate ciné imaging of valvular anatomy and function.

STATION 6.11a

Patient history

I am 53 years old and am a headmaster. I had a 'heart attack' 6 months ago. I saw the consultant cardiologist 2 weeks ago, who thought I should have a 'catheter' test to see how bad the damage is to the blood vessels supplying the heart. I have not been told very much but would like to know as much as possible. I am otherwise well and can lie flat in bed with no problems. I have never had any reactions to any medications.

[NB. Ask the doctor specifically about any concerns you may have.]

Assessment	Good	Adequate	Poor/not done
1. Polite introduction; establishes patient identity	❑	❑	❑
2. Establishes present understanding of the procedure	❑	❑	❑
3. Explains the procedure in a clear, non-jargonistic manner	❑	❑	❑
4. Mentions the following information: *Performed under local anaesthetic*	❑	❑	❑
Injection into the groin through which a thin tube is placed	❑	❑	❑
Contrast medium is injected through the tube/cine film is taken	❑	❑	❑
5. Explains common complications – reaction to contrast medium and bruising in the groin	❑	❑	❑
6. Explains the uncommon complications – femoral false aneurysm and rupture of coronary vessel	❑	❑	❑
7. Specifically explains the risk and benefits of the procedure – including mortality	❑	❑	❑

	Good	Adequate	Poor/not done
8. Invites patient questions and deals with them in an appropriate manner	❏	❏	❏
9. Establishes the patient understanding at the end of the explanation	❏	❏	❏
10. Asks patient to sign consent form	❏	❏	❏
11. Does all in a fluent, professional manner	❏	❏	❏

STATION 6.12

Assessment	Good	Adequate	Poor/not done
1. Polite introduction; checks the patient's identity	❑	❑	❑
2. Explains the procedure to the patient in a clear manner	❑	❑	❑
3. Checks that the correct equipment is available: needle/vacutainer or syringe, alcohol wipe, FBC bottle, tourniquet, gloves	❑	❑	❑
4. Performs the procedure in the following steps:			
Puts on gloves		❑	❑
Places tourniquet on the arm correctly		❑	❑
Selects appropriate vein to site cannula		❑	❑
Cleans skin with alcohol wipe		❑	❑
Connects needle/vacutainer or syringe correctly		❑	❑
Warns patient of 'sharp scratch'		❑	❑
Inserts needle at approximately 35–45°		❑	❑
Withdraws appropriate amount of blood (FBC 1–4 ml)		❑	❑
Releases tourniquet		❑	❑
Withdraws the needle		❑	❑
Covers puncture site with cotton wool or alcohol wipe, asking the patient to press on the area		❑	❑
Does all in as clean a manner as possible		❑	❑
Disposes of sharps appropriately		❑	❑
States would label the bottle correctly and fill in appropriate FBC form		❑	❑
5. Does all in a fluent, professional manner	❑	❑	❑

STATION 6.13

Assessment	Good	Adequate	Poor/not done
1. Polite introduction; establishes identity of the patient	❑	❑	❑
2. Explains the procedure to the patient in a clear manner	❑	❑	❑
3. Checks the right equipment is present (i.e. intravenous cannula, alcohol wipe, tourniquet, vecafix or similar dressing for cannula, normal saline flush, gloves)	❑	❑	❑
4. Performs the procedure in the following steps:			
Puts on gloves		❑	❑
Places the tourniquet on the arm correctly		❑	❑
Selects appropriate vein to site cannula		❑	❑
Cleans skin with alcohol wipe		❑	❑
Warns patient of 'sharp scratch'		❑	❑
Passes cannula through skin at 35–45°		❑	❑
Looks/obtains flashback into cannula chamber		❑	❑
Releases tourniquet		❑	❑
Inserts cannula whilst withdrawing introducer		❑	❑
Pushes on tip of cannula, or asks patient to elevate arm (to stop bleeding as introducer is withdrawn)		❑	❑
Replaces cap over end of cannula		❑	❑
Secures cannula with dressing		❑	❑
Flushes cannula using saline flush		❑	❑
Does all in as clean a manner as possible		❑	❑
Disposes of sharps appropriately		❑	❑
5. Does all in a fluent, professional manner	❑	❑	❑

STATION 6.14

Assessment	Good	Adequate	Poor/not done
1. Polite introduction; establishes the patient's identity	❏	❏	❏
2. Explains procedure to the patient in a clear manner	❏	❏	❏
3. Checks fluid prescription on chart, patient's details and fluid provided	❏	❏	❏
4. Checks that all correct equipment is present (e.g. normal saline + 20 mmol KCl, giving set and drip stand or equivalent)	❏	❏	❏
5. Puts on gloves	❏	❏	❏
6. Connects giving set to intravenous fluid correctly	❏	❏	❏
7. Runs through fluid so giving set is appropriately filled, removing air bubbles	❏	❏	❏
8. Removes cannula cap and attaches fluid correctly	❏	❏	❏
9. Ensures fluid is running easily into vein without causing pain/ burning sensation	❏	❏	❏
10. Ensures giving set is securely attached to the patient and cannula (may use a bandage)	❏	❏	❏
11. Does all in a fluent, professional manner	❏	❏	❏

STATION 6.15

Assessment	Good	Adequate	Poor/not done
1. Polite introduction; establishes patient identity	❏	❏	❏
2. Explains procedure to patient in a clear manner	❏	❏	❏
3. Checks that the correct equipment is present (i.e. saline flush, needles, syringes, antibiotic, mixing fluid)	❏	❏	❏
4. Checks the prescription chart, antibiotic and dose against patient identity bracelet	❏	❏	❏
5. Checks the patient has no known drug allergy	❏	❏	❏
6. Performs the procedure as follows:			
Puts gloves on		❏	❏
Removes seal on antibiotic vial		❏	❏
Cleans top of antibiotic vial with alcohol wipe		❏	❏
Draws up mixing fluid (e.g. water for injection)		❏	❏
Injects mixing fluid into antibiotic vial		❏	❏
Mixes antibiotic/fluid appropriately		❏	❏
Draws back antibiotic		❏	❏
Cleans cannula portal with alcohol wipe		❏	❏
Injects antibiotic slowly		❏	❏
Flushes cannula with saline flush		❏	❏
Closes cannula portal		❏	❏
Disposes of sharps and other materials appropriately		❏	❏
7. Does all in a fluent, professional manner	❏	❏	❏

APPENDIX A: THE OSCE MARKING SCHEME

The OSCE marking scheme

Traditionally, academic assessment has been 'norm' referenced, whereby candidates are compared to one another and are ranked from the best to the worst. In recent years the value of 'norm' referencing has come under question and 'criterion' referencing has become more accepted.

Criterion-referenced assessment is not new, the most obvious examples being the driving test and swimming life saving assessments. In both these examples a candidate must demonstrate a 'minimum competency level' for the given skills, i.e. driving a motor vehicle or saving a drowning person. Unlike traditional, norm-referenced assessment, there is no division of candidates into excellent, good, average, unsatisfactory and poor; there is only pass (competent) and fail (not competent).

Criterion referencing is easily applied to the OSCE format. A committee of examiners meets several months prior to the examinations and, through discussion, sets a minimum competency score, i.e. a passing score, for each given station. This score reflects what a candidate taking the OSCE should be reasonably expected to achieve, given their expected core knowledge, the time restrictions and the stress of the examination. These, in turn, should be reflected in the validity of the OSCE.

In volumes 1 and 2 the checklists are divided into three columns headed **Good**, **Adequate** and **Poor/not done**. These headings subdivide students into good, average and poor, where poor candidates do not demonstrate an acceptable level of competence, i.e. fail. However, in many medical establishments, the division of good and average candidates is regarded as old fashioned, regressing back to norm referencing and therefore the headings may read **Adequate or competent**, **Attempted but unsatisfactory** and **Not done**.

Some medical colleges apply weighting of individual items within a checklist. For instance, the initial item on each checklist – 'Polite introduction; establishes rapport', may have a maximum score of two marks if performed well, whereas another item, e.g. auscultating the four areas of the heart correctly, may carry 5 marks if performed well. Both would be given a lesser mark if performed adequately and 0 marks if not done at all. We have chosen not to weight individual items in our checklists. This is because:

(i) We feel that weighting of items in this way does not improve the discriminatory power of the examination.
(ii) We think students should be discerning enough to realise which are the important key points that will be more heavily weighted in a checklist.

We have, therefore, generally used 3 columns for our checklists, **Good, Adequate** and **Poor/not done**, carrying 3, 2 and zero marks respectively. Certain checklists, however, only have 2 columns, i.e. **Adequate** and **Not done**. These are typically items which are required to be named, e.g. risk factors for a DVT or contraindications to a given treatment. One can only mention them or not and for this reason a 'good column' is not applicable. In such cases 1 mark is given for adequate column and zero for the Poor/not done column.

To obtain the total score
For each station, minimum competency or pass mark is calculated by a committee of examiners/experts. If a candidate scores each item as 'adequate' this will equate to the 'pass' mark. A candidate should therefore aim to get an adequate or good for each item. If one scores adequate or poor/not done in the majority of items, this implies a lack of knowledge or areas of weakness and should be used to direct the student's learning.

In most OSCEs the stations are deemed to be as important as one another, so that the mean pass mark of the total number of stations is taken as the pass mark for the overall examination. If individual stations are important in terms of 'must pass', a weighting system may be applied to calculate the overall pass mark.

We have used one other style of marking whereby the station poses a series of questions to the student regarding an investigation, e.g. an abdominal radiograph, or a given scenario, e.g. management of a head injury patient. Examiners may consider that such answers should also carry serious consequences for the candidate, such as an outright failure on that question.

Establishing rapport with a patient is essential in a doctor-patient relationship. At the initial meeting, greetings and introductions help to put the patient at ease and ensure patient co-operation with the history and/or examination. In these stations, therefore, marks are allocated for such interaction. Positive criteria include empathy, putting a patient at their ease and establishing their confidence by careful listening and responding to verbal and non-verbal cues.

APPENDIX B: REVISION CHECKLIST

Use the checklist to monitor your revision. Mark off the sections you have covered so that key topics are not left out.

Neurology and Psychiatry
- ❑ Epilepsy
- ❑ Meningomyelocoele and hydrocephalus
- ❑ Hypothalmic and pituitary lesions
- ❑ Strokes
- ❑ Motor neurone disease
- ❑ Multiple sclerosis
- ❑ Parkinson's disease
- ❑ Cranial nerve lesions
- ❑ Peripheral neuropathy and nerve injuries
- ❑ Alcohol and drug abuse
- ❑ Eating disorders
- ❑ Depression
- ❑ Personality disorders
- ❑ Mania
- ❑ Schizophrenia

Ophthalmology and Otolaryngology
- ❑ Eye injuries
- ❑ The red eye
- ❑ Uveitis
- ❑ Glaucoma
- ❑ Cataract
- ❑ Otitis media
- ❑ Glue ear
- ❑ Chronic sinusitis
- ❑ Tonsillitis/pharyngitis

Cardiovascular diseases and Haematology
- ❑ Arrhythmias
- ❑ Cardiac failure
- ❑ Valvular heart disease
- ❑ Endocarditis
- ❑ Ischaemic heart disease
- ❑ Carotid heart disease
- ❑ Acute and chronic peripheral vascular disease
- ❑ Varicose veins

- ❏ Deep venous thrombosis
- ❏ Anaemias
- ❏ Bleeding disorders
- ❏ Thrombocytopenia
- ❏ Leukaemias
- ❏ Lymphomas
- ❏ Myeloma

Respiratory Medicine
- ❏ Bronchitis and emphysema
- ❏ Bronchiectasis and cystic fibrosis
- ❏ Pneumonias
- ❏ Pulmonary tuberculosis
- ❏ Empyema thoracis
- ❏ Traumatic pneumo/haemothorax
- ❏ Bronchogenic carcinoma
- ❏ Diaphragmatic hernia

Trauma and Orthopaedics
- ❏ Cerebral trauma
- ❏ Spinal injuries
- ❏ Thoracic injuries
- ❏ Abdominal trauma
- ❏ Pelvic and long bone fractures
- ❏ Bone dystrophies and dysplasias
- ❏ Bone tumours
- ❏ Spinal deformities

Ethics and Legal Medicine
- ❏ Patient's right to know
- ❏ Patient confidentiality
- ❏ Informed consent
- ❏ Sectioning psychiatric patients
- ❏ Organ donation
- ❏ In-vitro fertilisation
- ❏ Terminal care

APPENDIX C: RECOMMENDED READING LIST

Medical Texts

Hutchinson's Clinical Methods: Hutchinson R and Swash M, 20th edition, W B Saunders, 1995.

Davidson's Principles and Practice of Medicine: Edwards CRW, Bouchier IAD, Haslett C and Chilvers ER (editors), 17th edition, Churchill Livingstone 1995.

Clinical Medicine: Kumar P and Clark M, 4th edition, Balliere Tindall 1998.

Examining Patients: An Introduction to Clinical Medicine: Toghill PJ (editor), 2nd edition, Edward Arnold 1994.

Lecture Notes on Clinical Medicine: Bradley JR, and Wayne D, 5th edition, Blackwell Science 1997.

Surgical Texts

Hamilton Bailey's Demonstrations of Physical Signs in Clinical Surgery: Lumley JSP, 18th edition, Butterworth Heinemann 1997.

Lecture Notes on General Surgery: Ellis H and Calne R, 9th edition, Blackwell Science 1998.

The Washington Manual of Surgery: Doherty GM, et al., Little-Brown & Co, 1997.

Bailey and Love's Short Practice of Surgery: Mann CV, Russell RCG, Williams NS, 22nd edition, Chapman and Hall 1995.

Orthopaedic Texts

Lecture Notes on Orthopaedics and Fractures: Duckworth T, 3rd edition, Blackwell Science 1995.

Physical Signs in Orthopaedics: Klenerman L and Walsh HJ, BMJ Publishing, 1994.

Apley's System of Orthopaedics and Fractures: Apley AG and Solomon L, 7th edition, Butterworth Heinemann 1993.

APPENDIX D: MOCK EXAMINATIONS

Station	1	2	3	4	5	6
1	1.1$^+$	1.2$^+$	1.3$^+$	1.4$^+$	1.5$^+$	1.6$^+$
2	1.8$^+$	1.7$^+$	1.9	1.10	1.11	1.12
3	1.13	1.14	1.15	1.16	1.17	1.18/a
4	1.19	1.20	1.28	1.22$^+$	1.23$^+$	1.24$^+$
5	1.25$^+$	1.26$^+$	2.2	1.29	1.30	1.32
6	2.1$^+$	2.7	2.8	2.3$^+$	2.4	2.5
7	2.6	2.13$^+$	2.16$^+$	2.9	2.11$^+$	2.12$^+$
8	2.14	2.15	3.5$^+$	3.6	3.1$^+$	2.17
9	3.3/a$^+$	3.4$^+$	3.11	3.12	3.7	3.2$^+$
10	3.9	3.10	3.18	3.19	3.13	3.8
11	3.16	3.17	3.24	4.6$^+$	3.20	3.14
12	3.22	3.23	4.5$^+$	4.12	3.26/a$^+$	3.21
13	4.3$^+$	4.4$^+$	4.11	4.17	4.1$^+$	4.2$^+$
14	4.9	4.10	4.14	4.20	4.7	4.8
15	4.16	4.15	5.2$^+$	5.1$^+$	4.19	4.18
16	5.3	5.7	5.8^x	5.9^x	5.6	5.5^x
17	5.4^x	5.13	5.14	5.15	5.10^x	5.11
18	5.12	6.4/a	6.3/a$^+$	5.18	5.20	5.16
19	5.19	6.7/a$^+$	6.8/a$^+$	6.2/a$^+$	6.10/a$^+$	6.11/a$^+$
20	6.6/a$^+$	6.12*	6.13*	6.9/a$^+$	6.14*	6.15*

Each examination includes 5, 10 and 15 minute questions and takes 2 hours to complete. History stations (+) require a 'subject' to give the responses provided in the second half of the book. Questions with an '/a' include a preparatory station, questions marked (x) require a subject for examination and those marked (*) require a manikin of an arm.

PASTEST BOOKS FOR UNDERGRADUATES

PasTest are the specialists in study guides and revision courses for professional medical qualifications. For over 25 years we have been helping doctors to achieve their potential. The PasTest range of books for medical students includes:

OSCEs for Medical Undergraduates Volume 2
Visvanathan, Feather & Lumley
- Chapters covering history taking, examinations, investigations, practical techniques, making a diagnosis, prescribing treatment and other issues.
- Answers in a separate section so that students can assess their performance and identify areas needing further attention.
- Covers Endocrinology, Gastroenterology, Urology and Renal Medicine, Obstetrics and Gynaecology, Rheumatology and Dermatology.

Surgical Finals: Passing the Clinical
Kuperberg & Lumley
- 90 examples of favourite long and short surgical cases
- Syllabus checklist for structured revision
- 18 detailed examination schemes with action tables
- 36 tables of differential diagnosis
- 134 popular viva questions for self-assessment
- Recommended reading list and revision index.

Medical Finals: Passing the Clinical
Moore & Richardson
- 101 typical long cases, short cases and spot diagnoses
- Syllabus checklist for systematic revision
- Vital tips on preparation and presentation
- Structured examination plans for all cases
- Concise teaching notes highlight areas most relevant to finals
- Revision index for easy access to specific topics

Surgical Finals: Structured Answer and Essay Questions – Second Edition
Visvanathan & Lumley
- Prepare for the written examination with this unique combination of essay questions and the new structured answer questions
- 138 structured answer questions with detailed teaching notes
- 52 typical essay questions with sample essay plans and model essays
- Invaluable revision checklist to help you to track your progress
- Short textbook reviews enable you to select the best textbooks

Medical Finals: Structured Answer and Essay Questions
Feather, Visvanathan & Lumley
- Prepare for the written examination with this unique combination of essay questions and the new structured answer questions
- 141 structured answer questions with detailed teaching notes
- 73 typical essay questions with sample essay plans and model essays
- Invaluable revision checklist to help you to track your progress
- Short textbook reviews enable you to select the best textbooks

150 Essential MCQs for Surgical Finals
Hassanally & Singh
150 Essential MCQs for Medical Finals
Singh & Hassanally
- The crucial material for your exam success
- Extended teaching notes, bullet points and mnemonics
- Revision indexes for easy access to specific topics

For priority mail order service, please contact PasTest on FREEPHONE

0800 980 9814

PasTest, FREEPOST, Egerton Court, Parkgate Estate,
Knutsford, Cheshire WA16 7BR
Telephone: 01565 752000 Fax: 01565 650264
E-mail: books@pastest.co.uk Web site: http//www.pastest.co.uk